Jon & Pam Strain

spiritual
seeds

how to cultivate spiritual wealth within your future children

Toward building lives with Him...
Ps 127
because He gives good gifts!
Mt. 7:11

Jon & Pam
5/♡

elevate
faith

Scripture quotations taken from the New American Standard Bible®,
Copyright © 1960, 1962, 1963, 1968, 1971, 1972, 1973,
1975, 1977, 1995 by The Lockman Foundation
Used by permission. (www.Lockman.org)

Editorial Content: AnnaMarie McHargue
Cover Designer: Bobby Kuber
Interior Layout: Leslie Hertling

Published by Elevate Publishing, Boise, ID
www.elevatepub.com

Printed in the United States of America

ISBN: 978-1937498696

DEDICATION

To our four noble sons and our captivating
daughters-in-law—including those to come:
Bryant and Christina, Jason and Jenna, Jonny, and Sean,
we give you our best, praying you will reflectively share
the wealth with both physical and spiritual grandchildren,
blessing generations to follow.

"With insightful anecdotes, a breadth of Scripture, and a gaze fixed upon the Author and Finisher of our Faith, the Strains have produced an excellent tool to further the vision of Malachi, turning the hearts of fathers unto their children and that of children unto their fathers not just momentarily, but generationally."

Sage G. Dixon
Idaho State House of Representatives, District 1
Father of seven children

"In our quest to reach the Millennials more effectively, we must remember that their children will comprise yet another generation who must be grounded in values that promote both individual and corporate well-being. Incorporating their experience with Search Ministries and their own fruitful parenting, Jon and Pam Strain provide young parents (and those anticipating becoming parents) with genuine wisdom about how best to transfer that which is most valuable to one's children. I especially appreciated their emphasis on the necessity of partnering with God in this parenting process."

Randal Roberts, D.Min.
President and Professor of Spiritual Formation
Western Seminary, Portland, Oregon

"Reading *Spiritual Seeds: How to Cultivate Spiritual Wealth Within Your Future Children* is like sitting down with your favorite mentor for hours over a cup of coffee. It is entertaining, Biblical and very practical. Throughout the book there are several nuggets of truth that can be applied not only to every stage of parenting, but also to life in general. Every parent who wants to be intentional in raising their children should read this."

Jill Johnson
Co-Founder, Standing Together

Advanced Praise

"*Spiritual Seeds* is the book I wish someone had given me when I had my first child. It is packed with practical, Biblical wisdom for raising children to be the people God created them to be. *Spiritual Seeds* will challenge, convict, and encourage you to parent with godly intentionality. It had that effect on me. This is the book I will be giving to all of my friends who have young children!"

Blaine Larsen (and Sammie)
Hit country music artist and writer, Search Nashville

"When reviewing non-fiction books that I might want to read, I always look at the authors. What are their credentials? Can I have confidence that they are authoritative? Are they mature enough to have a certifiable track record of experience? I also want to know more personal information about them. Are their opinions, insights and research held in high esteem by their colleagues? Do they make as much sense outside of the book as they do in the book? Even more personally, if they are placed in a similar situation as mine (and that is why I am reading their book), how would they react to my difficult problems? Do they have the 'right stuff' to deal with my issues? I have known Jon and Pam Strain for a large number of years. I've seen them in action. I've heard their opinions voiced discussing problematic situations. I've been led by their thoughtfulness, sincerity, maturity and experience. I've seen their credentials. They've shared their walk. I know I can trust them. This book is *essential* for young families and equally important for single parents who are struggling with the 'How do I do this?!' Frankly, parenting is a far more important job than breadwinning. You can trust the Strains to lead you through this challenging and oftentimes overwhelming experience."

David S. Parsons MD, FAAP, FACS
Clinical Professor at both the Universities of North and South Carolina
[Retired from Charlotte Eye, Ear, Nose and Throat Associates, Dr. Parsons has been honored with multiple national and international humanitarian awards and research publication awards for Ear, Nose and Throat Advances in Children.]

Advanced Praise

"In *Spiritual Seeds*, Jon and Pam Strain give an inspiring blueprint for parenting and remind moms and dads that they don't have to do it all on their own. As parents, we can so easily forget to stop and ask God for help; I love the framework this book provides to Ask, Seek, and Knock so we can effectively raise kids to impact the world. Parenting is not an easy job, but it is worth every challenge and there is great joy in the journey. Jon and Pam's experiences and insights will encourage those who hope to be parents one day, as well as the moms and dads who already know the sound of little feet running down the hall."

Genny Heikka, Author,
Finding Mommy Bliss—
Discovering Unexpected Joy in Everyday Moments

"In an effort to impart spiritual and social wealth to our children and their children, Jon and Pam Strain have provided a blueprint for helping achieve that noble goal. Their purpose in writing this book is clear—to give pre-parents a tangible model and workable vision for growing their family with God's caring provision. It's also a legacy tool to invite our children and spouses to consider how they will build their home. Parenting is an exhilarating, gut-wrenching, often breathtaking journey that demands changing skills and lifelong learning. *Spiritual Seeds* should be a well-worn reference on every parent's bookshelf."

Skip and Virginia Hall
30-year college football coach, executive coach, speaker

"It's pithy. It's personal. It's practical. It is the conversation I wish we'd had 34 years ago!"

Davis Kuykendall, Search Charlotte
Past and Present Board Member, Charlotte Leadership Forum,
International Youth Commission and YMCA of Greater Charlotte

Advanced Praise

"Parenting is not for the faint of heart, it's hard work and getting harder in our technology driven world. Helping our children to grow up with Biblical values and keep them in a society bent on corrupting their character requires parents who are devoted to their kids. Additionally, parents need God's strength and Biblical resources to assist them in the challenges of raising their families. *Spiritual Seeds*, from Jon and Pam Strain, is just such a resource, available to help parents cultivate spiritual values into the lives of their kids. They practice what they preach and have seen God's blessings in the lives of the four boys they have raised into fine young adults."

Rev. Gregory Johnson
President, Standing Together
National Association of Evangelicals, At-Large Board Member

"Nearly 6 years ago my wife and I had the privilege of meeting Jon Strain. He is unique and unlike any minister I have ever encountered. Jon can take a punch, deal with resistance, and graciously roll back to the point. Before a person knows what happened, the crosshairs of an expert marksman are upon him, and the questions roll in, hitting home repeatedly while gently dislodging false suppositions in the heart. Folks like Jon assess desires, needs, and the primal angst that plagues people in a fallen world.

Jon and his wife, Pam, continue to hit the mark. They have masterfully addressed one of the greatest struggles people will ever encounter—parenting. In *Spiritual Seeds*, this couple has arrived on the scene as legitimate Christian practitioners who use Biblical principles, prayer, godly counsel and common sense to instruct parents, children, mentors, church leaders and anyone who works with young people. The book is well worth your time, and you'll find spiritual gold within. If you have been asking, seeking and knocking on God's door for help with your children and family or someone else's— this book just might be an answer to prayer. I highly recommend it."

Hakim Hazim
Owner, Relevant Now
Co-Founder, Freedom Squared

Advanced Praise

"If I were to describe Jon and Pam in one word, it would be *intentional*. Nearly everything they do has a purpose. From facilitating large outreach events, open forum discussions, adventure dinners, manhood ceremonies, etc., they have the intention of helping people to become more willing to examine God's love for them and God's desire to become their heavenly Father. Their intentionality is always tempered with leaving the ultimate results of their efforts to God. Like farming crops is the ultimate partnership with God (i.e. the farmer supplies the labor and God supplies the weather), spiritual farmers can relax since ultimately God is responsible for the crop!"

Jeff Klassen
Search Boise Advisory Team Member and former Idaho potato farmer

"A keen mentor of mine, Dr. Howard Hendricks, said in a Family Home class one ordinary day an unordinary statement, 'The greatest gift you can give your children is a marriage that loves one another.' Jon and Pam have lived that profound assertion. Therefore, we now benefit from wisdom fired in the kiln called home. *Spiritual Seeds* is practical and real. It is purposeful and Biblical. I like easy reads full of stories with insightful punch lines. I believe you will find this life work full of encouraging and helpful tools that will thoughtfully guide your kids to make a difference in their world."

Dr. Joel Housholder, Th.M., D.Min.
Dallas Director, Search Ministries,
Speaker with FamilyLife Marriage Conferences for 23 years
Former Regional Director, YoungLife North Texas

"Jon Strain has a knack for relating eternal truths to everyday life. He has been vital in my transition to life after college."

Grant Hedrick
Former Quarterback, Boise State University

"Jon Strain and I have served together on the staff of Search Ministries for more than a decade. Myrlane and I know that a real key to any staff member's success is what type of ministry asset is their spouse. Pam has been such an asset to Jon that she herself is now a full-time staff member. We first saw the effectiveness of the Search principles during my NFL days in Baltimore. Joe Ehrmann was a teammate who was impacted and has a ministry with a national footprint that led Joe to Boise a few years ago. Since our daughter and her family live in Boise, we make the trek regularly and are impressed by Jon and Pam's own footprint in their city."

Ken and Myrlane Mendenhall
Area Director, Search Ministries, Oklahoma City

"Our family used to play the 'Dictionary Game' where one would choose a little-known or unusual word and the rest had to guess its Webster definition from among a group of cleverly improvised definitions. Jon benefited from that exercise, for he is a true wordsmith. Coming from a heritage rich in artists, circuit-rider ministers and great storytellers, it seems quite natural those genes pooled in my 'little' brother. A self-motivated student of life and builder of relationships, in the spiritual realm he is 'jack of all trades, and master of pun.' Jon is an insightful storyteller, weaving Biblical riches, quirky humor and real-life illustrations into a handbook I wish I would have had when I became a parent.

Jon and Pam have written an artistic and vulnerably honest work rich in wisdom gleaned from their own experiences, from many mentors and from the Word of God. They are genuine, well-loved and respected, and consistent in their spiritual walk. For Jon and Pam, this is a labor of love: full of God's love, permeated with the love of a devoted couple, and the fruit of their love, four outstanding sons. As a grandparent, I am excited to share this book with those in the younger generation I know will benefit from its insights."

Patti Burt
Worship and Music Coordinator, Christ Church Anglican
Butte, Montana
Sister of Jon Strain

Advanced Praise

"This book is not a 'how-to' for parenting as much as it is a 'Why wouldn't I?' writing. While reading I kept finding myself thinking, 'Of course. That makes perfect sense.' Knowing Jon and Pam's sons a bit, the proof is in the pudding. The Strains created the atmosphere for each of those young men to flourish. *Spiritual Seeds: How to Cultivate Spiritual Wealth Within Your Future Children* invites adults to think creatively about parenting—not a fool-proof, add water and stir formula, but a big-picture view of what we really hope to be and do with our kids. Enjoy!"

Ken Schultz
Area Director, Search Charlotte
Former YoungLife Area Director for 17 years and church pastor

"The story of Jon and Pam's great marriage and raising four outstanding Christian sons just begged to be told. As the C.F.O. for Search Ministries, I also saw firsthand how Jon and Pam passionately trusted God as they raised financial support for their ministry and navigated the demands of the college years for their four sons. *Spiritual Seeds* should be a template for men seeking to raise their own children toward their unique gifting, successful adulthood, and spiritual maturity."

Gary Long, CPA
Search Ministries National Office
Baltimore, Maryland

"Becoming new parents this year has raised a lot of questions about what healthy family relationships look like. How hands-on is too hands-on as we help our daughter develop her world view? *Spiritual Seeds* skillfully highlights the joys and pitfalls of actively exploring these questions as a family, while maintaining the dignity and integrity of both parents and children. It's a must-read for parents who want a deep connection with their children throughout their lives."

Kurt and Stephanie Williams
New parents seeking to be intentional
Snohomish, Washington

TABLE OF CONTENTS

Introduction:
With God, We Can Grow a Socially
and Spiritually Wealthy House—If We A.S.K.   xvii

Part I: *Audaciously* ASK God to Enrich Your Soul Soil   1

Chapter 1:
DIRT IS MISPLACED SOIL: Parents Are Evil   5

Chapter 2:
RICH SOIL: Good God! Can It Be True?   11

Chapter 3:
ENRICHING SOUL SOIL: Why Don't We Ask?   17

Chapter 4:
SOUL SOIL ESSENTIALS: Ask for Everything   23

Chapter 5:
ENVISION FRUIT IN A SINGLE SEED:
Are Our Thoughts and Asks Large Enough?   31

Chapter 6:
SOUL SOIL TEST: How Our Past Affects Our Future   33

Chapter 7:
SOUL SOIL ANALYSIS: God Knows What We Really Want   37

Chapter 8:
GROWING PARTNERS:
God Enriches Our Dirt to Create Social and Spiritual Wealth 41

Chapter 9:
GROWER'S DIVISION OF LABOR: GOD'S PART; OUR PART:
Let's Quit Trying to Do God's Part   45

Chapter 10:
POINT THE PLOW: While We Do Our Part, Let's Put First Things First   49

Chapter 11:
CROSS-POLLINATION: Moving From Man-Father to God the Father   57

Chapter 12:
DISEASE RESISTANCE: Biblical Parenting Models Are Bi-Polar   67

Chapter 13:
ADD MANURE: Parents D-Constructed   75

Chapter 14:
GARDENS ARE FOR EATING: God's Good Gift of a Lover and Life-Mate   83

Chapter 15:
SOW BIG, REAP BIG; SOW LITTLE, REAP LITTLE:
God Is a Giver and the Maker of Givers   93

Part II: *Surgically* SEEK to Cultivate the Gift of Each Seed   101

Chapter 16:
GERMS-IN-MY-NATION:
Why Do We Make Small Things into Tall Things?   105

Chapter 17:
GERMINATION:
God Seeks Valuable Small Ones, Making Them Tall Ones   115

Chapter 18:
SEED GIFTS: Children Are a Gift from the LORD   121

Chapter 19:
GIFTED SEEDS: Children Have God-Given Special "Bents"   129

Chapter 20:
CULTIVATION IS A PROCESS: Patience for Free Agents   137

Chapter 21:
PRODUCE HARVEST:
Relaxed Vigilance—It's Between the Child and God   145

Chapter 22:
SPROUTING SEEDLINGS: Handle Parental Power with Care   153

Chapter 23:
WATERING: Eight Ways Parents Show Love   157

Chapter 24:
WEEDING:
How to Discern a Religiously-Confused Home
from a Christ-Centered Home   169

Chapter 25:
BALANCED NUTRIENTS: Teaching Children the Path of Life   177

Chapter 26:
FEEDING: Six Imperatives for Teaching Children   185

Chapter 27:
CROP BUSTERS AND DUSTERS:
Bring in "Air Support" and Cover Much Ground   197

Chapter 28:
CROP DISASTERS AND INSURANCE: Let's Get Praying   203

Part III: *Nobly* KNOCK on Doors of Opportunity & Share the Wealth 207

Appendix A:
SEED FOR FUTURE PLANTING I: Template for Parenting Target Letter 211

Appendix B:
SEED FOR FUTURE PLANTING II: Jon's Man-Ceremony Letter   217

Appendix C:
CROP YIELD I: Sean's College Paper, "Men of Virtue"   221

Appendix D:
CROP YIELD II: Jonny's letter to Sean, delivering him to college   225

Appendix E:
CROP YIELD III: Jason's "Case for Marrying Jenna" Letter
(written to her parents, Bob and Pam Harmon)   229

Appendix F:
CROP INSPECTION:
Bryant's analysis of this book and key applications (an epilogue)   235

Introduction:

With God, We Can Grow a Socially and Spiritually Wealthy House—If We A.S.K.

God has called us to populate the Earth. And, since the Earth has more than 7 billion people living on it, I would say that we are doing a pretty good job keeping that mandate. We also are called to teach our children well, but what qualifies us for the staggering responsibility of shaping these little lives? And, toward what end do we shape them? We know intuitively that there is shaping, but how much do we mettle? We have power and they need us, but what can be deemed an appropriate use of that power with these emerging free-will agents?

These are profound questions that require answers. After all, to do a good job, we need a plan, a well-thought out strategy to offer provision, protection and preparation for hopefully a really good life, whatever that is. These precious little ones are our life, an extension of us. It would be difficult to find parents who didn't want their child to have a better, more fulfilled, prosperous, and influential life than they themselves are having. No matter what kind of parent you are—whether a Darwinist, who believes in survival of the fittest and creating your own meaning since there is none ultimately, or a Creationist, who believes that each life has inherent value and is specially designed for something larger than this life, or somewhere in between—we are propelled toward staying alive and flourishing.

Dynamic Tension: The Over-Involved/Under-Involved Parent

As parents, we have an enduring sense of the power we wield over our kids. But there is a crazy-maker ingredient here: I want free will for myself and to determine my own destiny, but I also have some power to influence others. That influence can turn into ugly control and manipulation. Creepy, but some of us are really into it as a lifestyle. Others of us respect free will so much we back way off and appear indifferent or aloof, perhaps even irresponsible. Of course parents love their children; they would do anything for them. But is love controlling or passive? What does it mean to be a loving parent, especially when you have power over little lives? In many homes, there tends to be one parent on each pole of the controlling-passivity continuum. Occasionally, both will share the same pole, but opposites tend to attract. Children need protection and guidance, but where does parental influence cross the line by being over-involved or under-involved? To complicate matters, what happens when you sprinkle in the "God" question and how much you should influence your children's thinking here?

What Do You Believe?

Celebrating a friend's birthday, I met and was getting acquainted with a woman. I learned she is an attorney and had heard someone refer to me as "the Rev" in another context, so she assumed I must be a pastor of a church and asked which one. I told her I have pastored churches, but that I didn't think of myself as a "church guy." Even still, I was curious about her beliefs, so I asked, "What do you believe?" I thought I sensed her voice getting a little constricted, which I found curious, but since she was answering my question I dismissed her potential discomfort. She described that she and her husband had taken religion courses in college and decided they would raise their children in a manner that exposed them to all of the (main) religions and let them choose. I appreciated their fair-minded and objective approach with their children, but as I listened I realized that I still had no idea what she and her husband believed.

Many have not figured out where they are with God, so can't begin to guide someone else in it. Others have figured it all out and the rest of us damn well better listen to them, or else. Well-meaning people carry these views and everything in between into parenting. We are suspicious and condescending toward the extremes we see in others. Sometimes, God-people are controlling and use God to attempt to control other people—especially their children. Others are passive about God and don't offer to the child anything with grip. Aren't there certain things that we undoubtedly should share with them as they develop their own free will and grow into adults? Whatever your view of God is (atheist, agnostic, deist, Christian theist, etc.), let me invite you to take a glimpse at what God's involvement could look like. Our story describes a home bent on making intentional deposits in much-loved children that respects their free will.

Mingling Free Agents: Respecting Choices (of Parents, God and Children)

Let's face it. Ultimately we will do life with or without God. I opted toward the "with God" camp in 1978 and have stayed there. I'm more there than ever. I have many reasons for going with God: philosophical, scientific, moral, theological, historical, logical and experiential. My story is loaded with it. It all started when I came to grips with this fact: Being personal, God has intellect, emotions and free will; He does what He wants. Therefore, I can't control God. So isn't it to my advantage to know Him and what He wants? For example, it is to my advantage to know He is all-powerful and all-good, but honors human free will—that's why evil runs amok. He could (and will) do something about ridding the world of all evil, but if He did and, say, He did it at midnight, who would be left standing at 12:01? I'm glad He is patiently working the problem with his free-agent creation. God is very skillful at working with free agents run amok. This book is about how God influences (wins) our hearts and how we can adopt His perspective and practices. We learn a lot about who God is simply by being parents. It's a tricky business loving free agents, especially when they can sign with any team willing to offer them more of all they really want.

Clarifying the Division of Labor in Parenting: God's Part, the Parent's Part, the Child's Part

Attempting to answer these questions is what makes this book worth the effort for both authors and readers. Most of us have been in work settings or organizations where roles are confused, if not by job description, by action/inaction. People fight over turf (control) or abdicate responsibility (passive/not responsible). It's frustrating spending so much energy in dysfunctional "push-me-pull-you" behaviors.

When roles and responsibilities are clear, it's so refreshingly freeing! One of my most life-liberating experiences came in the midst of one of the darkest periods of my work experience, in a church. I was deeply concerned about a decision being made in the church. Not just the decision itself, but how the decision was made, not to mention the corresponding implications of the decision. I carried the "minority report" and found myself in a place where I couldn't go forward. And, of course, we couldn't go back. I had some pointed and clarifying conversations with parties involved, but found myself stuck in a world of no satisfying options. I could have moved ahead for myself, but felt responsible for the church. Several months of "being stuck" passed before I would have a conversation with a leader in the church. He heard my version of the story and offered these wise words: "Jon, it is not your responsibility to save the church." Instantly, I found I had been released from the burden of over-responsibility. I'm not sure anyone else would have carried the same weight in helping me sort that out. I read my resignation letter the following Sunday. This released me to be and do what I am eminently made for (my current role as an Area Director with Search) instead of trying to control something that was never mine to control.

The Division of Labor: Solomon and Jesus

The controlling and guiding ideas for this work come from two sources: Solomon and Jesus. At one time, Solomon was called the wisest man in the world. Aside from working with a few of his 3,000 proverbs, we will fillet and chew on one of his 1005 songs—Psalm 127. It's only five verses, but the imagery and message are loaded. I have pondered it for years and it is even at the heart of a letter we wrote to our sons when they were little toots, and it was still applicable the day we released them as men to create an impact in the world. In it, we describe and define the division of labor, especially discerning God's part and our part as parents. The wisdom in this literature provides transcendent perspective and is worth exploring, especially in three phrases most everyone has heard:

"Unless the LORD builds the house, they labor in vain who build it…"

Implied is that there is a house to be built. People build it. The LORD builds it. They must be co-laborers. This is the observation of the smartest and richest man in the world at that time. It makes sense that we should hear him out on the matter. The phrase "labor in vain" is used three times in two verses. It's possible we could work really hard as homebuilders, guardians/watchmen and provider/givers, but it could be for nothing! In three ways God has our back: Builder,

Watchman and Giver. The psalmist implies we are God's partners in building, watching and giving. But in all three roles, the human partner is **RELIANT** on the LORD.

"Children are a gift (heritage) of the LORD; the fruit of the womb is a reward."

In the heart of this five-verse Psalm is this nugget. Children are a gift (heritage, an ongoing gift), but a gift is something someone receives, the generosity of another who expresses value to the recipient. They receive something of value they did not pay for or earn. The LORD is the giver of the gift. Then why does Solomon go on to say the children are a reward? That sounds like something earned or merited. Likely he didn't intend this as an either/or (gift or reward), but a both/and (a gift from the start, but as it matures into "fruit" it becomes a reward). A parent doesn't merit the gift of children, but they sure work their brains out raising them. If I receive a flower or plant at the shoot stage, I plant it for proper sun exposure, and tend it with water, fertilizer, weeding, frost cover, etc. It will mature and bear fruit short of plant catastrophe: hail, drought, flood, farmer neglect. The "fruit" of the womb is the reward. He is likely speaking of the front and back side of parenting. Receive the gift; enjoy the mature outcome because of your labor.

Such enjoyment comes because we have opened the gift (each child) and we **RESEARCH** the nature of their giftedness to encourage them to be true to their God-given bent and calling.

"Like arrows on the hand of a warrior are the children of ones' youth..."

No pun intended, but what is the point of an arrow? To be released. Whether defending and battling in warfare or hunting for welfare, the arrow is created and crafted to be released to impact the intended target effectually. The warrior must **RELEASE** the arrow.

Corresponding to these three observations in Psalm 127 are three ongoing imperatives found in Matthew 7:7-11, words of Jesus in His famous Sermon on the Mount:

ASK: The action word for the person **RELIANT** on the LORD'S resources. We must remember that God can give one of three answers—yes, no or maybe.

SEEK: The action word for the person doing **RESEARCH** on the child-gift, understanding their giftedness.

(K)NOCK: The action word for the person preparing to **RELEASE** the arrow (child) to its intended target. It's the knocking that opens doors of opportunity. The play on the word knock/nock has to do with the fact that an archer, to steady an arrow on his bow, lands the arrow on an easy-glide notch, called a nock.

At first glance, one might not associate these present-tense, imperative verbs with parenting in particular, though broadly they could apply to everything. The context, however, is marinated in parent/child imagery, with the point to raise our view of how great a Father (and parent) God is.

Jesus presents an argument of "how much more" a life with God would be.

> "If you then, being evil, know how to give good gifts to your children, how much more will your Father who is in heaven give what is good to those who ask Him!" (Matthew 7:11)

If that's not convincing, the verses between ask, seek and knock (7:7-8) and their promised results give illustrations of those things essential for living that a child might ask a parent for, such as a loaf of bread or a fish. An imperfect parent doesn't answer such a request with giving the child a stone or snake! So why would you (parents) think God would do any less for you?! In fact, doesn't it make sense that we should assume that God, who has no corruption, would give exceedingly greater gifts?

You see where this is going. The only genius in the Strain family story is that we learned to ASK a lot in the early days, even before marriage and children. For me, there was a lot of rubble that needed to be worked through. In 1978, I made a huge pivot toward reliance on God and was naïve enough to believe He could and would build all my rubble into a beautiful house that not only would honor Him, but also would later win the attention of our four sons. This was a big deal for a young man who, because of a toppled house, learned fierce self-reliance and independence (big rubble).

Another piece of my rubble was that my childhood family managed in survival mode, and because of it, I fell through the cracks in terms of self-understanding. I did not have a sense of my gifts, strengths and contributions. Whatever my gifts were, they were not recognized or developed. I felt profoundly lost and had to wrap my life in false and pseudo-identities that appeared attractive or noble, but were not authentically me.

Soon after understanding the One whom I would ultimately rely on, I began to discover my value in Him, His gifts toward me and gifts imbedded in me that I could share with the world. This was the season of SEEK. It took years of seeking the truth of this to piece it together, researching how I was fearfully and wonderfully made and putting those gifts to work. Tools, experiences and feedback were invaluable. What once was confused identity "rubble" became a foundation stone in our family culture as we sought to un-wrap the gifts God had sent us, worked to understand them and then trained them up according to their bent.

Floundering into manhood, I was fortunate that God brought mentors into my life on critical fronts. I was KNOCKING on doors and God opened them, getting me where I was supposed to be. Each step has been a stepping-stone on what was "rubble" of aimlessness. There was no rite of passage, but with very resourceful people I was "heavenly Fathered" through His timely mentors. I figured a few things out just in time to set the table for a clear release of my sons into manhood. It felt awkward because it was unknown territory, but I knew it was right.

All of this led me to understand and believe that these three parts, ASKING, SEEKING, KNOCKING, were the foundation for readying my children to impact the world. In Part I, we will discover why parenting is learning reliance (daring to ASK of God). In Part II, we will see why parenting requires us to engage in research as we SEEK to understand the gifts of God toward us and our children.

Finally, in Part III, we uncover why the gift of parenting is to release our children so that they might KNOCK on doors of opportunity.

Parenting can be done with or without God. Clearly, we cannot imagine trying to do it without Him. Having reached the empty-nest stage, Pam and I have a great sense of satisfaction about accomplishing our role. God sure did His, but only because we asked.

Charlie Rose, American television talk show host and journalist, interviewed Jim Collins, the author of *Good to Great*. Collins said, "Every organization must ask itself this question, 'What are the brutal facts about our mission?'"

I couldn't agree more. There are many brutal facts on the parenting front.

In the following chapters, we will address one of the several brutal facts—both positive and negative—about our parenting mission. The negative is rubble—a picture of brokenness. The positive is mortar—a picture of what we can do to rebuild the rubble into a big, beautiful house surrounded by retaining walls.

PART I:

Audaciously ASK God to Enrich Your Soul Soil

Audacious = bold; daring; eager.

The tall Texas cowboy walked off the plane in front of Skip Hall, a 30-year college football coach. Skip had logged many travel miles, seeing many things over the years. Yet, arriving in Dallas, he found the cowboy first noteworthy, but, then, surprising. Noteworthy perhaps because the cowboy fit the stereotype: bow-legged, with the hat, the boots, the tight blue jeans (probably Wrangler), and a leather belt with a very large buckle. *A true Texas cowboy*, Skip thought to himself. They disembarked from the plane and entered the passenger boarding area. Skip observed the cowboy noticing something. Who wouldn't? It was a woman of uncommon beauty seated alone, apparently waiting for someone. Then came the surprise.

The cowboy, no match for this eye-grabbing beauty, took the shortest path to her. He removed his hat, placed it over his heart and asked her, "Ma'aaam, are you awaitin' fer me?"

Startled, she looked at the cowboy and matter-of-factly replied, "No. I'm not!"

With balled fists, bristled arms and wincing facial muscles the cowboy disappointedly said, "DAAAMN!!" Placing the hat back on his head he walked away.

The lesson: *You gotta ask!* How would he ever know unless he asked? He had one chance and nothing to lose. Sure he was audacious. This woman was out of his league. The application Skip had in mind for me related to fundraising for Search Boise. "Jon, *you gotta ask!*" Sure, the answer many people may give to a fundraising appeal will be *no*. But, if you don't ask you erase the opportunity of ever knowing! You've made the decision for them.

Audaciously, like the cowboy, I asked 100 people that year. And I was glad I did. It's been good for Search Boise, for us, and for our new donors. I would bet a cowboy's belt buckle that the big Texan was glad he asked, too. For no ask is a sure, "No."

"*Ask and it shall be given to you….*" Jesus said to His first century followers. If He intended to say *no*, He clearly wouldn't have invited us to keep asking.

I was naïve (even presumptuous) enough then to take Jesus at His word simply because He invited me (and you) to do so. I did then and still do. It's made all the difference on so many significant fronts. I invite you to be as audacious in your asking as I have learned to become. There have been "nos" and many "waits" for answers. Once in a while I realize that I'm not asking for the right thing and quit that request or adjust it. But I've learned to ask, ask big and ask often. I bet you will too after you're done reading this section and see things as I've come to see them. I've eagerly asked that you will.

It's important you understand why Part One—*Ask*—precedes Part Two—*Seek*—in the matter of cultivating wealth in a child. Part Two contains the nut and bolts, the perspectives and practices you hoped to glean from this book. But before we explore cultivating spiritual and social wealth in our children, we must make sure we have wealth to give. Part One is about our soul soil enrichment, which is essential to cultivating life in our children. Before we can be a wealth-giving parent, we must possess the wealth. We will not impart what we do not possess. Our premise is that God makes us wealthy by parenting us, the parents to be. In many ways, God "re-parents" us. God enriches our soul soil deficits. We are proposing that without Part One, Part Two will not have the resources to yield outcomes we long for, as illustrated in Part Three. Sometimes we don't even know what we are lacking... but someone does.

3

CHAPTER 1

Dirt Is Misplaced Soil:
Parents are Evil

"If you then, being evil, know how to give good gifts to your children,
how much more will your Father who is in heaven
give what is good to those who ask Him!"

—Jesus, Matthew 7:11

Shocking! Sweet, kind Jesus, friend of sinners, Messiah, Prince of Peace and champion (on some level) in most major religions seems to be saying that parents are evil. The nature of the statement reveals Jesus to be matter-of-fact, blunt and provocative. Though I've read it many times, it was like I read it for the first time. Heck, I even translated the famous Sermon on the Mount (Matthew 5-7) from Greek to English for my Reading Greek class project in graduate school. It appears Jesus is saying, "Parents are evil." What do you think? Read it again for yourself.

> *"If you then, being evil, know how to give good gifts to your children, how much more will your Father who is in heaven give what is good to those who ask Him!"*—Jesus, Matthew 7:11

Is He speaking to parents? It appears by the broad-stroke comment that at least the majority of His audience has children. Before I get too offended and dismiss Jesus or English translators reading Jesus in this way, I also observe that these parents, paradoxically, know how to give good gifts to their children. If they are

5

"evil," why would they "give good gifts?" Can parents be both evil and good gift-givers all at once? It seems Jesus is saying this as well.

Shouldn't we reserve the "evil" word for Hitler, serial killers, and antagonists of Austin Powers (ref. Dr. Evil)? Let's not confuse terms. Before I seek to define evil and provide further evidence that this is not a misread, let me suggest what I think the real trouble is. I want children, but I have profound pockets of darkness at work in me, the parent. That makes me uncomfortable. But it's even more troubling that others are that way. I don't like other people's dirt and stink. Yet, I'm entitled to be a parent and guess, to be fair, that I must allow others to be a parent as well. It's not like we have to have a degree in this. Just sex. That's what qualifies us to become the headwaters of our own peep-dynasty. The darkness in my heart does not disqualify.

And if it's true for me, then it's true for a serial killer. Where do we draw the line here on darkness?

Showtime produced an eight-season series called *Dexter*. I'm not recommending it, but simply using it as a convenient illustration because it reveals an interesting dilemma. How much darkness can we tolerate, especially when it comes to raising children? We all have it to some measure. . . we're not perfect, right? The main character, Dexter, is a blood spatter specialist, working on the forensics team for Miami homicide. He's very likeable, but quirky. He's got strange habits, but is really a gentle and intelligent soul and very effective at his job. By night, he's a serial killer, but with a code. He doesn't kill anyone, but only other serial-killer types who are beating the legal system or unreformed when they get out of prison. His is a vigilante system that saves lives. As long as he doesn't get caught and works to protect lives by cleaning up this kind of vermin from the streets, he is a valuable contributor to society. Furthermore, it's a way for him to channel what he calls his "dark passenger."

Before you condemn Dexter, you must realize that he is childhood victim, first watching someone kill his mother with a chainsaw, and then sitting in her blood and darkness for a couple days before a policeman finds him. Parentless, he is adopted by this police officer who identifies Dexter's dark passenger—a lust to kill—early on, and trains Dexter to channel it toward good, obeying a code. Dexter has morals and consistently keeps them. He is an efficient and moral serial killer making the most of his broken life. Hey, who are we to judge? We too, the viewers, have darkness, some coming out of our own mysterious inner place we seemingly cannot control, heightened by our broken backgrounds. We too sit in the blood and broken rubble of our family history.

My friend, Jim Cardillo, provided this spontaneous and apt quip one day. Dripping with his northeastern United States Italian sarcasm, he offered, *"We have our childhood, then we spend the rest of our lives trying to get over it."* Nailed it.

Getting in Touch with Our Dirt Bag

Former governor of Illinois (2003-2009), Rod Blagojevich, provided a frightening illustration of how many of us deal with our darkness—we spin it and pretend it doesn't exist. "Blago" was caught red-handed and, throughout his court case, repeatedly offered to the public explanations and justifications for his actions and motives. Every proclamation was perceived ridiculous. That is, to everyone except Blago.

Satirist Dennis Miller captured the governor's effort to cover his dark deeds with this statement: *"I don't think Rod is in touch with his inner dirt bag."*

Everyone has darkness and most of us work to deal with it. But it's the Blago bluff that scares us. The stuff we refuse to acknowledge. I'm actually refreshed by people who admit their creepiness, faults, fetishes and crap. It tells me they are grounded in reality—in touch with their inner dirt bag. The scary ones are those pretending nothing is wrong, wearing masks (especially religious ones!) that define hypocrisy. These are the guys who irked Jesus the most. He excoriated them, calling them snakes, white-washed tombs, blind guides, etc. (Matthew 23)

Should Dexter Have Children?

In the Showtime series, he did. He wasn't trying to, but, like I said earlier, the one qualification for being a biological parent is simply to have sex. He didn't want children because he knew they would complicate his night activities. And he wasn't sure that he wouldn't pass on his "dark passenger" to his child, let alone blow up his family if he was exposed. Eventually, he was persuaded to marry, have the child and adopt two step-children. The writers craftily bring the viewers to the realization that they are not that different from Dexter. Like him, they have desire to extend life through their loins, regardless of the discomfort they feel with their darkness and dark passengers. Like Dexter, the viewer is justifying oneself by the fact that they have a code and are not at all like those other serial killers out there. As the series goes on, Dexter selectively reveals for certain what he really is, but that rarely goes well. He so wants to be understood in context, but who can deal with "the monster"?

Samuel Johnson said, *"Every man knows that of himself which he dare not tell his dearest friend."*

What I'm saying is this: We know, and Jesus knows, these three things:

1. We all have darkness. Jesus calls it evil. Dennis Miller calls it a dirt bag. Dexter calls it the monster or dark passenger. We don't want others to see us for what we are inside-out because they wouldn't approve. Few of us are as bad as we can be, nor as Dennis Rodman's book title suggests, *"Bad as I Wanna Be."*

2. Yet, we still have children. We believe we can give them a good or better life than we had. We want to give them good gifts.

3. Jesus knows this about us. He's just honest about our nature. He says parents are evil.

What Is Evil?

Philosophically, evil is not a thing. It's the absence of something, a privation or deprivation. It is goodness and health in a diminished form. It's a corruption, rust, decay, deterioration or deficiency. We often put the prefixes "un" or "dis" in front of words to describe evil. *Disease, disinterested, unhealthy, unfulfilled,* etc.

Theologically, it's the absence of God's good in His created ones or creation. In Mark 7:18-23 (NASB), Jesus used two different Greek words that are translated "evil" or "bad" in English translations. In the New American Standard Bible, they are both translated *evil* in this passage. *Kakos* describes the quality of evil according to its nature—that is, it is inherently evil but not always outwardly expressed. *Poneros* is deliberate acting out in defiance to a moral law for selfish gain. Simply stated, poneros is the acting out of kakos. What is Jesus saying in the text? Is our corruption inside-out, or outside-in? The religious leaders accused the disciples of Jesus with having impure hands because they didn't wash them ceremonially before eating bread. He answered them, but now restates His teaching to the disciples with even more clarification for they are still swelling from the sting of the accusation.

"And He said to them, 'Are you so lacking in understanding also? Do you not understand that whatever goes into the man from the outside cannot defile him; because it does not go into his heart, but into his stomach and is eliminated?' And he was saying, 'That which proceeds out of the man, that is what defiles the man. For from within, out of the heart of men, proceed the *evil* (*kakos*—inherent evil) thoughts, fornications, thefts, murders, adulteries, deeds of coveting and wickedness, as well as deceit, sensuality, envy, slander, pride and foolishness. All these *evil* (*poneros*—breaks with the moral law for selfish gain) things proceed from within and defile the man.'"

Is Our Darkness More Due to Nature or Nurture?

Now, let's consider our application. There is no question that the home environment we were "nurtured" in has been hard on many of us. For most, it was a mixed bag. That was my story. With my parents trying to survive, I dropped through the cracks unnoticed on the "development" front (school, skills, etc.). My response was to go inward—into my corrupted nature for protection. Sadly, not upward—to God. More of this story will follow in chapters to follow. No one coached me to go inward; it came naturally. My mom was a regular church attender but it was not making a difference for the better in our life situation—at least that I could see.

My friend and Leadership Advisors business consultant, Phil Eastman, often says, "People are smart." I agree. People, including our children, see and sense more than we think.

Pam and I were preparing to teach a class on the spiritual formation of children, helping parents help their children take the next step toward finding God. The fallout rate for parents succeeding in persuading their children to embrace their faith is staggering. While there could be several factors, one is well documented: Hypocritical parents who say one thing and do another. We were standing in the lobby of a church to promote our class that we'd entitled, *I Can Do That, With My*

Children. An older gentleman walked up, sized up the class literature, looked me in the eye and said two words…

"*They know.*"

I knew exactly what he meant. Children know. Children are smart. They know if we are for real or when we are just talking. They know what our real loyalties are, even though we delude ourselves by saying something like, "God is first in my life." They know when we say their participation in a sport is for their development, but it's really for our image promotion through their (hopefully) successful play.

"They know."

They know before we do that we are not in touch with our inner dirt bag.

"They know" are two haunting words because of our darkness.

Like Jesus, they know parents are evil.

CHAPTER 2

Rich Soil:

Good God! Can It Be True?

"If you then, being evil, know how to give good gifts to your children,
how much more will your Father who is in heaven
give what is good *to those who ask Him!"*

—JESUS, MATTHEW 7:11

Suspended. What I felt when my sister mentioned to me my mom's observation of our family Christmas. Amazingly, it was the first time she spent Christmas in our home. There are many circumstantial reasons, but our sons being young adults and she in her eighties—well, it seems crazy that it hadn't ever happened until Christmas 2012. And that makes her debriefing comment to my sister even more suspending to me.

"Their Christmas is very different than what we did when you were kids." She was struck with how demonstrative the gift-giving culture was, especially between the boys. I love how we have spent our Christmas over the years, traditions and all, but I have to admit I've always felt a haunting detachment from the gift-opening part. Mom's comment provided a timely segue in to comprehending why.

What she observed—and this has gone on their entire lives—is a play-by-play, gift-by-gift celebration. It takes us forever to get through the gifts. It seems that after every gift, the opener will say, "Oh, this is awesome! It's exactly what I wanted...even better because_____ (they will fill in a detailed description).

Then the euphoric receiver will jump up, run across the room and lay a huge bear hug on the giver who scored a bulls-eye.

My sons inherited their Mom's gift for gift-giving. Like her, they spend months saving money, doing reconnaissance through the mutual sharing of gift ideas, then frugally chasing down just the right thing for each person. They are generous and dead-on. Everyone seems to find just the right gift. Then there's Dad. God help Dad; he's a little slow. I'm gift-giving challenged; a gift-dork, if you will. I seem to whiff annually and badly. They mock me for some of the stupid things I've wrapped up, such as the orange vest for my wife. (I get reminded of it every year.) I can still see the perplexed (even wounded and disbelieving) look on Pam's face (and their faces) when she opened it. There is no more sinking feeling. She wanted the WHITE vest, dork! Four young men look at me with searching eyes that ask, *What is your problem?* Talk about your stock falling ninety points in a matter of seconds. It's as if there is some secret knowledge they are all privy to and I'm locked out. To be balanced, I've done very well with giving my wife clothing gifts some years, but only when I begged a female store attendant for help. If I have the right sizes and categories, it usually works out. And, when it comes to the boys, I've always been the agreeable one to Pam's brilliant research and diligent retrieving. She makes me look good. I justify myself thinking that I earned the paycheck to enable the gift, but that's never celebrated that magic morning.

Like the guy said, *"They know."* Further shame sticks to me like salty sweat after a hot run in the foothills when I don't even make the grade of the evil parent. Those, Jesus said, ". . . know how to give good gifts to [their] children."

This is the gift-giving culture of my wife and four young adult sons that my mom observed. What was "different" about it is what left me suspended and explained the haunting feeling I've experienced over the years watching the perfect-gift-frenzy in my home.

To illustrate the suspension further, I came to possess some family pictures from my youth, including Christmas pictures. They provoked some emotion that will help me illustrate my larger point.

The early pictures, up to age 6, were warm and lively. Our entire family was there—Dad, Mom and seven children. Extended family, particularly grandparents on both sides, were there. Everyone was there. The tree was loaded, but moreover, I got exactly what I longed for, which at that time was Johnny West and his horse, Thunderbolt, and a zillion little accessories. A cowboy version of GI Joe was too good to be true. All of us idolized my dad, a cattle rancher and racehorse trainer. In a way, it was like I got to play with a miniature version of my dad and his horses. My active imagination could play out all kinds of scenarios.

We moved from Lewistown, Montana, to Hamilton, Montana, to get out of the cattle business and into a milder climate that would extend my dad's training season. Life turned chaotic and upside-down. The Christmas pictures from those years reminded me of the barrenness we experienced during that time. Missing from the pictures were Dad, grandparents and eventually older siblings as they started to leave for college. My dad was gone with the horses, racing back East or down South. In the summer months, he established a routine that included caring for a large stable of horses, when he trained and tested horses throughout the Montana racing circuit. Choosing the performers, he trimmed the travel team to a few. He would be gone all winter, leaving my Mom alone to raise seven children on a small forty-acre ranch. Resources were meager. The tree was sparse, and gifts were largely practical and often felt to be in the "need," not "want" category. This is no dig on my Mom; she was a master at making a lot out of a little, especially with food. She basically functioned like a single-parent mom for three to four years until she finally had had enough. I just missed my Dad. I was at an age when a son needed his father. During that time he would make monthly calls to talk to each child for a couple minutes. I recall being interrupted by the operator and listening to him pump coins into the payphone, which made it abundantly clear to me that time with him was precious…and costly. He tried to stay home one winter, but there just wasn't any work in the Bitterroot Valley. It certainly wasn't what he was passionate about and everyone knew it. As a couple and a family, my parents were simply trying to survive. During these years, I felt myself slipping through the cracks. We had a roof, meals, loving discipline and were sent to school, but there was a profound undercurrent of loss.

The divorce happened around the time I was nine to ten years old. The family frayed turned into the family torn. No one processed what was going on in our hearts. We retreated into our private rubble. The proud building and walls of protection were leveled. The new arrangement, while not that different since we still only saw my Dad in the summers, was worse than a death. At that time, my heart turned hard and dark. My own self-talk proved to be worse than my acting out or even the trouble I got into with the law and at school. I continually told myself, *"Everyone you care about will go away or be taken away. You can only count on you."* I became fiercely independent. Shamed by being stuck in my mom's world of church and denied being in my dad's exciting world of competition and toughness, I missed out on life skills. I found a substitute god in becoming fanatically attached to sports, both as a spectator and participant. I sought to excel.

Though it felt dark and broken, in retrospect the rubble would become the building blocks for a greater house. The divorce prompted my mom to move beyond being a nominal church attender to becoming a seeker of God. She discovered new resources for living for a God who loved and valued her for her and not just her religious performance. She began to live *with* God, and respond to the new reality that He was with her and could be called upon. Through her newfound living faith, model and prayers, one by one, several of her children began to discover God.

How *Much More* Does God Give Good Gifts?

Why do we, as parents, allow ourselves to roll through life thinking we are better gift-givers than God? I know I am guilty of this. The Jesus answer is that I am corrupted and catering to my darkness and not His light. (This is another way of explaining the word "evil" Jesus used.) When I catch myself suspended, I simply need to test myself with these questions: *Do I ask God for provision, guidance and intervention in my life needs? Once I ask, do I move ahead as if God will answer me, thus giving Him the chance to reveal His answer and me the opportunity to observe it?* (Even if the answer may be "no" or "wait?") *Do I live diligently and vigilantly in my prayerfulness?*

What this comes down to for me is choosing to live with God or without God. We are continuously invited in Scripture to put God first. Consider the first of the Ten Commandments: "I am the LORD your God. You shall have no other gods before Me." (Exodus 20) Consider the greatest of the commandments according to Jesus, "You shall love the LORD your God with all your heart, soul, strength and might." (Matthew 22) C.S. Lewis said, "Put first things first and you get second things thrown in. Put second things first and you lose both first and second things." There are only two choices:

Choice #1: With or without Him?

Choice #2: If with Him, where on the list does he fall? First, or somewhere much farther down?

Lewis's statement implies that the gift of God's presence dwarfs the gift of His presents. We know and experience His presents (blessings) through knowing God's presence. My mom and many of her children would come to discover many gifts of God, stemming from the fact that we can live life with Him and that He is with us! His gifts are all "on tap" for the asking. Here's some on my list, one that is foundational to how I want to roll, especially while I am parenting:

1. I am granted the gift of unconditional love and am highly valued as a special, created person. (Psalm 139)

2. I enjoy forgiveness, eternal life, leadership and wisdom for living. (1 Kings 3 & 4)

3. I am surrounded by mentors, coaches, disciple-makers and a spiritual family. (Matthew 28:18-20; 2 Timothy 2:2; 1 Corinthians 3)

4. I contribute through gifts creational and spiritual, with a kingdom calling and unique addition. (Solomon)

5. I am satisfied with a marriage partner, or singleness. (Psalm 37:4… Rebekah to Isaac)

6. I experience the gift and reward of children. (Psalm 127)

The Rule of the Kingdom of God Is ASK!

The gift-giving culture of our family Christmas is not an accident. It is intentional. It is intentional because God is a giver and we live life *with* God. It's not about the volume or quality of presents. It is about the people living in His presence—together! Our sons receive requested gifts (within reason) because they ASK! Because they are our sons, they already receive many gifts: love, shelter, food, clothing, guidance, education, play and recreation, etc. They have learned to ASK and we love to give. Sometimes we withhold for lessons to be learned or better timing. Sometimes we say no because it would be harmful. Most of the time, there is simply no good thing we would withhold from them, especially when they are conducting themselves in wise living. It is a household of liberality, honor and relational presence, not of scarcity, shame and loss. The difference between my childhood and my household is being *with God*.

Preceding Matthew 7:11 are four more verses you likely will recognize. In verses 7-10 Jesus invites us to Ask, Seek and Knock.

These verbs are imperative and present tense. It's a command that we are to live by continuously. Another way to say it is: always keep asking, always keep seeking, and always keep knocking, as each phrase is accompanied by a promise:

Ask...*and it shall be given to you.*

Seek...*and you shall find.*

Knock...*and it shall be opened to you.*

Then Jesus asks two rhetorical questions that illustrate and expose the reason you could, should and would do this. "If your son asks you for a loaf, do you give him a stone? If he asks for a fish, do you give him a snake?" Does that even require an answer? Of course not. We give that which is good. We want to give them what they ask for, unless they are asking for the stone or the snake, which we might refuse, for their good.

The Jon and Pam family story is one of God's honoring presence and provision because we chose to live with Him and ask for provision on all six fronts above. That is the subject of the next brutal fact: We need to ASK. But to ask, we need to be with Him, both for the asking and receiving. This is the continental divide between blessing and breakdown.

CHAPTER 3

Enriching Soul Soil:
Why Don't We Ask?

". . .how much more will your Father
who is in heaven give what is good
to those who ask Him!"

—JESUS, MATTHEW 7:11

God the Father Uses Our Children to Raise Us

As we raise our children, God is using our children by parallel experience to raise us. The "how much more" argument Jesus makes in Matthew 7:11 uses our own goodness toward our children (though we are corrupted, full of our own darkness and therefore evil parents) to make a difficult-to-refute statement about asking.

In the past several years, a handful of friends have sold businesses and profited a gazillion dollars. I've had the inside track in hearing about their experiences with this. While one part of me thinks, *Wouldn't it be nice…?* another part of me observes the burden of wealth that I frankly don't have the bandwidth to handle. One challenging dynamic is the sense of entitlement to that money friends and relatives seem to have, simply because they have access to or "know" the gazillionaire by blood or proximity. People want help with their debts and life hardships, business start-up ideas, investment opportunities, ministry/mission-funding, blah, blah, blah. Sometimes their own children take for granted what they have, not realizing how unusual it is to be in that position, nor understanding what it took to build that wealth, let alone having a sense of what wealth is for.

All these gazillionaires found themselves withdrawing from people. It's hard to say, "No," especially when you have it, they know it, and you certainly *could* meet the request. One said to me, "I felt like I should just put a sign out in front of my office that read, 'The First Bank of [his name].'" He shut off his cell phone and told people the only way to contact him was email. All of them had to put boundaries up and wrestle through their sharing values. Though they had a lot by the standards of most people, that amount was a finite number. All were generous (and "tithing/offering") people well before they ever earned the mother lode.

The difficulty was that the requests came from people who made them feel like human vending machines. Those making the appeals made them feel obligated (and therefore, not cheerful) and didn't take time to ask them what their values and causes were, or even what mattered to them. I happen to know they have all been spontaneously generous, but there is a strong sense of stewardship about the resources they hold.

Most importantly, and this is my core point, most of them want to be ASKED, but in a certain way. It must be personal and clearly connected to what's important to the giver. So the one asking must ask that first. This is also true of foundations, who usually publish what is important to them and give clear procedures on how to ask. Again, they all have priorities and hot buttons, and they all must be asked. Similarly, God wants us ASK Him, too, but He wants us to recognize His desire and His will first.

Why We Don't Ask

Why is it that we ask the wealthy person with his finite resources, yet do not exercise the same reconnaissance and persistence in asking the infinitely wealthy creator God? He is the one who invites us to do so without limit on any front. I've had to think about this a lot because I fundraise for a non-profit ministry. Fundraising is hard because asking is hard, especially for a fiercely independent guy like me who grew up in the intermountain region and who has always leaned toward being frugal, self-sufficient and resourceful.

My stepfather, who prayed before every meal, was also often heard to say, *"Don't bug God with the small things."* My mom would then retort something like, *"They're all small things to God."* So we can thank God for our daily bread, but not ask God for our daily bread? Wouldn't you do both?

Another reason we might not ask is that we know we have a dirt bag and feel unworthy to ask. Let's not forget that Jesus already called us evil, but it's not about our goodness; it's about God's goodness and His desire for us to ask Him. He commands us to continuously ask, seek and knock, because He is a gift-giver.

We are post-moderns and it's normal for our generation to question things. *Did Jesus really say that? Does the Biblical record accurately reflect what Jesus said and the way He said it? Is Jesus really God in the flesh and a legitimate spokesperson for God? If yes, is this meant for us moderns and post-moderns or was it for a more primitive and less-enlightened culture?* I need to be thoughtful in how I answer these questions because the logical answers leave us in one of two places: living with or without God.

For the reader struggling with these kinds of questions, I recommend *I'm Glad You Asked* by Boa and Moody. Many have found their treatment of these kinds of questions (and others) logical, well-illustrated and explanative of how it is more plausible (reasonable) to believe in, trust and live with God than without God.

Ask Small, Ask Big, Ask Often

These words are on my strategic plan. It's something I've been learning the whole time I've been in relationship with God. He has come through big and small, whatever is appropriate to the situation. Ministry funding is still hard to ask for, but I'm practicing the discipline of the daily ask…at least asking for God's provision. Somehow we are still floating 13 years into Search Boise. Search creates opportunities that serve as spiritual conversation catalysts. Such conversations open doors to deeper dialogues addressing the great questions of life. We enable Christ-followers to winsomely share the good news of Jesus Christ. This begins with learning a lifestyle of drawing on the resources of Jesus Christ—otherwise, there is nothing to talk about. So, we pray for open doors and open hearts as a lifestyle.

A few years back, the President of Search, Larry Moody, asked the staff, "Do you pray daily for your funding?" In my head I answered, *Not daily, but regularly.* As if he read my mind, he strongly exhorted us, "You need to pray daily for your funding." He didn't say why daily, but since he was fully funded and I was not, I thought his idea of daily was better than my method of regularly. But did he really need to say why we should pray daily? Jesus already addressed that when the disciples requested that He teach them to pray. Part of that model prayer was, "Give us this day our daily bread." Most of us live so far beyond our daily bread that we are lulled into a self-sufficient slumber about our asking. So, I started to pray daily for our funding, amongst other things, and we've been in the black since, sometimes in ways that defy explanation. God has not answered exactly as I ask...that it come from Boise-area donors in the form of many large residual monthly pledges and one-time gifts. He always provides in ways that I can't take credit for, using outsiders, irregular gifts and unlikely donors to let me know that He is our provider.

People often tell me that they could never do what we do, especially living with the fundraising challenge. It definitely confirms our calling. If God doesn't provide through generous people, we are belly-up. Furthermore, I'm amazed that Pam and I have lived this way nearly our entire adult lives.

Bold or Timid...Just Ask!

One of my sons, Jason, is very bold in asking for what he wants. There were times through the years when he would ask for something and I would have a two-fold reaction. Part of me would think, *Well, why are you so special to be considered for that above the others (sons)?* He wasn't. Then again, just because I, or my other three sons, or most people, might not have presumed to ask for it, *he did!* My mild offense would turn to a smile on my face, because I wanted to give to my son—not just because he was my son, but because he knew he had a special place with me and dared to ask for what he really wanted. I was always amazed that I would so willingly say yes. What a lesson in reverse. If I, being evil, know how to say yes to my son (he's evil with corruption, too), then how much more would my heavenly Father say yes?

The Christmas lists are another striking example of this. Though I'm resistant to make a list, I'm not resistant at all to seeing the very long lists our sons turn in to Mom. Fortunately, there are stars next the really high-priority items. We have a budget, but Pam is brilliant in figuring out how to get the most with that budget for each valued son—and they are never disappointed. Again, "If you (evil parents) know how to give good gifts to your children, how much more…"

"Unless the LORD builds the house they labor in vain who build it… He gives to His much loved ones even in their sleep." (Psalm 127:1a, 2b)

Is it time for you to start asking God to build your household His way?

Ask about everything!

Ask big!

Ask daily!

A father saw his son trying to move a huge boulder from one spot to a desired spot. He was struggling, maneuvering and grunting. His father finally asked him, "Son, are you using all your strength to move that rock?" The exasperated son affirmed that he indeed was using all his power. His father said, "No you're not. You haven't asked me for my help."

What does it look like to be a big-help asker? Parenting is a huge job which no one is qualified for. Thrice in Psalm 127, Solomon used the word "vain" as related to house building. All three times, it is measured "vain," because the LORD isn't included in the workload alongside us.

CHAPTER 4

Soul Soil Essentials:
Ask for Everything

". . .how much more will your Father
who is in heaven give what is good to those who ask Him!"

— Jesus, Matthew 7:11

Overwhelmed! This is the word that comes to mind when I ponder my 35-plus year history doing life *with* God. Gifts, great and small, populate the landscape of my memory. These packages of God's goodness are very tangible and historical. I have lived better than I deserve. Much better. Pam sees our history the same and we would wish these gifts on anyone, especially our own sons. This fuels, informs and guides our parenting of them. The reason is simply this: I asked; a lot!

The big pivot for me came at age eighteen when I turned to God with a whole heart and asked for the house—forgiveness (amazing grace), His presence forever (the gift of eternal life) and His leadership in this life, starting now! Though my early years revealed more of a hard and dark heart bent on doing its own thing, I had enough Bible exposure and life examples to suggest to me that I could ask for these things. Moreover, I firmly believe when my mom's prayer life focused on me, Heaven released its hounds to put me up a tree where God the Father could make me an offer I couldn't refuse. I believed He was good and willing to share His good gifts with me. So I pulled the spiritual trigger in my Palm Desert apartment, June 1978. I bent my will toward God and dared to ask.

For now, it's time to imagine and consider what "asking" looks like in real life, especially real-life parenting. It starts and ends with being "parented" by God. It starts with knees on the ground, and then a race through the day firing "arrow prayers" in the midst of the battle. I started a pivotal habit a few years back—hitting the ground with my knees, right out of bed, before my feet hit the ground. It's a symbolic, but physical, way to ground myself in humble dependence on God for the day. I go to the throne first, but I don't stay long because I'm usually under pressure and need to visit the other white throne. I don't mean to be crude; I'm just a practical man.

Pam's parents, renewed in their spiritual journey with God, started their own knees-on-the-ground approach when their high school daughters started dating. Their spiritual growth happened to coincide with this season. Young men arriving to pick up four pretty teenage daughters will do that to you. They have lamented not doing things earlier in their daughters' lives, but they did the right thing by picking up where they were. They couldn't go back, but this season created spiritual urgency and vigilance they have carried throughout their lives since. And all of us have enjoyed the benefits. To this day, they begin every day in prayer for their concerns and their family, and read a short devotional together over their breakfast. I have admired and envied them for this, as our conflicting schedules don't allow for that approach. So we have found other ways.

Similarly, my mom's spiritual growth hit its stride when my older siblings were in high school. A broken marriage and meager resources produced many needs. She learned to live and move with God and found ways to give us the most important things in this new season: love and care, prayer and timely words.

I suspect that the good gifts we experience now, that we don't deserve, came to us because of parents who dared to ask God for good things as they learned to live life with Him. Out of this foundation, I'd like to share the good gifts I have dared to ask for and can clearly show that I have received. What I'm hoping is you will follow suit and persist in it over your life, asking big, wide and long.

Good Gift #1—Spiritual Rescue and Relationship...*because I asked.*

I know we have covered this, but it's so foundational it must be included as the pivotal basis for all the rest. During my youth, from age 10 to 18, my hardness of heart wouldn't allow me to respond properly to the message of my family's church home. I saw it through the eyes of pain, being stuck in my mom's "church" world when I wanted to be in my dad's world—one of livelihood on the line, competition, excitement and risk. Church for me was underwhelming: the world of children, women, old people and bored men. No thanks. Testosterone flowing through my system, I felt emasculated and my motto was, "I gotta get out of here!!" And I did every chance I could, especially during my high school years. I'd find summer work opportunities somewhere in Montana away from home. I threw myself obsessively into sports during the school year.

After graduation from high school, my "gotta get out of here" script put me on the road to southern California for work. It was in Palm Desert where my spiritual regeneration (birth) occurred, and where I would be transformed, inside-out, by an application of "amazing grace."

Good Gift #2—A Transformed Heart and New Resources for Relationships...*because I asked.*

I discovered afresh the community of Jesus—ironically in the same church denomination I grew up in.

Alone in my Palm Desert studio apartment, I calculated my guilt and need for forgiveness. I calculated my concern about what would happen when I died and the "gift" of eternal life. I calculated my aimlessness in life, though I was enrolled at Idaho State University the next fall. I was exposed to gated community wealth and realized that even in a most desired place to live, people were bitchy, whiny and apparently unfulfilled. I saw this firsthand having a job where I was in and out of their homes all summer.

I didn't know the term then, but I was an existentialist, out trying to create my own identity and meaning. Existentialists run on two tracks. Nihilism (total despair), where the logical thing to do is commit suicide because life is hard and then you die. Or, hedonism ("pleasure is the only good"), which became my drug of choice because it was more optimistic and helped make the best of my broken life. The Schlitz Beer motto sold it to me by the can: "Go for all the gusto, baby, because you only go around once." You've likely heard a similar sentiment in the statement, "Eat, drink and be merry for tomorrow we die." The previous April (1978), a conversation in the Hamilton, Montana Riverview

Cemetery with my non-Christian girlfriend exposed the shallowness of my worldview. She did it with one well-placed question free of malice or religious motivation. After philosophizing about her view of death, she split me wide open by asking this question: "What do you think will happen to you when you die?" Church boy knew the options, but also knew his heart was hard and far from God, medicating in all things "this world." It was like she threw a cup of gasoline on an open flame—EXPLOSION. I answered, "I don't know, and I'm tired of this conversation. Let's get the h_ _ _ out of here." End of conversation. But her question hounded me for the next two months, following me from Hamilton, Montana, to Palm Desert, California.

One June afternoon, I traded my guilt, fear of death and aimless life of existential drivel for a life invested in God. In His world, I was objectively valuable, having been created in His image, worth dying for to pay off a large load of spiritual/moral debt, and full of potential to live a full and meaningful life. I had it on the good word of Jesus, the most credible person who walked planet Earth. For around two broken and prayerful hours, I made a great exchange: my dark, pitiful, stupid life for His infinitely creative, loving and valuable life. No evangelist or organ music, just me and the Holy Trinity. I knew John 3:16 and it was enough to debt-dump and say to God, "I'm your guy now; do with me what You want."

I had no idea what I had just asked for, but I was at peace with God and myself. God and I carried on a continuous dialogue. I felt forgiven, knew I had eternal life and sensed God's guiding presence and provision. We began to talk about everything. I had a voracious appetite to hear His voice, especially in the Bible. I spent a lot of time in the Psalms, which I later realized mentored me into a rich, emotional relationship with God as well as expanding my view of who He was. Debts forgiven, I began to sense forgiveness and empathy toward others that transcended me. I became open to others and their counsel like never before. I met a wide variety of other youth who had a similar experience with God, ironically in the same church denomination where I had been so underwhelmed. I observed that there were a lot of people in church, like me, who were living without God, or not experiencing His resources in their lives. I found myself flailing to describe what was going on in my life, including to my girlfriend in

Montana. I failed on several attempts to explain to her, and to others, what was "going on in me." We broke up through mail. The next fall, on the way to ISU, I was traveling with a childhood friend who was carrying on about all the fun and partying we were going to enjoy. Finally, I broke in and said, "Bill, there is something I need to tell you. I've given my life to the Lord." Nothing else was said between us for the next three hours to Pocatello. I knew that there must be a better way to say this. I asked God for help in explaining to others that I cared about what has happened to me. He delivered more thoroughly than I could have ever imagined and in a way that would shape my entire life of work and parenting.

Good Gift #3—Mentors, Models, Disciple-Makers and Leaders . . . *because I asked.*

The late Zig Ziglar spoke often about his "Wall of Gratitude." He commemorated people who made big deposits into his life. I could write an entire book on the people who have made huge deposits in my life. I have written tributes to many of them. God connected me with them, in part, because I asked. Arriving at Idaho State, I asked God to help me find some like-minded believers. He initially answered in the form of another student, Rich Brown, who invited me to play football with some other Christians. That morning, I would meet three people who, over the next several years, would make grand deposits in my life. They were fun, interested in me, encouraging and initiating. And to meet them playing something I loved and didn't associate as a "Christian activity"—football—was amazing. These three Campus Crusade for Christ (CRU) staff members, along with Rich, were instrumental in introducing me to many others who made further deposits in my life.

One player, Mark Moselle, began meeting with me weekly, making deposits into my spiritual growth. He invited me to leadership training classes where I learned how to articulate my faith to others, which I began to do with good effect. He also challenged me to consider Jesus' words to be a disciple-maker by taking all I received and sharing it with others. I simply did what Mark did. He also gave me a ride to church with him every Sunday. There, he introduced me to Pastor Bill Knepper and his wife, Sue, who would make a huge deposit in me, modeling pastoral ministry, a Christian family, and how to be good-humored in all of it because it was hard work. Bill would have a huge effect on my Bible study and communication skills. He modeled a regular deep study of the Word, how to mine its truths and how to communicate it with style—winsomely and truthfully. Bill and Sue opened their home to me for mentorship over one summer during a break from college. Many of the people in the Inkom church adopted ISU students and shared their lives with us.

My first year of college, Mark invited me to live with him and some other students and provided regular life-deposits, modeling life in Christ and ministry, having fun and so much more. The other two CRU staff members I met playing football that day, John and Dayle Rogers, poured a foundation of leadership DNA, modeling strategic, relational leadership in public and in the home. John is an understated great leader and thinker. He framed my thinking about how to motivate people and lead a Christian movement. These men gave others and me the opportunity to grow as leaders and influencers, including speaking and teaching, as well as many other fronts. Dayle set the bar for encouragement. She had a knack for finding good in anyone doing anything, including a dopey Montana redneck. Her verbal affirmation of me in very specific ways, even in the smallest things, put oxygen in my lungs and promoted growth in underdeveloped areas.

The Rogers recently watched their youngest of six children graduate from college. When we met, they had no children. In some ways, I was one of many other lucky students to be on their practice squad in preparing for their family. I know what their children got, even though we watched their family grow from a distance over the years. John has huge responsibility in CRU, but he doesn't wear it. He's the guy everyone wants to work for. Dayle is the original "talent on loan from God." She has put that aside to make the most important deposits one can ever make—into her children. Their children are obvious influencers.

My wall of gratitude is rather large. I cannot possibly mention all the names here, but it is tempting. They have enabled me to think better, lead better, live better, husband better, parent better, work and serve better, invest better and on and on. God used the broken rubble and built a wall through these people, which I now stand on to support still others, especially our four sons. All of this leadership investment in me came because I saw my need and dared to ask God.

In the chapters to follow, my "Good Gift" list grows.

A great wife…*because I asked.*

Parenting mentors…*because I asked.*

Man-building mentors…*because I asked.*

Provision and giving…*because I asked.*

Open doors in mission…*because I asked.*

CHAPTER 5

Envision Fruit in a Single Seed:
Are Our Thoughts and Asks Large Enough?

". . . ask Him!"

—Jesus, Matthew 7:11

Adventure Dinners are a Search event where we provide a fun and safe place to explore the great questions in a long dinner format. We bring a chef into a home and use dinner course themes to prompt conversation. The theme of the third dinner course is meaty/hearty. We invite the group to consider this question: *"If you could ask God one question and get an answer, what would it be?"* Usually, the answer each provides is a window into the vortex of their disillusionment and pain about life. My colleagues in Search Ministries like to say we are into "street apologetics," exploring great "everyman" questions. We work hard at seeking to master these questions so that we are capable trail guides who help others explore. We are mindful that our role is not just to dispense correct answers. These are big mountain questions with serious implications. We also say that it is our role to answer a life and not just a question. Seeing (and answering) a life question in context is very important. So we spend a lot of time building relationships characterized by trust and respect, earning the opportunity to explore. Most often, residual opportunity springs forth to continue chasing answers and figuring out what that means. One desired outcome is progress made in someone taking the next step toward God.

Let's put a twist on this. What if God came to you and made this offer: **"Ask what you wish Me to give you."** Our cute answer to the similar genie-in-the-bottle question is, "I would like 10 more requests." But seriously, what do I want? Some serious contemplation leaves me suspended about my answer. I don't want to blow it on something lesser. Again, what do I really want? Really!?

Immediately, I realize I have settled for much lesser-thing pursuits in life. Most people I pose this question to (including myself) will give an answer that has to do with the welfare and influence of their children. We will do anything to enable our children to have it better, do it better and go further than we have. It's a source of great parental pleasure when children do and parental pain when they do not.

Solomon was given this very offer, recorded in 1 Kings 3. We know he was the smartest and most influential man in the world during his life. Was he wise because he asked God for it, or did God ask him the question because He knew he was (somewhat) wise already and knew exactly what to ask God for and why? Maybe it's not either/or, but both. Solomon provides a terrific model for us to consider in the realm of parental influence and building a house for (with) God.

CHAPTER 6

Soul Soil Test:
How Our Past Affects Our Future

"If you want to know your past — look into your present conditions.
If you want to know your future — look into your present actions."

– CHINESE PROVERB

In Solomon, we observe things that will be the subject of the next few brutal facts:

- One whose life is seen in context, both by the person and God

- One who was responsive to God's offer in the form of a continuous imperative to ASK

- One who discerned the division of labor in building a house: God's part, the leader/parent's part and the follower/children's part

- One who didn't heed warnings required to stay on the path to the end

God responds to **our life in context. We need to see our life in context, too.** We have a sense of our rubble and darkness, but how many have received a sense of our family history and legacy? Moreover, how do I/we fit into the panorama timeline of God's movement in the world? On these fronts, we tend to carry on both vices and virtues, gaffs and gifts, corruption and contributions.

I have gained a greater sense of myself by reading the history of others, particularly the Jewish people. I see myself in their story. I have adopted them as my surrogate family tree because Paul said Christian "Gentile" believers are grafted into Israel. (Romans 11:17-18)

It's possible that I have some family tree from among the "ten lost tribes of Israel" who were dispersed following the Assyrian invasion, 722 B.C. Since that appears to be a dead-end in terms of family tree, I'll stick with the story of the remaining two tribes referred to as "Judah." Since my earthly father was adopted and records were sealed and said to be lost, I'll learn from the ancients I'm grafted into (in Christ) and reboot the dynasty. There are a bunch of characters I really resonate with in the positive (Joshua, Nehemiah, Joseph, etc.) and I definitely share in the descriptions of evil traits as well. Want me or not, these are my people because I know their God and I'm so much like them.

Some of you may be saying, "Great idea, Jon. I could be a part of the Bill Gates family and plan to attend the next family reunion." Have a great time and let me know how that works out. That's not a family I want to get in on, because their family charter does not include this statement: "Through your [Abram/ Abraham's] descendants I will bless the whole earth." (Genesis 12:3)

The kingdom of Israel was established in the hands of Solomon, following the death of his father, David. In front of him were ambitious building projects: the Temple, a palace, and a home for his new Egyptian wife, the product of an alliance with the king of Egypt. Kings did this for political alliances and security. And, she was his first. There was a downside in that she was a foreigner and there was a warning from Moses about kings collecting foreign wives (Deuteronomy 17:1-6). Furthermore, the people were sacrificing on the high places because there was no house built for the name of the LORD yet. Solomon then sacrificed at Gibeon, the great high place, offering 1000 burnt offerings on that altar. The commentators wince at the good-willed compromises, but seem willing to tolerate a youthful mistake.

Yet, this 20-year-old king put first things first (by making generous sacrifices to the LORD) even though he didn't get it all right or perfect (location). The LORD responded to the man, not to the technicalities. The writer tells us:

> Now Solomon loved the LORD, walking in the statutes of his father
> David, except he sacrificed and burned incense on the high places.

> The King went to Gibeon to sacrifice there for that was the great
> high place; Solomon offered a thousand burnt offerings on that
> altar. (1 Kings 3:3-4)

These sacrifices were good, and made to the LORD. Yet, in the location of the former pagan high place, this is not so good and warned against by Moses.

Immediately following the report of Solomon's mixed-bag sacrifices (right act, wrong place), just when we are fussing about his youthful mistakes, we read:

> In Gibeon [the wrong place], the LORD appeared to Solomon in
> a dream at night [the wrong revelation method; why not read the
> Law of Moses?]; and God said, "Ask what you wish Me to give you."
> (1 Kings 3:5)

Solomon's response shows that he sees his life in a larger context than just, "Hey I'm the powerful King of Israel. I'm the boss and this wealth and power is all for me." Far from it! He answers God, personally acknowledging God's lovingkindness (kesed) shown to his father, David, and the fact that God put Solomon on the throne. Twice he calls it this "great lovingkindness" that God has shown David, that "You have given him a son to sit on his throne." (3:6) His placement is grounded in God's sovereign love and stewardship. Thrice, he refers to himself as "Your servant" in verses 7-9. He sees himself as one among many ("in the midst of") of God's "chosen" and "great people." He also says, "Yet I am but a little child; I do not know how to go out or come in." (3:7) Put another way, he said, "I don't know squat!"

CHAPTER 7

Soul Soil Analysis:
God Knows What We Really Want

The LORD appeared to Solomon in a dream at night;
*and God said, **"Ask what you wish Me to give you."***

—1 KINGS 3:5

God strongly invites us to ask for what we really want. We continually have a choice to respond.

Given all the life-context discussed in the previous chapter and perspective, Solomon answered God's question with this request (v. 9): "So give your servant a hearing heart to judge your people to discern between good and evil." Then he answered the invitation with his own rhetorical question, "For who is able to judge this great people of yours?" (A twenty-year old?)

How endearing is this? What a wise, humble and grounded response! The request in context "was pleasing in the sight of the Lord." (3:10) Verses 11-13 show God affirming the content of his request, essentially saying three times, "Already done, little bro!" It is a prayer God delights to answer exceedingly:

"Behold, *I have done* according to your words…" (v. 12)

"Behold, *I have given you* a wise and discerning heart…" (v. 12)

"*I have given you* what you have not asked both riches and honor…" (v. 13)

God's delight to answer Solomon sounds so much like Jesus in Matthew 7:7-11. *"Keep asking…keep seeking…keep knocking…If you then, being evil, know how to* *give **good gifts** to your children, **how much more will your Father who is in heaven give what is good to those who ask Him!***"

Here's a most intriguing thing. Under God's affirming and generous leadership, Solomon eventually figured out the proper location to make sacrifices.

> Then Solomon awoke, and behold, it was a dream. And he came to Jerusalem and stood before the ark of the covenant of the Lord, and offered burnt offerings and made peace offerings, and made a feast for all his servants. (1 Kings 3:15)

God responds to a life in context. He invites people who don't have it "just right" to ASK, boldly. The asking becomes bold, when we see ourselves in relational context: reliant on God, positioned by God to serve God's valuable people under our charge and influence.

Brent Southcombe was a five-star hotel chef in Brisbane, Australia. He would say, "Ten miracles later, God has relocated me serving refugees and other at-risk people in Boise, Idaho, training them in culinary skills." He drills them in fundamental perspectives and skills that will enable them to break into the job market. Others do this kind of training, too, but then release the trainees to fend for themselves. Not Brent. What makes Brent unique is that his Create Common Good trainees have a 99-percent job placement rate once he has worked his magic. He runs a tight kitchen, but he is watching, affirming and breathing life and encouragement into his students. He gets to know them, their stories, their ticks and strengths. He believes in them and proves that he does by how he trains and serves them.

Early in their training, Brent looks each trainee in the eye and says to them, "God has a job for you. I am praying for you and the special job God will provide." Presumptuous is he? Messing with them, is he? What can they say? They hope he isn't just blowing smoke at them, yet they have nothing to lose by waiting and watching to see what happens. Most Christians would be uncomfortable with praying so openly like this. I am, but I'm not Brent. Only Brent is Brent. As their training progresses, Brent is asking God for contacts, job openings and wisdom about whom he should take where. "God impresses things on me about employers to call and trainees to promote. God brings people and situations to us." Prayed up, he vigilantly and diligently starts scanning the community. He puts feet on pavement on behalf of his valued and vulnerable students. They won't get an even break in a competitive job market because their English is often sketchy and their résumés are thin. They are minorities and unknowns who, otherwise, have small chances of landing the job.

Brent becomes a passionate street-fighter for them. He gets the interview through the unconventional. He rarely follows employment protocol because, though orderly, his trainees won't get a look. So he promotes and sells their skills and attributes to employers. He has even lobbied for higher pay than what is offered. God, working through Brent, brings just the right job for each trainee in every class. You can't reproduce this. It's the "x-variable" in Create Common Good's portfolio, which I hope and pray will franchise all over the world in due time. But is there a Brent Southcombe in every community?

Brent is an all-in man who has learned to ask God for specifics to the benefit of those under his leadership. If he is whole-hearted, deploying his gifts, time and knowledge for the sake of others in need, why wouldn't God answer, when He cares even more for these valuable ones than Brent does? He does answer and He cares.

If you've lost track of the point, let me explicitly say it again. The point is that Brent and his family have learned to ask God, ask big and ask often. Every story has its own unique details.

1 Kings 4 describes the multi-faceted ways God provides resources to match the task He entrusts to Solomon, and *to us*, especially as we live out the sacred role of parents who are preparing the vulnerable and valuable for a challenging world. A partial summary of this is found in 4:29-31a:

> Now God gave Solomon wisdom and very great discernment and breadth of mind, like the sand that is on the seashore. Solomon's wisdom surpassed the wisdom of all the sons of the east and all the wisdom of Egypt. For he was wiser than all men.

Solomon asked for wisdom and God responded greatly! Why wouldn't God be pleased to answer that request?

CHAPTER 8

Growing Partners:
God Enriches Our Dirt to Create Social and Spiritual Wealth

God can use our broken-rubble past, mixed with present mortar,
to partner with us in building a wealthy, big-house future.

Many people strongly reacted to President Obama's chide of the American people when he made the point about government building the highways we drive on and bridges we cross over (to name two). Technically what he said was true, but many listeners argued, saying, "Wait a minute! The government is made up of elected and appointed servants of the people, paid for by the people for the common good. We didn't personally build that highway or that bridge, but to say that government provides the highest-end good is nonsense. The government provides nothing without the people, their leadership and their revenue." Actually, *both* government and people "built that."

In 1 Kings 5 and 6, Solomon began to engage his role as a co-builder with God. ". . . [I]n the fourth year of Solomon's reign over Israel…he began to build the house of the LORD." (6:1)

God had been providing for a long time through David. With peace on every side, new resources were brought to bear through David's network of friends, such as Hirum, King of Tyre, who provided cedars from Lebanon. Much silver and gold were in the treasury of the LORD, the product of the spoils of war and steady gifts of God's people. Before the Temple was completed, there were special offerings from within Israel and from outsiders.

With stockpiles of building resources at hand, Solomon launched an ambitious building campaign. It took seven years to build the House of the LORD and 13 years to build Solomon's palace. His priorities were right to build God's house first, before building his own. The workforce described in 1 Kings 5:13-18 was staggering: 30,000 forced laborers, 10,000 a month going to Lebanon in relays to float the logs by sea. Stoneworkers numbered 70,000 transporters and 80,000 hewers in the mountains. He had 3,300 chief deputies who ruled over the workers on these various projects.

Do you get the idea that Solomon had plenty to do staying in front of this machine? Throughout the chapter, there are phrases repeated that show Solomon's part in the division of labor:

- "he built" (6:5, 7 [3x], 9, 10, 12, 14, 15, 16 [2x], 36, 38)

- "he made" (6:5, 23, 31, 32, 33)

- "he prepared" (6:19)

- "he overlaid" (6:20, 21, 22 [2x], 28, 30, 32, 35)

- "he carved" (6:29, 32, 35)

Did Solomon personally do all that these verbs indicate? No; he led chief deputies who led the people.

Did Solomon make all of these resources: the trees, the stone in the mountains, the costly granites and marbles, the gold and silver? No; God provided these resources through the Earth and various human agencies that discovered them, harvested them and prepared them for alignment in the building project.

Many times during the dedication of the house of the LORD, Solomon says and prays things like, "I have surely built You a lofty house, a place for your dwelling forever." (8:13) Eight more times the phrase "build a (the) house" is used of Solomon and it is not contested by the LORD. Solomon's part is weighty and sacrificial, the effort significant.

God will not diminish His servant's role by saying, "You didn't build that! I provided my resources to you during a period of peace on all sides! You didn't build that! Your skilled and forced laborers did it, led by your chief deputies; they actually put their hands on the materials. You didn't touch a single stone! And by the way, who gave you that wisdom and world recognition?"

It is clear in the benediction offered by Solomon at the dedication of the House of the LORD, that he has first things first as exhibited by his bodily posture before the altar, "On his knees with his hands toward heaven," and by his expressed motive, "so that all the peoples of the earth may know that the LORD is God; there is no one else. Let your heart therefore be wholly devoted to the LORD our God, to walk in His statutes and to keep His commandments, as at this day." (8:54, 60-61) This is accented by Solomon's sacrifices offered to the LORD, which numbered 22,000 oxen and 120,000 sheep. (8:63)

For a household in our day, How would one show this kind of "first things first" response? What disciplines would need to be in place to remind of Who holds us, where we came from, where our resources came from and to Whom we owe our very existence?

CHAPTER 9

Grower's Division of Labor:
God's Part; Our Part—Let's Quit Trying to Do God's Part

"Unless the LORD builds the house they labor in vain…"

—Solomon, Psalm 127:1

God wants us to build a house with Him. While we are parenting, we must discern God's part, our part and the child's part.

But what kind of house is Solomon referring to? Among the Psalms of Ascent, assembled to facilitate the Jewish pilgrim's journey up to Jerusalem, some have suggested it refers to the Temple residing in the Holy City. In 2 Samuel 7, the writer uses the Hebrew word for house (*bayith*) in different ways:

1. A palace. (2 Samuel 7:2) e.g. Solomon's palace

2. A temple. (2 Samuel 7:5b) e.g. Yahweh's temple

3. A dynasty or family line. (2 Samuel 7:11b,16; Genesis 16:2) e.g. David's dynasty

4. A family (people) who dwells together. (Psalm 127:1-5).

5. A house can be a physical structure and/or a people, literal or metaphorical. The physical structures are built to serve the people in relationship with the LORD.

These passages show a house to be built by both God and man. They are co-builders. We would say a developer/owner, a building contractor and a framer (to name a few) are co-builders, each contributing something valuable and unique to the building process. Psalm 127 implies that God, parents and even children (in a later season) are co-builders of a household of people. The key questions for the reader to work through are:

1.   *What is God's part?*

2.   *What is the parent's part?*

3.   *What is the child's part?*

Conflict and trouble break out when each does not do his own part or one starts trying to do the part of the other. When God made his covenant with David, He was very clear about the division of labor. Let's observe this carefully, because it provides clarity for our household co-building.

In 2 Samuel 7, King David anticipated building the LORD a permanent house—a Temple. Why should God the King live in a mobile tent when King David lived in a house of cedar? While God affirms David's desire, he speaks through Nathan the prophet that David's son (who we will later discover is Solomon) would be the builder of the house of God. David was the warrior-king who won the land. Given that, he had too much blood on his hands. God told David that though he would not be the hands-on builder, God would make his dynasty (house) the builder and his name would be great through his descendant.

> When your days are complete and you lie down with your fathers, I will raise up your descendant after you, who will come forth from you, and I will establish his kingdom. He shall build a house for my name, and I will establish the throne of his kingdom forever. I will be a father to him and he shall be a son to Me; when he commits iniquity, I will correct him with the rod of men and the strokes of the sons of men, but My lovingkindness shall not depart from him... Your house and your kingdom shall endure before Me forever; your throne shall be established forever. (2 Samuel 7:12-16)

David is very satisfied, even pleased, with this covenant/promise. When we observe his prayerful response to God in 7:18-29, we see that he is clearly energized, and decisively dedicates to the LORD the spoils of war (such as silver and gold) in Chapter 8. In years to come, David, zealous for the LORD and for his son's success, will begin networking and stockpiling resources like wood, stone, gold, etc. to expedite the Temple building project.

Two things about this are noteworthy:

First, consider that God knows what is most important to a parent. *Parents want their children to have a better life and greater opportunities than they had.* Greatness for a parent is being associated with this even though they will never see it. Just setting the table is satisfying.

Second, note that **God promises to be a father to that son** (7:14). There is a "co-fatherhood" in the design. Whatever the human father situation is, children have a heavenly Father to whom their trust is ultimately to be transferred, as is strongly implied in Matthew 7:11. A human father must be mindful that it is his job to help his son/children make this transfer. As John the Baptist said of Jesus, "He must increase, but I must decrease." (John 3:30)

Immediately following David's death, his son Solomon fired up the Temple project. He had a strong sense of the covenant the LORD made with his father and his descendants. (1 Kings 2:45) It made him decisive in the face of corruption. When God asked Solomon, "Ask what you wish Me to give you," he immediately reviewed the lovingkindness of God, considered his youthful ignorance, the greatness of God's people in stature and number and asked for a "hearing heart" to shepherd God's people.

Upon hearing this, God loaded him up with many enabling gifts that exceeded his request, but matched resources and opportunities to match and illustrate his God-given abilities:

1. Wise and discerning heart between good and evil to judge fairly.
   (1 Kings 3:9-12; 16-28; 4:29)

2. Riches and honor. (1 Kings 3:13)

3. Peace on all sides. (1 Kings 4:24; 5:4)

4. Breadth of mind. (1 Kings 4:29-34)

5. Strategic alliances for resources. (1 Kings 5)

We believe Solomon's story is included, in part, to show God's desire for us to build our house with Him. Solomon clearly implies this in Psalm 127, speaking of a household with children. We parents must discern God's part, our part and the child's part in the building process—womb to tomb. Such a house is a gift from God and can be built with God in wisdom if we ask. Is it really so audacious to ask God for something He appears delighted to support us in? What He requires of us is a "hearing heart" to shepherd well His people—the children who are gifts from Him.

CHAPTER 10

Point the Plow:
While We Do Our Part, Let's Put First Things First

*"**Put first things first** and you get second things thrown in.*
Put second things first and you lose both first and second things."
—C.S. Lewis, "First and Second Things," from *God in the Dock*

Before Stephen Covey or C.S. Lewis was God. God, revealed in Jesus, exhorted us to keep first things first.

> "Do not be anxious…your heavenly Father knows you need these…
> Seek first the kingdom of God and His righteousness and all these
> things will be added to you."—Jesus, Matthew 6:32-33

On the dark side, this chapter could be entitled, "Stupid Is the Smartest Man in the World." The brutal fact is we don't know what "first things" are, or struggle to keep them such, like the smartest man in the world. We are to learn from Solomon—both from his amazing wisdom and from his tragic mistakes made later in his life. Our part is to figure it out, remember and guard our heart on this matter.

There are many ways we can get our ball lost in the weeds. This chapter is an amplification of the "dirt bag" hypothesis at work in parents. "Parents are evil," as you may recall. Knowing correct answers doesn't get it done. Adolescence is already filled with confusing perils for children. But parents who are not in touch with their dirt bag, pretending to be about "first things" but who are really about "lesser things" will reveal themselves. As the man hauntingly said, "They know."

Sometimes parents don't even know what the "first things" are, or are in hot pursuit of "lesser things" without apology. Though forthright about this they are headed for trouble. To the adolescent, and some of the more observant children of any age, it appears parents are stupid, regardless of whether the parent is practicing "first things" or not.

When my older two sons were in junior high, I led a group of boys through a study of Proverbs and manners. We named the class "Wise Guys." One week I showed up with a prescription pill bottle and with a serious face put forth my confession. "Men, I don't know if you are aware of this, but when you turn thirteen your parents have to start taking a prescription pill. It's known as the 'stupid pill.' We have to take this for all the years you are in your teens, until age 19 or 20." I paused for a little drama and let the thought sink in. (So far, they thought I was telling them the truth.) Then they lived up to the class name, grins starting to break on their faces, realizing I was being a wise guy.

Holding with the pill metaphor, I'd like to explore some of the 'stupid pills' we parents swallow that don't work out for anyone's good—even though they seem cool at the time.

Seated at a wedding reception dinner, I listened in on a discussion between two former classmates as they were catching up. One guy revealed to the other, "A few months ago I decided to become an atheist." His friend, without any guile or emotion, asked, "Well, how is that working out?"

"Not so well," he confessed.

I marveled at the brilliance of both the honest question and its tone. It was asked without any judgment—just mild curiosity. He might have more bluntly observed, "That's your choice and we all know that we have to live with our choices. Are you getting what you want?"

If one has a choice to do life with God, why would you do it without God? Asking the question, I'm not picking on atheists and agnostics—they have their reasons. I'm asking people who have or lean toward belief in God. Why would I do life, especially parenting, without God? Why not at least give yourself the benefit of the doubt? It's tragic when I say I believe in God and then live as if He doesn't exist.

Without God, there is no one to thank, ask or go to for an objective, larger perspective. There is no one to complain to about (perceived) evil that does not exist without transcendent good rooted in moral law. There are merely inconveniences. There is no one to blame. Atheists have values; they just have nothing but self-smart opinions to anchor them in. But is the "believer" who lives without God somehow better off?

Solomon explored the life cycle on earth without God and cried, "Empty! Useless! Vanity of vanities is life under the sun." In Ecclesiastes, he shared about all of his life opportunities and experiencing the best of the best, and how empty it all is at the end of the day. Solomon enjoyed peace on all sides, best-selling books, the honor of being the smartest man in the world, hundreds of Miss Universe wives, wealth coming out his ears, building projects, horticulture projects, etc. He observes, "Behold, I have found only this, that God made men upright, but they have sought out many devices." (7:29)

People have sought anything and everything but God. In some ways, I inadvertently discovered Solomon's recommendation after my short existential spin in hedonism, trying to create my own reality and meaning through pleasure seeking. He said, "Remember also your Creator in the days of your youth, before the evil days come and the years draw near when you will say, 'I have no delight in them.'" This is what I observed in the Palm Springs gated community and it scared the hell out of me.

Solomon spikes it with 12:13-14: "The conclusion, when all has been heard, is: fear God and keep His commandments because this applies to every person. For God will bring every act to judgment, everything which is hidden, whether it is good or evil."

I was not a declared atheist at that time, but I lived just like one. I lived without God. Worse than an atheist, I used God for my own ego enhancement. I asked him to put me on sports award podiums and even had the audacity to say, "for Your glory" before the contests, knowing full well it was only for mine. I did not thank or acknowledge Him in private or public for the victories, nor thank Him in any setting. I beat my chest.

In the Palm Desert apartment in 1978, it was as if my friend God asked me about my life trajectory: "How's that working out?" I didn't like what I was getting and decided to fire the incompetent junior management in my life (me, the dopey 18-year-old) and get some new life-giving leadership on the scene. That was a great decision and the hire of a lifetime, eternally.

Drayton Nabers, in *The Case for Character,* includes a thoughtful hypothetical example for the "self-made" and the self-determined to ponder. It's a letter to a hypothetical Heisman trophy winner about how and why he is holding the coveted award. These days, the winners all seem to be well-coached in their speeches and credit-giving so they don't come across so full of themselves. Some are grounded in true humility. Some are not. The dirt bag in all of us seems to cloud perception of where we came from and how we arrived where we are. Nabers writes:

> Let's take the example of a tailback who wins the Heisman Trophy. This Heisman winner gets his name in the paper and his face on ESPN. But where did he get the DNA that created the strong body? And where did he get the great coordination that helped him win the prize? How many of the one hundred trillion cells in his body did he create?

> We are told that for each of these cells there is a bank of instructions more detailed than the thirty-two volumes of the Encyclopedia Britannica put together. Does this tailback understand even one of these instructions? (For that matter, does even the smartest doctor or biologist in the world fully understand the marvel of a single human cell?

> "But I worked so hard," the tailback might say. I went to the weight room. I practiced harder than anyone else on the team."

> To him we could reply: "But who taught you to work that hard? Who built the weight room? Who bought the equipment? Who built the

university, including the stadium you played in? Who cut the grass there and laid out the lines and boundaries? Did you hire or pay your coaches? Did you recruit your teammates? Did you open up those holes in the line that you ran through?

If this tailback has humility, he will express nothing but overflowing gratitude when he wins the Heisman—to his parents, to his teachers, to his coaches, to all the players on his team, to everyone who helped him along the way. Most of all, time and time again, he will express gratitude to God.

. . . Humility is a form of wisdom. It is thinking clearly. It is simply being realistic. It is knowing who really deserves the credit and the glory for what we do.

Another wise man, raised in the palace of the most powerful monarch in the world, had the foresight to warn future kings of Israel about the snare of accumulating for themselves, horses (military power), wives (political alliances) and gold (highest symbol of wealth). Moses, immersed in the king's world in Egypt, envisioned Israel in the Promised Land. He knew how intoxicating the environment was. Solomon had access to these words and no doubt let them guide him for most of his life. (Deuteronomy 17:1-6)

Fast-forward to the summary of Solomon, which the writer of 1 Kings penned during Solomon's last days. The words are haunting, especially when he had been described as "whole-hearted" toward God and His law in 1 Kings 3. Is it accurate to say that he became the most stupid smartest man in the world? Consider these selections in Chapter 11:

- 11:1-3—"Now King Solomon loved many foreign women...Solomon held fast to these in love...and his wives turned his heart away.
- 11:4—"For when Solomon was old, his wives turned his heart away after other gods; and his heart was not wholly devoted to the LORD his God, as the heart of David his father had been."

- 11:6—"Solomon did what was evil in the sight of the LORD, and did not follow the LORD fully…"
- 11:9—"Now the LORD was angry with Solomon because his heart was turned away from the LORD…"
- 11:10b—"… he did not observe what the LORD commanded."
- 11:11—"So the LORD said to Solomon, 'Because you have done this, and you have not kept My covenant and My statutes, which I have commanded you, I will surely tear the kingdom from you, and give it to your servant.'"

The kingdom would divide in a civil war, the by-product of his divided heart. God raised up adversaries (11:14, 23) and gave the throne to a servant (Jeroboam, who rebelled against the king), and not a son. This outcome ought to strike fear in the heart of anyone desiring to be a whole-hearted God-follower all the days of their lives. Wasn't it Solomon who wrote, "Watch over your heart with all diligence, for from it flow the springs of life"? (Proverbs 4:23)

Whew! I have to decompress and take a shower.

On a lighter note, a story went around in the 1970s about an airplane trip that included a hippie college student, a successful businessman, a pastor and Dr. Henry Kissinger (Secretary of State for President Richard Nixon and a Harvard professor. At the time, Dr. Kissinger was thought to be one of the smartest men in the world).

The small plane encountered some serious troubles. The pilot was heard over the intercom.

"Gentlemen, I have some bad news and some good news. The bad news is that we have serious mechanical failure and this plane is going to crash. The good news is we have parachutes! I'm going to model putting it on and how to jump out of the plane. Please don't waste time: do as I do." With that, the attentive passengers watched the pilot put on a parachute, pull the cord and jump. The businessman noted to the others that they were one parachute short and seized the first one. He justified, "I've got hundreds of employees counting on me for their livelihood and a huge business deal to close on. I'm also a father of three and I'm not ready to die." He jumped.

Dr. Kissinger said, "I'm the smartest man in the world and people are counting on me for negotiating world peace." With that he jumped. Stunned, the pastor and hippie student looked at each other. The Pastor said, "Son, you take the last parachute. I'm an older man who has raised his family and settled where I will spend eternity by the amazing grace of Jesus. Please, take the parachute and jump. All I ask is that you remember this gift God has extended to you." The hippie student stared in unbelief. Pondering the generous offer, he noticed two parachutes left. He said, "Pastor, that won't be necessary. We can both jump. The smartest man in the world just jumped out of the plane with my backpack!"

Moses warned that we could become arrogant, not realizing where our abilities, gifts and our very life originated. He reminded the Israelites that God provided for them the forty years of their wilderness wanderings and He gave them the promised land of plenty—loaded with resources (crops, trees, homes, precious metals, etc.) they did not grow, build or mine. It was enough to inherit these things, but when the resources began to multiply and the people were increasingly satisfied by them, the creep of a proud heart began to get root in their soul. They began to reason, "'My power and the strength of my hand made me this wealth.' But you shall remember the LORD your God, for it is He who is giving you power to make wealth." (Deuteronomy 8:17-18)

I'm not different than the Israelites or a Heisman trophy winner. I can become the stupidest man in the world very quickly. Being firmly and daily anchored in relationship with God the Father slows me down reaching for backpacks at 30,000 feet. It is a father's job to teach the difference between a backpack and parachute.

CHAPTER 11

Cross-Pollination:
Moving From Man-Father to God the Father

"We had earthly fathers to discipline us…as seemed best to them,
but He [God the Father] disciplines us for good
that we may share in His holiness."
—Hebrews 12:9-10 (NASB)

Dads have god-like power in the lives of their children. Such power is used for good or harm, usually a mix of both. This chapter is about the perplexing mix.

Father's Day found my youngest son, Sean, and me at Merritt's in Boise. It's an old Boise icon in terms of breakfast. The waitress was too cute to be working at a place like this. She replaced the "I've had a hard life" waitress and seemed right at home. She was sporting a T-shirt that read, *"I got sconed…at Merritts."* Sean and I would purchase similar T-shirts to wear home.

We had climbed Table Rock, another Boise icon, early that morning, working up a Sunday morning appetite. Omelets, hash browns and a ridiculously decadent scone were the perfect answer to a fresh spring morning hike. I realized Merritt's was a surprisingly perfect Father's Day place for me as I took in the ambiance.

The wall by our booth was loaded with pictures—pictures of horse racing wins. This was something very familiar. My dad had hundreds of these pictures from many years of horse racing, and I explained to Sean that he had binders and binders loaded with them.

"This is the kind of place we often went to when we were on the road with the horses," I said.

Seizing the moment for him to look into a window of the life of the grandfather he never met, I elaborated.

"During the summers, we hit all the race meets across Montana. My dad would use the summer to train and test the race talent in his stable. By the end of the summer he would have thinned out the ones who would not likely be producers and take the 'money horses' down South or back East for the winter months. Larger tracks were more expensive and competitive, so Montana racing was a valuable filter. Generally, he would have only a handful of his own horses, but mostly he trained horses for other people. Horses are an expensive hobby when you consider feed, vet bills, stabling, travel, racing fees, etc. No one really makes money at it. It's an addiction owners fool themselves into thinking is an investment (at least that's what they tell their wives). Mostly, it's an expensive hobby. A few horses make money for their owner, but to find the money-makers you go through a lot of wild cards—and cash."

Sensing my sentimental moment on Father's day, Sean showed interest. So, I continued. "Merritt's is a 'trackers' restaurant, being this close to Le Bois, Boise's horse racing track. On the road, we ate at these kinds of places all over Montana. A cup of coffee was 15 to 25 cents! One summer, my dad had 24 horses in the stable. It was all-hands-on-deck in the mornings when they exercised and we cleaned stalls. I've mucked out more than my share," I reflected.

I went on to describe some of the chores I cut my teeth on, as I learned to work in the family business. I can still smell and feel it. We would clean the stalls out, refresh the bedding consisting of either straw or woodchips, scrub out the feed buckets, fill the water buckets, then throw some hay in the corner of the stall, and on and on. In the afternoon there were casual chores to tend to. We could be found watching my dad shoeing the horses, fixing tack or purchasing hay, oats and straw.

This was a new world for my son. He and his brothers never had the opportunity to meet Bob Strain, their grandfather. It seemed honoring and right for Sean to get to know him a little better through me—on Father's Day. He was killed in an accident in 1981 just shy of age 52. I was 21 years old—in college. I'm now two years older than he was when a falling oak tree took his life. Both the way he died and me being older than he was when he did seemed odd.

Even though keeping and training horses was hot, stinky, itchy work, I loved it. It was our livelihood and my dad was recognized as a very good trainer. It was the family sport and I was exhilarated to be a part of it. It was horribly disappointing to miss out, which we did most of the year when we were in school and my dad was on the road with the horses without us. I was the self-appointed family statistician, keeping my own records on every jockey and horse on the Montana circuit. I knew their breeding, form record, their race times, almost everything in print. There was nothing more exciting than race days, especially big ones, when we had horses running. Our Super Bowl was winning futurities or derbies—the big races for two and three-year-old horses at most race meets. Someone would claim bigger purses, trophies, blankets and other symbols of racing success. I loved listening to my dad strategize and commentate on race situations. His post-race reports would find our ears on fire to know "what happened" and why a horse had been so disappointing, or won running away from the others.

While jockeys were consumed with keeping their weight down, not too many others around the track were. My dad was a contrast. He was a fitness and nutrition zealot who regularly filled our head with insights about vitamins and food. He was always looking for the competitive edge with the horses and he trained himself like he trained the horses. He lit a fire in me with his passions.

We would watch the former Marine work out daily. He would inspire us by his example and offer challenges with incentives. "If you can run around the track in such and such time by the end of the month, I'll buy you _____. If you can do fifty consecutive pushups, the first twenty on your fingertips, and 100 sit-ups, I'll buy you a $50 savings bond." And so on. He had a diverse workout regimen including dumbbell weights, distance running and classic core routines (pushups, sit-ups) to keep in tip-top shape. He became a Kenneth Cooper disciple. Dr. Cooper was the aerobics guru whose research and writing took the nation by storm in the 1970s.

Dad was god-like to us; he was invincible. He was fiercely independent and self-sufficient. Taking care of stuff was a matter of pride. Why he had to be away so much for a few winters we could not comprehend, but we assumed it to be for our livelihood. The divorce was mind-bending and awkward, and put a little rust on Dad's armor. I wanted to be in his masculine world, but felt stuck in my mom's feminine world. In the long run, this would prove to be for the better because his physical and masculine invincibility would be shattered by losses and death itself.

Through Mom, I discovered the ultimate resources for life in Jesus Christ. Total forgiveness, assurance of the gift of eternal life, and the ever-present, wise, daily leadership of God prompted me to share the wealth with those closest to me. I began to pray for family members and friends who had not discovered such resources. Included in my regular prayer was asking God for an opportunity to discuss this with my dad, an opportunity would come one year later—the next time I saw him in person. Headed for Ocean City, New Jersey, for a summer leadership project, I rode a bus from Montana to Shreveport, Louisiana, where he was running horses. I spent three days with him, my grandparents and my brother, Kim.

Curious about my summer in Ocean City and what prompted such an adventure, I shared my story of coming to faith in the Palm Desert apartment and consequent changes. Both my dad and brother sat in rapt attention, with little comment. Three years later, my brother shared at our wedding rehearsal dinner something surprising. Though he could hold mom at a distance, rebuffing her spiritual counsel, he couldn't explain me. He knew me! We worked together during my summers in high school. He could see the presence of God in me. My dad didn't say it, but I have reason to believe he observed the same. They politely allowed me to share the *Four Spiritual Laws*, a concise summary of the Gospel message, with them. I even led a sample prayer recorded in it. My hope was that they would receive Christ. Kind of bold on my part (even presumptuous!), but it was sincere and clarifying.

The sum total of my dad's spiritual instruction with me up to this point (aside from mentioning God and Jesus' name a lot when he was angry with the horses) was one humorous story he told me as he was leaving our Hamilton ranch to go on a long road trip with the horses. I waved to him as he was pulling out of the driveway and he yelled for me to hop up on the side-step of his truck. I was hanging onto the side mirror and listened with great anticipation to his story, just for me. He said, "There was a little boy out walking one day and he found a wee little willy worm. He saw it and said, 'Ah, look... a wee little willy worm!!' He picked it up and began to stroke it with his finger saying, "Ooooh wee little willy worm, so soft and cuddly. So alone...and nobody loves him. But I love you wee little willy worm, and Jesus loves you! Wanna go see Jesus?"' CLAP! My Dad smashed his palms together and began to wipe the imaginary guts off of them.

He mussed my hair, said good-bye, and was off to the races. I analyzed this parable, seeking to discern if there was moral and spiritual nutrition wrapped in it, but no, it was just a wicked-funny little story that was the sum total of my dad's "theological instruction" deposit in me.

Dad simply had nothing to do with church except taking one for the team on Christmas and Easter. He liked the Presbyterian minister in Hamilton; Rev. Sherwood was a man's man. My dad did some reading and was amused by the occult and other forms of alternative spirituality. He had spiritual hunger and curiosity, but simply didn't see an answer for himself in mainline Christianity.

Over the next two years, Dad would be stripped of everything he had clung to and would experience quirky things that would expose him to the message again. Among them, freakish accidents that ended the racing careers of valuable horses, the failure of his second marriage, and his much loved pit bull named Buddy freakishly dying of a twisted gut. At the same time, he contacted a psychic for "counsel" and freakish specific historical information was revealed to him that no one (especially randomly in another part of the country) could have possibly known, apart from God Himself or demonic sources. This was creepy, he later confided to my Mom. We later learned of many people who were praying for him and who engaged him in spiritual conversations. Even his in-laws and the Christian owners of a truck stop he frequented when moving horses had something to say to him about his spirituality. It was as though there was a furious battle going on for his spiritual life. This notion was amplified later in Lewistown.

Running horses and managing a Charolais cattle ranch in Arkansas, he had occasion to drive through our home state of Montana to attend my sister's graduation. His truck needed repair and so he would be delayed in our family history home of Lewistown for a couple days. My brother, Kim, who had begun a relationship with Christ since the three of us had conversed in Shreveport, was working in a nearby town. He came to spend some time with my dad. Seated in a café, they noticed a man they both thought looked familiar. My dad left for the restroom, and curiosity prompted Kim to do what he normally would not. He walked over to the man and asked, "Are you Herb Hofer?" The man said, "No, I'm his brother, Pete." Kim met Herb once when he visited a rural Bible study for remote ranchers and farmers. Herb introduced Kim to Christ that night! His brother Pete was a TV artist evangelist in Great Falls. My dad returned and Pete joined them and immediately turned his focus to my Dad. Quickly sizing up where my Dad was spiritually, he introduced him to Jesus Christ in the restaurant in the midst of his old cronies.

Now comes an even more amazing part. Pete was in Lewistown by freak chance. He was very discouraged about his ministry in Great Falls and couldn't help but feel that God had given up on him. Discouraged and distracted, he climbed into his car that morning and started driving, anywhere and nowhere in particular, because he was lost in his prayerful pain trying to work out his disillusionment with God and discouragement with his situation. He ended up in Lewistown— randomly in that particular café, randomly, mistakenly "recognized" by someone, randomly approached by a shy cowboy—unlikely; shared Christ with a man who shouldn't have been there—unlikely; introduced a proud, self-reliant man to Christ—*very* unlikely; on his own turf—surreal! So random, yet so on time.

The event would save Pete's ministry as God let him know with resounding affirmation that He was not through with him. We learned this years later through my sister, Patti, who was the worship leader at St. John's Episcopal Church in Butte, Montana.

> Our brother, Kim, made a statement I have found to be true: 'The longer I live and the more I learn, I realize there are so many times our encounters with people are by divine appointment.' One of those encounters happened as I was working at the church one morning; it's not by chance that I was there alone. Normally our secretary would have handled it, and I would never have seen the man who came to the door. His name was Pete Hofer, with 'Advanced

Fire Protection.' He was there to check our fire extinguishers. As he worked he asked me a few strange questions, which eventually led me to understand he had the heart of an evangelist, and was testing me to see where I was spiritually, if I really knew the Lord. (I think his job was actually trying to keep people from the fires of hell.)

I asked a few questions of my own, because I remembered his rather distinctive name from a story my brother, Kim, had told me years ago, relating to my father's salvation. As my mind was flashing back 15 years, I asked him if he had ever been in Lewistown, MT. When I told him what I knew of the story, he was astounded....yes, it was he and his brother who had prayed with my father and brother. Pete told me he had been in a T.V. ministry with his brother in Great Falls. They were at a low point, spiritually, when Pete ended up in the café in Lewistown. He said he had told the Lord, "Whatever I am, wherever I go, I am willing for you to use me in whatever small way You desire, Lord."

One of the things Pete recalled was asking my father if he knew Christ. Dad replied, "No, but I have been looking for Him." I started to weep as I recognized God's divine appointment to let Pete and I see His love, so great and His mercies, so kind, that extend to a thousand generations.

In a way, God the Father rescued two men that day in the diner—the evangelist and our dad.

A few months after the chance meeting in the Lewistown diner, my very fit Dad lay in a hospital bed in Arkansas fighting for his life. Stopping by his brother-in-law's house, Dad told him, "I am SO proud of how my children have turned out." He then said the only thing he had left to do was cut down a huge oak tree threatening to fall on his new horse barn if a bad wind should come up. An oak tree on a slightly (too) windy day bested him, or should I say busted him: two broken arms, two broken collarbones and severe swelling on the brain.

Amazingly, he lived several days. They didn't know what condition he would be in if he survived and there was a high likelihood he would never be normal again. The Lord chose to take him. It is a twist of redemptive irony these words would be his last— captured and reported for the comfort of his seven children. His children doing well is all a dad wants; his affirmation is what his children want. I would not learn of these words until fact checking this. It has left me in puddle of tears thirty-four years later. Dad power. Whatever the deficits and losses we suffered, he finished blessing his children.

I was out of the country, in Malaysia, that summer when he died. With communication difficult, I didn't get word of his death in time to return for the service. Six of the seven children were with him together, as Christ-followers, a few weeks before the accident. Instead of arguing about horses, he and my brother, Kim, instead argued about the role of baptism in salvation. Some things don't change, but my dad was a changed man. My dad's new church emphasized baptism, so in our last time together on Earth, he took special effort to care for our souls, systematically going around the circle asking each son or daughter if they had been baptized. Only when he was convinced about each one would he move to the next.

My grandmother on my mom's side told me later (and she knew him for almost a lifetime), "The moment I looked into your dad's face I could tell something happened to him." She was a mainline Methodist and not one given to such a way of explaining something like this. She saw a transformed man.

Twenty years later, I would visit his grave in Amity, Arkansas. Attending a conference in Little Rock, it was my first opportunity to be in proximity. Twenty years! I couldn't believe how quickly time had gone. Walking through a cemetery in the midst of a cattle pasture, I thought to myself with satisfaction, how fitting a setting. My eyes searched for his site among my stepmother's family name. Then I saw it—with flowers all over it!! What? I broke and fell to my knees sobbing twenty years of grief and loss. Here was tangible evidence that the "invincible" one was not, but simultaneously, here was consolation by the promise of amazing grace and the presence of God forever for those who put their trust in Him. My dad entered the kingdom of heaven as a little child. He, too, had a heavenly Father. I realized that the same amount of time had passed between his death and the total number of years I had known him on Earth. I missed him. I wished my sons could have known him. They'd be doing a lot more pushups than they do now, including on the fingertips.

It's a father's job by design to point a son to the ultimate Father, his heavenly Father and prayerfully make the handoff. In my case, the role was reversed. I am not a better man than my dad. I just came to be better off because I found huge resources early in life that he never knew. Along with an army of other people praying and sharing Christ with him, he embraced the wealth for himself and learned briefly what it was like to do life with God, and not without God.

Father's Day at Merritt's Café with my son unlocked a lot of raw memory in this dad who is a son...a son of Bob Strain, the horse guy, and a son of the eternal Creator/Redeemer Father God.

For three years I asked the eternal Father for my Dad's salvation. He roughed up the rough guy to get his attention—and in the nick of time, wouldn't you say? Is it really surprising that my ministry is helping dads (and all men) take the next step toward God?

Unfortunately, most parenting role models in the Bible are less than stellar, particularly fathers. This can leave a child with a distorted view of God. They can project a poor experience with Dad onto God the Father. Stephen Colbert satirically framed one form of father-failure this way:

> "A father has to be a provider, a teacher, a role model, but most importantly, a distant authority figure who can never be pleased. Otherwise, how will children ever understand the concept of God?"—Stephen Colbert, *I Am America*

In our search for models, you may want to strap on a seatbelt as we take a roller-coaster ride through the ups and downs of Biblical parenting. In my assessment, Colbert got it wrong about God being a distant authority figure who cannot be pleased. Then again, I think he got it right that mankind perceives this to be true of God and demonstrates displaced anger and distance toward God. How do you see it?

CHAPTER 12

Disease Resistance:
Biblical Parenting Models are Bi-Polar

"There are three kinds of men: the ones who learn by reading.
The few who learn by observation. The rest of them
have to pee on the electric fence for themselves."

—WILL ROGERS, HUMORIST

Since you are reading this, the odds of avoiding the parental "electric fence" Will Rogers refers to increases. Yet, let's exercise caution. Let's not take a victory lap yet. The history of parenting is chronicled with hazards. Parenting models in the Bible are mostly negative. But, there is gold to mine in the dirt. Here's a gold nugget in the dirt to observe: as we are seeking to raise our children, God uses the experience to raise us. Grab your pick and lantern, and let's enter the dark "Bible parenting" mineshaft together.

Parents unintentionally pass their dysfunction and darkness (corruption and evil) on to their children. *Yet, we don't stop having children!* Does anyone not see this?! Or, do we simply convince ourselves that we are the parents who will do it better? We think to ourselves: *I have the power (and right) to procreate, so I will. And I cannot possibly screw it up more than my parents did.* But, of course, then we do.

Being the son of a cattle rancher, racehorse trainer and breeder, I have a jaded (or shall we say *earthy*) sense of humor and perspective about all this. We would never do to people what we do with horses: pen up the stud for starters: "No *access, bro! You procreate when we say so, and with whom we say. In fact, if you don't have a high likelihood of producing winners, we will 'fix' you.*" How many times did I hear my dad say, "I'm about ready to cut that SOB!" Often, it was in reference to a young stud horse acting out on the racetrack. Testosterone is useful when under control, but look out for the knife, big hoss, if you are a troublemaker. My dad would work with the situation, giving them every chance, but he only had so much patience when our livelihood was on the line. I digress, but horsemen know something. Fortunately, God has moved toward us procreators in a much wiser, more patient and redemptive way. Yet, in Biblical history, do we not see that humanity has crossed the line at times, where our darkness just can't be turned back? It appears so. God attempts to "pen us in" and present constructive opportunities, but we jump the fence and act out.

The Bible has "up" statements about parenting to be sure, but it's matched with a load of "downers." It's manic. Shouldn't it be more positive?

Perhaps God gives us the negative record of parenting (and human behavior) to help us get in touch with our dirt bag and see our need for Him. Maybe we will ask for help. Maybe we will be more thoughtful, prayerful and vigilant about this amazing challenge. Indeed, I have learned much about the heart of God through becoming a parent of free-will agents. And it has made me desperate. It almost has turned me into a desperado at times, ready to revolt and bolt. I can almost hear the Eagles singing their hit song: *"Desperado, when will you come to your senses…"*

Let's do a quick hill run through Biblical parenting history, to get a diagnosis of our manic attack. Then, we can prescribe meds. You might take Dramamine before you start reading, as it will be "wavy."

As we jog, ask yourself, *Should we keep having children or should we simply put ourselves out of our misery?"*

UP: God had something in mind for humanity on Planet Earth, starting the first cast of parents giving them clear instructions (including the commission to procreate!) in a pristine garden environment. (Genesis 1-2)

DOWN: God's children, the first couple (Adam and Eve), went AWOL almost out of the blocks. He allowed painful consequences, but put a plan in motion to restore right relationships. (Genesis 3)

UP: Children! Going forth to multiply! Two sons. "Children are a gift of the LORD." (Psalm 127:3)

DOWN: The first murder: Cain deep-sixed Abel due to sibling rivalry/ jealousy.

UP: Good thing the first parents had another son, Seth, because Messiah would come through his line.

DOWN: Everyone goes dark.

UP-DOWN, UP-DOWN, TO-GO-UP-AGAIN: God hit the reset button through choosing one righteous man (Noah) and his family. Flush. Reboot. Crap: now we have free will again. These people are really good at creating disasters and now they are doing it through community organizing (Tower of Babel). Scrambling their radar (languages) God closed the one-big-city gate, guiding them toward open pasture to "fill the earth." (Whew! I'm feeling nauseous already. I strongly recommend the Dramamine.) *Let's try this again…*

UP: God calls into being a "covenant family" through the descendants of one man (Abram) that is conditioned only on God Himself to fulfill promises to them (Genesis 12:1-3). God makes the covenant with Himself, perhaps thinking, *They don't have the resources to get it right. All they have to do is trust Me, the creator of the universe, to do it for them.*

DOWN: This family line became quite adept at making wealth but the trust (faith) thing was sketchy. The generations, father to son…father to son… seemed to transfer a fair amount of what we have come to call dysfunction. Stuff like taking matters into their own hands helping God keep His promises (Abram/Sarai), child favoritism (Isaac/Rebekah), children doing desperate things to gain parental blessing and approval (Jacob), and selling siblings into slavery (sons of Jacob and Joseph), to name a few.

UP: God answered the prayers of these women who seemed to have fertility issues, "The fruit of the womb is a reward." (Psalm 127:3b)

DOWN: As her son reached the age where he could have his own children, Rebekah complained to Isaac, "I'm tired of living…if Jacob takes a wife from…the daughters of the land [not their people] what good will my life be to me?"

UP: The children of Israel are dramatically delivered from slavery in Egypt.

DOWN: Four hundred years as slaves in Egypt, followed by a great deliverance (Moses), didn't seem to stick. They still won't trust God to possess the Promised Land. Another forty years of wandering in the wilderness to prepare to enter the land…another woodshed of discipline just doesn't get it done. That generation died off. Their children, plus faith-filled Joshua and Caleb, got to enter.

UP: God graciously gives the Israelites a reboot to prepare them for the land of blessing. The Mosaic covenant, a great future-casting sermon giving clear household rules, is recorded in the book of Deuteronomy. Moses projected how to live in the land. He gives everything they need to know and do to make life as the LORD's covenant people work. Perhaps they will get their act together when they have their own place.

DOWN: They took ground under Joshua's leadership, but bowed to other gods, stalling out after he died. God raised up a new leadership model/ structure, the judges, who would deliver and rule Israel. It did not take; Israel would still do "what is right in their own eyes." (Judges 2:12-16; 21:25) They wanted a king, like all the other nations. They rejected God as their King.

UP: Barren Hannah asked God for a child, whom she dedicated to the LORD's service. She named him Samuel ("because I have asked him of the

LORD"—1 Samuel 1:20, 27-28) who would become a great prophet, trained by the High Priest, Eli, to hear the voice of the LORD and anoint the coming kings of Israel.

DOWN: Eli tragically could not train his own sons to hear God's voice, but rather they used their leadership role in the Tabernacle to use people. "Now the sons of Eli were worthless men; they did not know the LORD…thus the sin of the young men was very great before the LORD, for the men despised the offering of the LORD…they lay with the women who served at the doorway of the tent of meeting…they would not listen to the voice of their father." (2:12, 17, 22-24) Eli honored his sons above God (2:29-30).

UP: "And the glory [weight] of sons is their fathers." (Solomon, Proverbs 17:6b)

DOWN: After his adultery with Bathsheba, who would become Solomon's mother, David's family became characterized by sexual scandals, deceit and conspiracy—all finding their genesis in David misusing his power to take another man's wife, engage her sexually, attempt to cover it up with deceitful tactics, then having Uriah (an honorable warrior) deceptively murdered on the battlefield. Absalom, angry with his father for not acting justly toward his brother (David's son) Amnon raping their sister Tamar, revolted. He deceitfully conspired against his father and died at the hands of David's military. Upon receiving news, David grieved his enemy son's death. "The king was deeply moved and went up to the chamber over the gate and wept. And thus he said as he walked, 'O my son, Absalom, my son, my son Absalom! Would I had died instead of you, O Absalom, my son, my son!" (2 Samuel 18:33)

UP: Solomon wrote, "A wise son makes a father glad." (Proverbs 10:1b) God could not have been more proud of Solomon's request for a "hearing heart" to shepherd God's people when asked what he wanted from God. (1 Kings 3) In this, he followed his father's model. (1 Kings 3:14)

DOWN: Full circle, Solomon would illustrate in full display the temptation Moses warned Israel and its kings about in Deuteronomy 17:14-20. To accumulate horsepower (military might), wealth (gold and silver) and women (political alliances by marriage) would invite idols and false gods to gain their trust and lead them from their covenant God. Solomon had every advantage and still ended his life with a divided heart. His divided heart led to a divided household, followed by a divided kingdom and a civil war. In 722 B.C. the Assyrians provided "the knife" to cut away the ten northern tribes of Israel and disperse them beyond recognition throughout the Earth. Though they lasted 250 years longer, there would be another woodshed for the "more obedient" tribes of Judah and Benjamin, transport provided by the Babylonians under King Nebuchadnezzar (586 B.C.).

***

So much more anecdotal information could be included to illustrate the ups and downs of parenting, especially Father God seeking to bless His children, Israel. He procreates, blesses, leads, disciplines and loves. They get out of control and find themselves in a weed patch, such as experiencing captivity in Babylon for seventy years. His children are His pleasure and pain. He longs to give good gifts, but their own evil and waywardness, choosing to live life without God instead of with God, limits the realization of the Father's longing.

This cursory history reveals realities and modeling about parenting free agents who break toward the darkness too easily. It's not what it ought to be. It's not what it will always be. But it is our inconvenient truth. It is a history and current reality of ups and downs. To rectify it, God brings on the scene of the crime an obedient Son. Ironically, this scenario is full of more ups and downs.

UP: "This is my beloved Son in whom I am well pleased." (The Father speaking of Jesus at His baptism, Matthew 3:17.)

DOWN: Jesus's mother, Mary, at the foot of the cross watching her son die and hearing Him say, "My God, My God, why have you forsaken Me?" And, "It is finished." (John 19:25-30)

UP: God the Son dies on a cross, a perfect sacrifice for sin, rises from the dead, ascends to heaven and is seated at the right hand of the Father, a position of authority and power. (Hebrews 10:10, 12; 12:1-3)

DOWN: Now He is the prodigal God who waits for wayward children to return to Him, even though they have sold out on Him and considered Him dead to them. (Luke 15:11-15)

UP: In this parable of Jesus, God sees the silhouette of a son returning in the horizon and runs out to greet him, hug him, put a ring on his finger and cloak on his shoulders. This son who was dead is alive, who was lost is found.

DOWN: The older son is infuriated that his irresponsible brother has returned to spend the responsible son's share of the inheritance, starting with the fattened calf. He cares only of the stuff, not his brother, not his father. Wouldn't you think he would at least be happy for his father's happiness? Now the father realizes he has lost another son…this time to materialism.

UP: Paradise is restored in the new eternal city…no more tears, death or sin. All things are new for people who chose to live with God.

DOWN: Some choose to be apart from God, forever. They want nothing to do with Him here, or there. C.S. Lewis said, "The gates of hell are locked from the inside," and that "there are two kinds of people: those who say to God, 'Thy will be done, oh God,' and those to whom God says, 'Thy will be done, oh man.'" Again, we choose to live with or without God. Some make it permanent.

Many sons and daughters of God, by creation, will reject his Fatherly love. Made in His image, they are his pleasure; rejecting His presence, they become His pain, but He will not violate their free will. The ultimate parent honors free will, though He is infinitely creative in winning hearts and lovers.

I have chosen God because He made an offer too good to refuse. He is the ultimate God-Father. My wife, Pam, has done the same and this brings us together (a gift) to procreate image-bearers of God (gifts) and thus free agents (also a gift). We enter into a battle zone for their lives. We hope, work and pray they choose the path we did, but it's ultimately between them and God. They are our pleasure and our pain.

If you are single, it's not too late to stop yourself. The best birth control is spending a few days watching someone else's children. Parenting is not for lightweights. It is bi-polar and manic. It can be the highest of highs and lowest of lows. Yet, we can't help ourselves; most of us *must have* children.

CHAPTER 13

Add Manure:
Parents D-Constructed

"Having children is like living in a frat house—nobody sleeps,
everything's broken, and there's a lot of throwing up."

—RAY ROMANO

Leadership is getting people from where they are to where they ought to be. Parenting is leading at its most fundamental level. We must quickly realize we are both builders and battlers, requiring us to be diligent, vigilant and prayerful. Parenting is leadership that can "D-construct" us, leaving us: Discouraged, Despairing, Destroyed, Devalued, Distracted, Divided, Dark and Done!

Some people think the state bird of Montana, my home state, is the middle finger. That is incorrect. The state bird of Montana is the meadowlark, which has a very distinct melody when it sings. True, both birds exist in Montana. The one who sings got the nod to be our state symbol. Here's why. Though dark and challenging times are inevitable, good and beauty can spring forth in parents and children who learn to battle through personal obstacles and threatening circumstances. Birds. Singing. Montana. They all remind me of one of my favorite stories. Consider the story of a third bird.

As normal birds were leaving Canada to fly south one winter, one decided to forgo the trip and stick out the cold. How bad could a Northern winter be compared to all that flying? As the air turned frigid, the bird started having second thoughts. This could be a really long winter. He made the decision to go it alone and head south. "Dang, it's cold!" he chirped out loud. Maybe flapping would get him warmed up. After a while, it began to rain and he began to feel numb. The water was freezing on his little wings, so he flapped harder. He needed to get south as fast as possible to get into warmer weather or he was not going to make it. Working hard, crossing over the Canada/Montana border, he was starting to have doubts. He started to feel himself drop in altitude and could no longer feel his wings.

Mind over frozen feather, he commanded himself to flap for his life. Over Lewistown he found himself in rapid descent, realizing he was going to crash in a barnyard. He landed with an awkward face-plant into a mix of mud and manure. *Is this what it has all come to?* he asked himself. *I'm going to die alone, frozen to death.* A cow standing nearby wandered over and stepped over the top of the bird, paused and dropped a huge plop right on him. "Oh _____ !" exclaimed the bird. "I'm going to die and now THIS to add insult to injury."

Wait a minute, he thought as he experienced a warm sensation begin to hug his little body. *That feels pretty good. I think I can feel my wings.* Moments passed and the warmth penetrated all parts frozen.

"I think I'm gonna live! *I'm gonna live!!*" The bird began to sing at the top of his little bird lungs, songs of thanksgiving. Happy songs.

Meanwhile, passing through the barnyard, a cat heard chirping songs and came over to inspect. *Strange*, the cat thought. *The sounds seemed to be coming from that pile of plop.* The cat cautiously sauntered over and brushed the plop away only to find…a bird!

So he ate him.

Morals of the Story of the Bird
1. Plop happens.

2. Not everyone who drops plop on you is your enemy.

3. Not everyone who cleans it off is your friend.

Humor aside, the real lesson relates to how we respond to the parenting plop. Just as rubble can be used to build walls and manure (plop) used to turn things green and fruitful, parents can use the entire "D-constructive list" to realize growth in lives. There is plenty of plop in our family of origin and in our current family. How do we harness the negative, broken and stinky and turn it into something redemptive and good? Parenting is very personal, relentless and requires our best even when we are at our worst. Lives depend on us. It's both the beautiful and brutal. Did I say it's manic, bi-polar?

We've read our share of parenting books over the years, but the best material and counsel has come from other realms of life, including general leadership models. Most all of our models will find their way into this writing effort eventually, but I will magnify one source here. It gets me fired up every time I read through it, which is often. It's a book of the Old Testament—Nehemiah, a profoundly insightful model of leadership. The fact that it is in the Ooooold Testament might make some yawn.

One might ask, *Why would I read a 2500-year-old leadership story when I can read Drucker or Collins?* Taste and see. Need more? Consider Nehemiah's résumé. He was the most trusted man in the presence of the most powerful monarch during the Persian Empire, Artaxerxes. The breadth of this empire's reach would require some great leadership, and being the King's cupbearer, Nehemiah was privy to it. He was the last line of defense to keep the king alive. Poison was the top-rated way to get rid of a king.

Nehemiah has always resonated with me from the very beginning of serious Bible reading. One can measure my excitement about the books I read by how marked-up the text and margins are. Yes, I mark them up profusely, interacting with the author and digesting the goodies. These markers help me return quickly for references I want to review or teach. I have several old Bibles on a shelf at home. In these old buddies, the pages of Nehemiah are littered with my handwriting. Nehemiah's leadership lessons transcend culture and time. Not bad for over 2500 years old!

The story starts with rubble—a formerly glorious city wall leveled. The Babylonians left no stone on top of another when they sacked and plundered Jerusalem in 586 B.C. They carried its valuables and marched most of its inhabitants to Babylon. We remember dump trucks carrying rubble out of "the hole" in downtown Manhattan after the 9-11 attack on the Twin Towers. For months, truckload after truckload carried it away, leaving a giant hole in the ground. It was surreal to ride the train under the harbor and only to see an empty, epic hole.

Hearing the report of Jerusalem's condition, Nehemiah was crushed. He was a covenant-informed man who knew the LORD. Serving the king in the capitol city of Susa, he went immediately into a season of prayer about the condition of God's city. He knew the Jewish people were in the "woodshed" for their sin and disregard of God's covenant. He also knew that the discipline period was concluding and he was in a position to be a difference-maker because of his place of influence. He asked God for an open door with the king to bring up the issue. I suspect he saw himself as an agent of change for the Holy City in its humiliated state. I know this because of his recorded prayer in Chapter 1 and ready response when God did open the door with Artaxerxes. It was sudden and frightening.

Asked why his face was so sad one day, Nehemiah immediately responded, "Long live the King," a very wise thing for the cupbearer to say when the king wonders why his face is a little intense. The king may be asking, *Did you just poison me? Are you about to poison me?* Nehemiah was prayed-up and vigilant enough to hit the hole with his request. Straightforward honesty is usually the best policy. Nehemiah answered that of course he was down since he heard of the condition of his father's holy city.

Moving on, the king asked, "What do you need?" Nehemiah prayed again, shooting an arrow-prayer to his heavenly King as he looks the human king in the eye.

Beyond *prayerful*, Nehemiah was *vigilant* (watchful) to recognize the divine moment of opportunity. We realize that for several months he had been diligently preparing for this question by planning exactly what he needed to engage Jerusalem's rubble. He had been *diligent* and produced his list of everything needed in terms of travel, resources and time off to lead the project. He didn't just ask, he prepared and watched for an answer.

Prayerful. Watchful. Diligent. The three attributes go hand in hand for the leader or parent who wants to do God's building project, whether building a wall, a palace, a household or anything for God's people. Perhaps Nehemiah had pondered Solomon's proverb, "The king's heart is like channels of water in the hand of the LORD; He turns it wherever He wishes." (Proverbs 21:1) Nehemiah's influence began in private, talking to the King of the universe about the king of most all of the Earth.

4 x 4—A Four-part Definition of a Man for Four Sons

Nehemiah shows masculine initiative here that is so worth noting. Men, by nature, tend to be passive on the spiritual/social front. The first man illustrated this passivity in the Garden when he was "with her [Eve]" as the serpent seduced her into acting in open challenge to God's counsel. Adam watched Eve commit spiritual suicide and then drank the poison potion himself. (Genesis 3:6)

For years I had wrestled with what a man was to be. Having four sons, I thought a lot about it and how it was to be handed off. My dad's physical distance (not emotional) left me with a dropped baton in the man race. My own rubble moved me to press for a solution about how to build the man-wall in my own life as well as my sons' lives. I am not a better man than my dad, but I knew I was better off because I had access to mentors who thought long and well about this. I also had a Father-God who I could ask for help in answering this. And I did ask—a lot!! I eventually adopted a working definition from Robert Lewis that was imbedded in deep Biblical theology, yet succinct and memorable. A real man:

- *Rejects passivity*
- *Accepts responsibility*
- *Leads courageously*
- *Invests eternally*

I thought I might wordsmith my own definition, but chose to use Robert's until I had something I liked better. I could never improve on it. It became the hitching post for my man-interactions with my sons. It's what I told the man in the mirror every morning. I palm a keychain throughout the day that has the definition written on it, reminding me to connect the enduring substance of manhood to key responsibilities. This definition has found its way into the ceremonial rites-of-passage in which I've engaged my sons. It's also been a significant additive in the man-food I serve up in my personal ministry, year round.

My point: Nehemiah continually illustrates and models this definition. Threaded through his account of rebuilding the wall of Jerusalem is the man-definition expressed through prayerfulness, diligence and vigilance.

When Nehemiah entered Jerusalem, at night he privately surveyed the wall rubble. He then told his story to the leaders and invited them to engage in his ambitious task in 2:18-20.

> (18)"Then I related to them how the good hand of my God was on me and what the king had said to me. Then they replied, 'Let's begin rebuilding right away!' So they readied themselves for this good project."

> (19)But when Sanballat the Horonite, Tobiah the Ammonite official, and Geshem the Arab heard all this, they derided us and expressed contempt toward us. They said, 'What is this you are doing? Are you rebelling against the king?'

> (20)I responded to them by saying, "The God of heaven will prosper us. We his servants will start the rebuilding." But you have no just or ancient right in Jerusalem."

The final frame is described in 6:15-16:

> "So the wall was completed on the twenty-fifth day of Elul in just fifty-two days. When our enemies heard and all the nations who were around us saw this, they were greatly disheartened. They knew that this work had been accomplished with the help of our God."

Here is a summary of observations about the start and end of the project:

1. God gave the resources and ability to Nehemiah and the workers for the work to succeed.

2. Nehemiah and the Jewish people engaged in the hard work. They did their part.

3. From start to finish Nehemiah faced enemies and agents of D-construction. Rubble rascals! These boulder bullies had a nasty bag of tricks and were relentless in punches thrown.

Corresponding to these observations were Nehemiah's three actions throughout the project. All three of these were meant to function together all at once. It wasn't just about hard work. It wasn't just about prayer. And it wasn't just about perceptive eyes and perspective. It was all three. Let's dissect all three and then survey Nehemiah 4 where they are vividly on display.

1. **Prayerfulness (Asking).**

   There are several very personal, first-person prayers recorded by Nehemiah, often including, "Remember me O God . . ." Four things are certain: Nehemiah knew the character of His God, what was important to God in terms of the covenant and Jerusalem, that God would listen to him for the sake of God's people, and that *he was not afraid to ask*. Nehemiah always took his issues to God first. He talked back to his enemies but never let them get him off of the work. He spoke truth that put them in their place.

2. **Diligence (Hard work).**

   "So we built the wall…for the people had a mind to work." (4:6)

   ". . . then all of us returned to the wall, each one to his work." (4:15b)

   "So we carried on the work." (4:21)

3. **Vigilance (Watchfulness).**

   The opposition that mobilized against the workers, the "rubble rascals," were ministers of D-construction. This may be considered D-ranged, but consider their five-fingered-fist that can and will D-liver a powerful jab, knocking well-meaning workers/parents off of their feet. Ask yourself if this list isn't a recipe for parental dis-ease. Everything but the kitchen sink was pitched at those engaged in God's good work.

   - *Discouragement*—Demoralized, demeaned & disparaged. (Nehemiah 1; 4:5; 6:9)

81

- *Distraction*—Off the best thing(s), focused on the lesser or good (4:12, 16-17; 6:3-8)

- *Division*—Conflicts that divide us: immaturity, core values and sociopath evil. (Nehemiah 5)

- *Discredited, Dismissed and Despised*—Dishonor is painful. (2:19-20; 4:1-5; 6:10-14)

- *Disturb and Destroy* (4:8, 11; 6:1-2; 10-14)

The point? We are not only builders, but battlers.

You want to see a spiritual street brawl? Pull out a Bible and read Nehemiah 4. It captures concisely everything I'm saying here. Watch the interaction of the D-constructionists with the Nehemiah-led wall builders who were praying, working and watching. Trowel in one hand, a sword in the other, alarmed by a watchful trumpeter, we build and battle.

A parent, married or single, who seeks to turn life-rubble into life-building materials, must engage all three disciplines to move ahead *with* God in the home:

Prayerfulness. *ASK!*

Diligence. *WORK!*

Vigilance. *WATCH!* (For God's response to your asking that directs your work.)

CHAPTER 14

Gardens Are for Eating:
God's Good Gift of a Lover and Life-Mate

"Delight yourself in the LORD
and He will give you the desires of your heart."
—David, Psalm 37:4

By now, a theme should be coming through loud and clear. I have learned to ask God for the big and small things. It's not my nature to ask for help, but when in over my head and someone with resources has invited me to ask, well, I ask! It's safe to say this has paid off in ways unimaginable. At every wedding I officiate, I quote C.S. Lewis: "Put first things first and you get second things thrown in; put second things first and you lose both first and second things." This truth has been highlighted in my marriage to Pam. The result—a "garden" in which I could "eat its choice fruits." (Song of Solomon 4:16b) Was it presumptuous that I should trust God for such a great gift? Evidence points to not at all.

It was my intention that my sons sense that I treated their mother (and my wife) as a gift. I hoped they would be excited and hopeful about marriage, possessing a basic confidence about their treatment of women in general and clear-eyed about the kind of woman they would pursue.

I asked God to bring just the right woman to me at just the right time. I suspected that because I wanted to be married, he must have someone out there for me. There were times in my early Christian life in college that I longed for that person. In my yearly reading through the Bible, I would note that God brought Rebekah to Isaac. God provided the right girl at just the right time and He was very involved in the details. My assumptions about God's involvement on this front were multiple:

1. He put desires in me that He most likely intends to fulfill. Psalm 37:4 always caught my attention, "Delight yourself in the LORD and He will give you the desires of your heart." How could I possibly know the depth and duration of that?! God knows. If I put "first things first" seeking Him first and foremost, He either will meet my desires or change them.

2. He invented marriage and it is his default plan for the majority, of which I'm a subset.

3. He cares for me and the details of my life. He invited me to ask.

4. He is infinitely creative and wise in His timing, so I don't have to "make it happen" but I do need to be watchful and give things a chance.

5. In the meantime, He is as much committed to making me "the right guy" as He is to helping me find the "the right girl."

6. Having been exposed to a broken marriage and rough second rounds for my parents, I needed to gain new models and understanding and have a good grip on God's design for marriage and family. Plus, I needed to be a student of women and learn how to treat them well—all of them— whether I'm married to them or not. I remember reading books to start figuring this out, such as *Letters to Philip*. The book is an accumulation of letters a father wrote to his newly married son, helping him to learn how to treat a woman. I read a chapter each day, pondering the wisdom and retraining my mind.

These assumptions had a huge effect on how and whom I would date. Actually, I spent most of my time encouraging the sisters involved in our ministry, whether I had "interest" in them or not. Usually I didn't chase unless I was sure it was someone I really liked.

Along the way, I really enjoyed hanging out with the Campus Crusade staff women. They were all "older" than me, so there seemed to be a safe distance, but I wasn't shy about catching time with these marvels. I knew I wanted to be locked down long-term with someone like that, a Great Commandment/ Commission playmaker for life. It wasn't that I was "interested" in any one of them in particular: I just knew that I wanted to commit to a woman who did as they did and who understood that:

1. God would be number one and I would be number two. My reasoning here is that putting God first would raise the bar on how they treat others, including a less-than-perfect husband. No one person can possibly meet all the needs of another person. Only God can do this, but He uses a variety of people in our lives.

2. They needed to take care of themselves so that they were more able to care for others.

3. They were committed to something bigger than us: God and His kingdom for starters, but also being a tangible part of a movement of people helping others take the next step toward Jesus.

Somewhere along the way I communicated to my mentor, John Rogers, my intention not to involve myself with anyone who was not a "mature and godly woman" of the nature I've just described. John moved into another ministry leadership role out of state, but returned to Idaho for a visit a year or two later.

I was dating a new Christian, someone I was influential in introducing to Christ. He pulled my own statement out on me saying, "I thought you said…" Stinger. There was nothing wrong with the young woman I was dating; she was a tremendous person, but she was the unfortunate proof of my compromise. I was jumping the gun and trying to make something happen. I was not where I knew I needed to be, including Psalm 37:4. In my heart of hearts I knew it wasn't the right thing and I had to discontinue it. That was brutal, but it was the right thing to do before heaven.

John was kind of a menace to me on the other end as well. Actually, I owe him twice. There was a very sharp student friend who did meet all the criteria, who had just broken up with her high school sweetheart. He was also my good friend and the three of us were in the leadership circle in campus ministry. I didn't know the details, but I knew they agreed to "break up and were free to date others." Tim was doing just that, so I declared my interest to John in pursuing Renee. He looked at me and said an emphatic, "No! Don't do it." It was one of those moments where you know someone knows something they can't say. I thought Tim was crazy for letting Renee become a free agent, but now that she was, she really wasn't. What the heck. It was sort of weird to consider anyway. I chose to trust John's firm counsel to back off. Really good call; Tim and Renee would re-emerge in due time and marry as we all thought they should have all along. They are also our very close friends to this day. Pam and Renee are particularly close.

Then came Pam. She emerged on the scene a few months after the other breakup, but in direct response to another honest "ask" on my part. My good friend, Bill Howard, and I climbed Red Hill overlooking the campus of Idaho State. Bill had joined Campus Crusade staff and I was soon to after another semester of school. Standing on a bench in front of the "Greek-Roman looking columns," he asked me what I wanted to ask God for. He said, "I want to pray that I will not be satisfied." He meant that in the sense of not being mediocre or half-hearted about life. I appreciated that, but my honest prayer was that I *would* be satisfied by the woman God had for me. I was cautious about being susceptible to a rebound, but that's why I was asking. I felt compelled to ask. God answered both prayers. I met Pam a few days later and Bill would not get married (or be satisfied) for several years. We always have a good laugh about that. Be careful what you ask for. Terri was worth the wait for him.

With Pam, it was apparent early she was "the one." It was just a matter of due diligence and verification that came clearly after an all-night chat on a retreat we both attended. We connected on all sorts of fronts, but the clincher was when she shared Psalm 37:4 with me and said, "My part is to delight myself in the LORD and trust that He will give me the desire of my heart in terms of relationships."

She could have cited many Bible verses that night and none would have arrested my attention as Psalm 37:4. This was too quirky to be coincidence. Things up and running, we began to spend some time together. Engaged in five months; married within a year of meeting.

To appreciate her path to Psalm 37:4, one story has to be shared. I was looking through her binder of photographs from her previous years at Ohio State.

One picture was of a cake in the form of the United States, accompanied by the caption, "Happy Boy Day!" On the cake were several locations with men's names written on them: Gary from Nebraska, Mark from Columbus, Russ from Colorado, another Gary from San Diego, to name a few. *What the heck is this?!* I was stunned and lost in wondering if I was another dope-on-a-rope. "If you can't be with the one you love, love the one you're with," or something like that. She assured me that they were all history and a large part of her journey to Psalm 37:4. A couple guys in her robust dating history had even told her it was God's will for her to marry them, which was perplexing because God had not told her!

The next few months, I met several of these guys. They were all great guys, but I think I got the prize because I was praying for her since 1978 and my prayers preceded their best moves. Gary from San Diego was particularly humorous when I was introduced as her fiancé. I think he was a little underwhelmed. He pulled me aside out of earshot of Pam who was in another conversation and said, "You?!!!" in the most incredulous unbelieving tone. Then, in a more serious and teachable voice asked, "How did you do it?" I just smiled and said, "Amazing grace, I guess." In retrospect, I would add, "I asked first." (God, that is.)

Thirty years later, I'm writing as if it just happened. It's hard to believe we are empty-nesters with four sons released as gifts to the world. Our two married sons were selective and they were graced by marrying women who are nothing short of diamonds. To watch the friendship Bryant shares with Christina and that Jason shares with Jenna is immensely satisfying. We prayed for these women from the start; we learned the same was true of their parents, who prayed for the men their daughters would marry.

Delighting and asking. Desires met in the right time and right way. I feel suspended and living beyond my pay grade just saying it. One of the best gifts we have given our sons is the reality that they can do both (delight and ask) with us because I hope they see it in us, and more importantly with God. It appears that is the case.

We are including a letter written by Jason to his new in-laws, Bob and Pam Harmon, asking for their daughter Jenna's hand in marriage. Jason already asked them in person, but told them to watch for his letter with a more detailed explanation. Let's not overlook the obvious. Jason delighted. And Jason asked

God, Bob and Pam, and, of course, Jenna. And we prayed for him and counseled with him through the whole process. Tell me you wouldn't want a letter like this (see Appendix E) from a prospective son-in-law who has put first things first. Jason and Jenna, whom we refer to now in the hybrid form "Jenson," became "Team Jenson" in August, 2013.

If you think our story is a quirk and that it's really up to us to find our spouse with our own genius and finesse, then this story will mess you up. It features the same God, same family line, same creativity, but it's a unique story. I can tell the same kind of sweet story about Bryant and Christina. However, Jason and Jenna's story has some extra dimensions pertaining to themes in this book. There is room for one story in this chapter.

To more appreciate Jason's letter, some historical context should be provided. The spring of Jason's junior year of high school, he arrived home and offered this information:

"Dad, Jenna's parents were asking about our last name and they think they might know who we are."

Curious, I asked, "What is her last name?"

"Harmon," he answered.

I pondered . . ."Are her mom and dad named Bob and Pam?"

"I don't know. I'll ask."

It was my best (and only) guess. Unlikely, I thought, however, as I would certainly know if they lived in Eagle. Bob was a childhood friend from the fourth grade on. We ran in the same pack of friends and played several sports together, including Babe Ruth baseball. His dad was the coach. I barely knew Pam, but I certainly knew of her. She was the cute girl who transferred to Hamilton High from Victor. She and Bob had been high school sweethearts, though she was a year behind us.

Word came back from Jason, "It *is* Bob and Pam Harmon."

I was stunned. I discovered that they had lived in Eagle for *six years*. Eagle is not that big and our children went to the same schools—junior and senior high. How could we have not run into each other in six years?! Or become aware of each other through multiple high school friends? This was crazy.

A few weeks later, Jason and Jenna became more than part of the same circle of friends. They started spending "special time." This was really bizarre, but really cool. We loved Jenna. We secretly thought, *Wouldn't this be amazing if their relationship went somewhere?* (Don't say it and jinx it.)

We had some gatherings with the Harmon family, watching Boise State football, etc. A new place in life, it was fun to get re-acquainted and explore the gaps. I will say that we also knew each other from the ground up, so there was a brotherly rapport between Bob and me. Some things didn't need to be explained. We were both rednecks at the core.

Sometime later, Bob's parents visited Eagle. I couldn't wait to see his dad and share the effect he had made on my life as a baseball coach, and as a man. To put it in a nutshell, Bob, Sr. noticed me at a time when I was vulnerable to the "dark side." He gave me a chance, spending amazing time and energy coaching me. More than that, he would always take a special interest in me, perhaps because I was in Bob, Jr.'s circle of friends. Whenever we came into the Penney's clothing store he managed, he would always take time to show personal interest and visit with my mom and me. Bob, Sr. put some of his minor league baseball knowledge to work, coaching what became a two-time championship baseball team.

I loved baseball and softball, and was much better at the latter because of hours of opportunity at school. The baseball (hardball) opportunities were limited because I would miss too much of the summer season over the years due to traveling with my dad around the Montana horse racing circuit. So, I was platooned in the outfield and rarely got any real coaching. I was in the junior high years, feeling lost and invisible. Life was hard after the divorce. Everyone was in survival mode, so anything extracurricular meant I was largely on my own to fend for myself and to get myself to and from sports practices and games. I was very motivated so I welcomed the extra mileage by pedal.

One day, Bob, Sr., likely frustrated with our catcher's inability to throw the ball to second base and catch base-stealers (one could clock the guy's throws with a calendar), approached me. He said, "Jon, you have a pretty good arm. Have you ever caught?" I said, "Just playing in the backyard. I've never put on the gear." He helped me put on the gear and gave me the do's and don'ts of catching. I was the new catcher after one outing. It seemed he was coaching me up with every pitch for the next two years: affirming, teaching, kindly correcting (a lot!), yet always believing in me. Somebody noticed and cared. I can't say I was really conscious of it, but I sensed it. Years later, I came to realize that it was huge. I was slipping away and somebody saw something in me. I was starting to get some wins under my belt at something I loved. He worked with me on hitting and I began to strike some good balls. He even bought me a thick sponge to insert into my catcher's glove because of a bruised hand.

One very hot July day, we were in a game that couldn't end. Every batter reached base on either a walk or an error. It was miserable—especially for a catcher. I was working hard. Each team put up points that rivaled a football game: in the 30s. We went through what seemed like our entire team taking a turn on the mound and no one could find the plate.

Finally, Bob, Sr. came out and asked, "Jon, have you ever pitched?"

"Just in the yard, Mr. Harmon, but never in a game," I shyly offered. He said, "Take the gear off. You're on the mound." Well I was certainly warmed up from playing catch with the entire team, not to mention five to seven hundred knee bends. I was too shy to show a full wind-up, but I threw strikes and got us out of the game from hell.

Bob said, "Jon, you have good control. You're in the pitching rotation from now on." You cannot imagine what that did to me. Bob began to give me pitching pointers, such as how to do a full wind-up.

My crowning moment, small to everyone reading this, but huge to a lost-in-the-cracks junior high boy, came toward the end of my second season. The main umpire was a gruff guy named Red. He also coached the Ravalli County all-star team that would play around Montana. I'd heard stories about Red. He was tough. One day, during a game between innings, he asked me, "What are you doing the rest of the summer?" I said, "I'm headed out to be with my dad, who is racing horses." He said, "I'd like you to be my catcher for the all-star team." I was stunned. In two years, Bob, Sr. had coached me up from very lost in the outfield depth chart to an opportunity to be the county all-star catcher.

This is not a tribute to my great athleticism, but to a man who noticed a young man who needed to be noticed, discovered and cultivated. He changed everything for me. Little did he know, this kind of DNA would be passed on through the catcher to the young man who would marry his granddaughter one day. Small world; things come full circle. It was my honor to honor Grandpa Bob at the wedding rehearsal dinner for "Team Jenson."

Jason and Jenna showed amazing restraint, patience and maturity as their relationship stretched into college and through the college years, often marked by distance when Jason went to Boise State and Jenna finished at Eagle High School, and then again, when Jenna attended Washington State University. They enjoyed a couple years at Boise State together, but distance stepped in again when Jason moved to Seattle for his first real job and Jenna finished her accounting degree at BSU. Everyone knew they were right for each other.

Read it and consider:

"... *how much more does your heavenly Father give good gifts*" *to those who ask...*"

Bob and Pam asked.

Jon and Pam asked.

Jason asked God.

Jason asked Bob and Pam.

Jason asked Jenna, of course.

Jenna already asked God... So, how could the giver of good gifts say, "No?"

And the story we didn't tell about Bryant and Christina; they both asked God for their future mate.

Christina's parents, Harold and Carrol—yes, they asked too—a lot.

Will you ask? For yourself? For your children?

Go ahead; be audacious. Do it now. Do it again.

CHAPTER 15

Sow Big, Reap Big;
Sow Little, Reap Little:
God Is a Giver and the Maker of Givers

"I shovel out the money, and God shovels it back to me—
but God has a bigger shovel."
—R.G. LeTourneau, inventor of earth-moving machines,
who reached a place of giving 90 percent of his income back to God

We are designed to be conduits of God's good gifts through giving, living and asking. We tend to resist testing God the giver in how we use money. Yet, God invites testing (Malachi 3:10) and gives leadership on this front. Perhaps my story will reveal why people break one way or the other. I hope you will choose to give God the benefit of the doubt.

Graduating college, I was debt-free, but my net worth was less than $200. My parents contributed $300 to my college effort, bailing me out at the end of my first year to get me home. That's it. How did I do this debt-free? Little cash, attending an out-of-state university, served three summer mission or leadership training experiences, virtually no help from my parents (I didn't ask them) and minimal scholarship monies that were used up the first year. How did I graduate from college without debt? My calculations for part of the answer include:

1. I was a Resident Advisor for most of my time at school, which covered room and board and a very small stipend each semester ($100).

2. I lived frugally, certainly not on the cutting edge of fashion. I didn't own a car until my last year and a half. I walked and found other ways to get around.

3. I had occasional odd jobs and summer jobs paying minimum wage.

4. I had some aid, covering modest tuition fees, but only during the first year.

How did I manage to come through with what I needed, no more and no less? The math (or memory) seemed to transcend or escape me. I learned three things during this season that have marked my entire life related to giving, living and asking:

- First, I gave off of the first-fruits of all my (meager) income.

- Second, I lived within my means and never went into debt. In my mind, it wasn't even an option.

- Third, I asked God to provide for what He called me to do, where and when He called me to do it.

Daring to Give

Having good role models on this front (my mom and stepfather, O.D.), knowing what the Scripture taught on giving, plus being in over my head, I calculated that I had nothing to lose by giving off the top.

Seriously. It was my discipline to write at least a ten percent check, giving off the top of my meager income. It was on the level of the famous widow's mite that Jesus championed, but that inspired me. I wanted to give as unto the LORD.

How much my Mom and O.D. gave, I did not know when I was living under their roof. Yet, occasionally I would observe them writing checks to give to our church and was aware of many other organizations they donated to. Later, I learned they were giving away 40 percent of their income, living mostly on Social Security. They were debt-free, had a large garden from which they were able to be very generous, had the home paid off, etc. They were simple, frugal, hardworking and generous. Modeling matters.

Part of my pursuit of autonomy was healthy in that I learned to work hard and pay my own way. Part of it was not. I would learn to live dependently on the LORD first, then interdependently with others. The last one has been the hardest to learn.

Jesus and all of Scripture is unanimous on the act of asking and giving. I learned to ask, seek and knock. That means I would ask for provision, seek His answer and ways to do my part and jiggle doorknobs for answers. Yes, God provides for the birds, but the birds spend a good portion of their day out picking it up. I learned that I was a conduit of God's life, provision and blessing. In the words of R.G. LeTourneau, the creator of large earth-moving equipment, *"I shovel out the money, and God shovels it back to me—but God has a bigger shovel than I do."* I started learning this early. In my case, it was a spoon. God invites us to test Him in Malachi 3:7-12, so I did and found that I couldn't out-give Him. He is infinitely creative in providing for us.

Giving is multi-faceted. I'm a giver with the checkbook and very attentive to the larger budgetary giving we do. Pam is a giver in the sense of showing special value to each person, always finding the right gift for each one. We have learned more about God's attribute of giving by living together. My giving is very faith-oriented and took her breath away early in our marriage. She would often say, "We are doing this on YOUR faith." She has been my teacher on studying the needs and desires of people and knowing, through the exact right gift, how to say, "You are very special." Christmas, birthdays, weddings, whatever the occasion may be, Pam has the appropriate idea. She often consults with me on the amount, but she always gets the most from whatever our ability is. Gift-giving is her love language.

Putting our first budget together was a struggle because the special gift category was not reflected in it. I put traditional categories in it, including my style of giving: first-fruits off the top. For several months, I worked at trying to get the perfect budget, but Pam would turn her nose up at each version. It was getting tense because we had a limited amount of money, some fixed categories and some flexible categories based on our living values. As I listened to her one day, it came to me that a budget is an expression of our values and ours didn't express her value of special gifts. *Lights on!!* We fixed that and have experienced harmony ever since.

Daring to Live a Simple, Debt-Free Life

In college, loans were not that common or easy to get, especially for someone like me. So I hunkered down to work and pay for things as I went. This discipline would pay my dividends for the rest of my life. We certainly have more discretionary spending than those days, but my demeanor is the same.

Aside from our mortgage, we have never carried debt. Even with the mortgage, we have assets to match. It really bothers me when I have to pay interest on anything. I'm a fanatic about this to be sure.

We keep track of our spending down to the dollar, keeping a handwritten ledger of our budget categories accessible to record each purchase. Our discipline is to collect purchase receipts and record them every day or two. It's a little extra work, but we always know where we (as in "we together") are with budget categories and cash flow available. Some have heard about this and feel suffocated by the thought. I say to them, but we are free and rarely have financial spats that come when the right hand is unaware of what left hand is doing. The shared ledger is our shared reality.

An older friend of ours, Terry Kester, once commented that he taught his children not just how to save or give, but also how to spend. I like his common sense notion that all money will be spent ultimately and reflect the larger values of our lives. To teach our young children what can be done with money, we used a Larry Burkett bank, which was a transparent plastic container in the shape of three buildings: a bank (saving), a church (giving) and a store (spending). When they made money, we coached them to deposit some into each section, 10 percent, 10 percent and 80 percent. We wanted to introduce them to basic categories and practices of how money can be used. It seemed to take. Each son developed his own budget once he left for college. Bryant did it first with the on-site help of a college mentor and we encouraged him to share what he developed with his brothers. They are all budget-savvy at their stage of life.

Daring to Ask

Jesus taught us to pray, *"Give us this day our daily bread."* I pray this every day, but let's be honest here: we live with means so beyond this simple request. I tell people that I am one of the richest missionaries in the history of the Christian church based on when and where I live. That said, it takes a lot to stay alive and not become a burden to others. And if you haven't heard, it's very expensive to die! In fact, an absurd percentage of one's total life expenditures will come at the end of his life, especially if medical care is required.

So, we pray and ask (more often thank) God for our daily bread. I also have learned to ask God to raise up donors for Search Boise. We get paid a set amount determined by Search, but if we don't develop our funding, we don't get paid or reimbursed for expenses.

How many nuts should we put away for the winter season of retirement? This is a crazy-maker for my retiring or retired friends. How does one calculate this not knowing how many days one will have? Ultimately, we have to trust God with the answer and details. In general, with respect to saving, we take our lesson from *both* the ant of Proverbs (Solomon) and the bird of the Sermon on the Mount (Jesus). The ant saves while he can; the bird is out picking up food most of the day, though Jesus said God provides for the birds. Many things could wipe out our nest egg: catastrophe, overwhelming medical challenges, being defrauded, etc.

So again, we practice asking, seeking and knocking. "Unless the LORD builds the house" applies to the financial piece as well. Most of the time it is our challenge, whether we are in prosperity or adversity, to say with Paul, "I have learned to be content in all circumstances." (Philippians 4) I don't want to be a burden to others. So, I may have to live on less.

I had several opportunities to learn asking, seeking and knocking in finances while I was in college. The first was applying for in-state tuition. It appeared that I would have to return to Montana to school, but I felt strongly that I was supposed to stay at Idaho State. Stressing about it, I surrendered this to God, but said, "LORD, I think you want me at Idaho State. Will you work through the application for in-state tuition, even though I don't have a strong case apart from threatening to leave the school?" He did, because I asked.

I felt His nudge to participate in a summer mission project in Malaysia. The fundraising part was unnerving. I sent letters out to a number of people I knew who might be open to participating. Two weeks out from the deadline, I had about half of what I needed. The letter trail had grown cold, no doubt, and I felt that I might need to widen the circle of asking. But, with whom? Cold calls? On top of that, I was heading into dead week and finals and had no time to do both. I remember well one Sunday night, feeling pressed by the obstacles in my resources that I could not see a way to overcome. I expressed this burden to the LORD and said, "If You called me to this, You must come through. From what I see, if You don't do something, it won't happen. Will You make it happen?" I simply asked, then waited as I attacked papers and finals, resting in His provision if there was truly a calling. Several days went by and a couple more small checks arrived. Then I opened a letter from wheat farmer friends I worked for through several harvests. The letter explained their excitement about what God was doing in my life and the opportunity at hand. Then Anne wrote, "Louie and I prayed about this independently and the LORD put this number in both of our minds." Enclosed was a check for $1000, exactly what I needed.

It wasn't just the large check, it was the way they had come to a number together, asking, and God speaking into their hearts exactly what I needed deadline week. This would be a huge building block for a lifetime of what some refer to as "faith risk" fundraising for ministry. In fact, I've only spent two years drawing a "normal" paycheck in my entire adult life, and that was in the midst of a faith risk church plant when the church grew enough to be able to support both pastors. It was a huge building block for what God was calling Pam and me to. It is something He has used to affirm our calling. We have missed paychecks here and there, but the LORD has always made up for it later after He reminded us that He holds our lives and calling in His hands. I don't think that is different for anyone, though others don't have to go through a hiring process, only to be told, "You need to develop the funding to get paid."

A few months into our first year with Search (2002) we missed paychecks for almost two months. I can be good for nothing, but I just can't do it for very long. We were letting our need be known and had a little reserve for buffer, but for how long? During this time, Pam and I recorded our devotional life in our journals. An amazing gift came in, the largest single gift we have ever received in ministry. We were gifted a night away (from children) so we took our journals and read our entries in consecutive order. Amazing to me was that my more security-oriented wife didn't panic through this period. Neither did I. In a strange way,

God used that period to confirm our calling. I experienced freedom from a firm conviction that it wasn't about the money or security. I resolved that if we ended up having to sell our home and move into the low-rent trailer park, we still would do Search. We hoped and prayed otherwise, but were willing. This confirmed our calling like nothing else could have.

It seems that God has us in a socio-economic place to reach into a lot of worlds, both up and down. He enabled us to put our sons through college. We have just taken it day by day, month by month, asking for our daily bread. That's what Jesus taught us to pray for, our *daily* bread. I thank Him for the abundance beyond what we need that day, but I also ask Him to raise up donors and money for Search Boise on a daily basis. I have learned to do so. I've also learned to be content in whatever circumstances we find ourselves. We are the same in abundance or tight-belt seasons. We have chosen to do finances with God because He has shown Himself to be faithful through so many years. We have learned to ask and this makes us better people and parents.

Howard Hendricks was often in the home of a very wealthy family. One day he was visiting one of the adult sons and made an observation. He said, "You are immersed in wealth and yet seem so detached from it all. How is that possible?" The man replied, "My parents raised us to understand that wealth could be either a tool or an idol."

Like the man said to me about our children: "They know." They know what we love and serve ultimately. Do we? Or do we fool ourselves? What do we need to do to put first things first?

> *"I have held many things in my hands and have lost them all.*
> *But whatever I have placed in God's hands, that I still possess."*
> —Martin Luther

99

PART II:

Surgically SEEK to Cultivate the Gift of Each Seed

Glenn was frustrated. I was frustrated for him. He so badly wanted to communicate the rich resources of Jesus Christ to two man-groups where he was a participant. One was a group of retired surgeons who labeled their gathering "The RODEO" (Retired Old Doctors Eating Out). The second was a cancer support group, MACHO (Men Against Cancer Helping Others).

Doubly frustrating for me is that for a night and a day, Glenn heard "the best of Search" at our Search35 Conference in Dallas. Buttressed by two strong keynote speakers, including Lee Strobel, 450 men were immersed in the dynamics of a relational and winsome style of communicating their faith in Jesus. As Search staff, we brought our best, but apparently the "stick" factor wasn't there for Glenn, at least not yet. I prayerfully puzzled over this while listening to his outreach challenges at dinner on Saturday evening.

Glenn is a retired surgeon living in another state. He attended the conference at the invitation of his (also) surgeon son, Kevin. Surgeons are a special breed: very smart, sure-minded and confident—perhaps this is why they are "the cowboys" of the medical field. Glenn is discovering the vast riches in Jesus Christ later in life and is passionate for men to know and experience Christ as he does.

"People are dying around me and there is so little time!" he exclaimed to me. With the same intensity he has applied himself to save lives as a surgeon, so now he does as a Christ-follower. One hitch: his good intentions are rebuffed. The typical demeanor of a surgeon is candidness. They don't have to be diplomats. People listen because their life is on the line. This has limits, however, in taking the Gospel to the remotest parts of a fearful heart. Glenn is re-tooling for soul-surgery.

A breakthrough came Sunday morning when Glenn recounted to me the following story. On the surgery table lay a man with multiple punctures in his abdomen from the knife blade of an enraged girlfriend. Glenn was finding and binding up puncture after puncture, mopping up hemorrhaging holes between each suture. After several hours of surgery they were losing the patient and getting desperate. They were running out of blood and out of time. Glenn simply couldn't locate the last puncture. He prayed for eyes to see. *BINGO!* He finally located it and the man's slide toward death was halted. *BINGO,* for me! As I listened to Glenn's story I believe God gave me a "sticky mental picture" to share with Glenn.

"Glenn," I asked, *"what if you were to approach the men in your groups like you approached surgery? On a spiritual life-saving mission you cannot see the wounds in each man's heart that are spiritually life-threatening and creating fear-based rebuffs toward your initiative. What if you prayed for 'eyes to see' and for 'skillful hands,' entering each man's soul with the special care and precision you would in surgery? No incision larger than needed, every caution taken to avoid dangerous bacteria, etc.? Prayerfully, diligently, patiently you explore with God the person's emotional, intellectual and volitional barriers until God shows you what to do?* **What if you did 'soul surgery' with men like you did physical surgery throughout your career?** *I have a passage of Scripture I'd like to pray for you (and myself):* 'So he [David] **shepherded** them according to the **integrity of his heart**, and guided them with his **skillful hands**.'" *(Psalm 78:72)*

With the new application of this familiar image, Glenn's vision was released to move into men's hearts in a new way under the guidance of the Great Physician. It is our hope that the following section will help you "surgically seek" your valuable children under the guidance of the Great Father. Like surgery, it's a science and art requiring eyes and heart.

CHAPTER 16

Germs-In-My-Nation:
Why Do We Make Small Things Into Tall Things?

*"Seek first the Kingdom of God and all these things
will be added to you. Seek and you shall find."*

—JESUS, MATTHEW 6:33; 7:7

Action words fill the language of Jesus as He instructs parents in Matthew 7:7-11.

Ask.

Seek.

Knock.

Incentive is added by repeating the action words and connecting a promised outcome.

Ask and it shall be given to you.

Seek and you shall find.

Knock and it shall be opened to you.

Urgency permeates these three verbs in the imperative form. They are commands. They are strong statements. A command is usually employed when the one receiving it tends to be neglectful or passive about a matter. Jesus doesn't want us to be indifferent or slothful about asking, seeking and knocking.

Evidenced by the fact that they are present tense, these three verbs embody persistence as Jesus means for A.S.K. to be repeated, continuous and ongoing.

Exasperated with myself, I ask, *Why don't I?* What does Jesus know about me, and us, that He has to use imperative, present-tense verbs with amazing outcomes promised? We are corrupted. We are not doing what we were made to do. Live life with God; all of it! Remember, evil is the word He uses to describe the parents listening in. *"If you being evil know how to give good gifts to your children…"* Evil is a not a thing. Evil is a privation, such as a corruption or corrosion, of something "good." It is my tendency to live life without God, but I fool myself thinking things are okay because I am able to give goodness, especially to my children.

Remembering the first section of this book, recall His invitation to ASK! If you do, it will be given to you. Though I amply illustrated the good gifts that permeate my life and our family because of asking, I am still a sloth in relation to asking. God help me to ask more, more often for more good gifts. Living on the same block is the sister of ask. Her name is *seek*. The essence of the lesson she brings to us is that we are not to sit idly after we have asked. We move to go out and collect the answer.

Parents Are to Seek

Providing us a visual from nature, in Matthew 6, Jesus tells the listener to learn something from the birds. Getting to the point, He is warning against becoming anxious about what we shall wear or eat. Look how well God dresses the flowers and how He provides for the birds. He knows you need food and clothing. Jesus asks, *"Are you* [human image bearers of God, including parents] *not worth much more than they?"* (Matthew 6:26b) Not just more, but *much* more! Well, the correct answer is a resounding *yes*, but we have not bought into this view of our value to God. We would rather be worried because we are not sure about God's goodness toward us.

Back to the birds, exhibit A, from nature. Birds are not farmers, sowing and reaping. They do not have barns to store crops. *"Yet your heavenly Father feeds them,"* says Jesus. (Matthew 6:26a) We are not sure we are worth much more than they so we become anxious or worried (divided in the mind) and we act like people who do not know God. We are like the Gentiles (those who do not know the LORD) who *"eagerly seek for these things."* Jesus says, *"Your heavenly Father knows that you need all these things. But seek first His kingdom and His righteousness, and all these things will be added to you."* (Matthew 6:32-33)

Observing birds, I have not noticed their barns, but I have noted they spend a good deal of their day picking up food God has provided. That seems to fit well with what Jesus just taught the disciples to pray: *"Give us this day our daily bread."* (Matthew 6:11) Well, then, isn't that "eagerly seeking"? Yes, in a sense, but it's more just picking up what you need. We live so beyond what we need daily that the discussion seems moot. To be clear, what I read Jesus to be saying here is:

1. God cares for the birds and provides their daily needs, which they go out and pick up.

2. God cares for people a lot more and they can ask for their daily needs and seek to pick it up.

3. In so doing, I seek God as my first priority (the King of the kingdom) and His way of living (which includes me asking and picking up what I need) and He answers my request to provide. The birds and flowers show that God feeds and clothes His image-bearers well.

Stomach acid kicks in and sleepless nights occur when I start to fuss about this at the next level. I begin to live life without God when I:

1. Begin to store up treasures on Earth and not lay up treasures in Heaven, thereby serving mammon (wealth) as "first" and not God. (Matthew 6:19-24)

2. Finding my life and livelihood in wealth or a standard of living that I calculate adds to my value and importance. *"And who of you by being worried can add a single hour (cubit) to his life?"* (Matthew 6:27) A cubit is a measurement. It's ambiguous whether Jesus is referring to time or physical stature, but both fit this context. I will not live longer or be taller in the eyes of myself or others from worrying about what I wear or what I will eat.

It's not wrong to work hard. "Seeking" to pick up God's provision is hard work. It's not wrong to save or store for coming months or years. In Proverbs 30:24-25, Solomon invites the reader to consider the wisdom of the ant, who stores for the winter season. Savings, wealth and abundance are not condemned, but instead God provides a strong warning to those with misplaced priorities. I am prayerful and ask for my daily provision. I am diligent to seek for and pick up God's provision. I'm vigilant about what is going on in my heart and what I am trusting in for my livelihood and personal value. What is first? Who is first?

Is God not more good-hearted and energetic to provide for my family and me than I am to provide for my family? Children want provision, but more, they want to be valued! Remember what the man said: *"They know."* Over time, they become what we are and not what we say we are.

Crisis of Will: What Do I Really Want?

What do you seek? What do you really want? Be careful what you want ultimately, Jesus said. If your treasure is something someone can steal, or rust can break down or death can separate from you, then where will you be when that happens? Things will corrode and others will take possession of your stuff at death, if not before. Things don't make very good gods. (Matthew 6:19-21)

In my seeking, Jesus would rank "first things" this way:

1. God and His way of living.

2. The value of people who bear His image.

3. Hard work for those seeking to pick up God's provision to sustain livelihood and share. Manage wealth to honor God (#1), value and care for people (#2), and sustain creation's resources (#3).

The Priority of Seeking God First

Casually reading the Bible, one observes a consensus of the writers of what the person who desires to live "with God" will seek first. Seeking God first is paramount. Consider here the Old Testament.

Moses, in Deuteronomy 4, forecasts what is needed to attain and sustain a prosperous life in the Promised Land the people of Israel are about to enter:

"For what great nation is there that has a god so near to it as is the LORD our God whenever we call on Him? (4:7) "You will seek the LORD your God, and you will find Him if you search for Him with all your heart and all your soul." (4:29)

God to Solomon, in 2 Chronicles 7:14:

". . . and my people who are called by My name humble themselves and pray and seek My face and turn from their wicked ways, then I will hear from heaven, will forgive their sin and will heal their land."

Hosea to unfaithful Israel, in Hosea 10:12:

"For it is time to seek the LORD . . ."

Seeking God First Requires He Be Our First (and Foremost) Love

Watching the falter of one of our national icons, the Twin Towers, on 9/11 left us riveted to the television. Someone came into our meeting room in the Search Ministries national office and told us an airplane flew into one of the towers. We chased down a television and watched the second airplane/tower collision. We watched with morbid unbelief as each tower collapsed. It was surreal... unthinkable!! It was something we never imagined could or would happen. Not only the Twin Towers but the Pentagon, not to mention a third target—the White House itself. We were sitting in Baltimore at the Search office, 30 minutes from the Pentagon and only 90 minutes from New York City. Watching on television, it all seemed like it was a world away...on the other side of the globe.

That morning, we had just finished engaging in a devotional Bible study, three defining chapters in Luke's gospel, stretching over three mornings. Luke 14, 15 and 16 are all "red letter." The passage is a continuous discussion by Jesus, with some historical "connective tissue" so that the reader discerns whom Jesus is speaking with. Always, the disciples are listening in. He includes the Pharisees in the conversation twice. The 9/11 experience would galvanize in my mind the message(s) that evolved in these chapters. It would mark me in a new way about what really matters and how I was to spend the remainder of my days on Earth:

Luke 14: Count the cost: Love Jesus pre-eminently. (Three conditions to be a disciple of Jesus.)

Luke 15: Seek the lost: Love people proactively. (Three parables teach the value of each one.)

Luke 16: Invest eternally: Use wealth to make friends for the eternal future.

These three chapters have everything to do with parenting. Parenting is about passing on what really matters in the long run. It's about modeling and coaching the most important people in our life about the most important things in life including:

1. Who will your master/leader be? Everyone follows someone.

2. Who will you choose as your mate?

3. What will be your mission? Everyone lives for something, even if just for self.

Run the calculations. What should you consider? Can you afford to go to with God? Can you afford not to? In Luke 14, Jesus gives three conditions for being His disciple:

Condition #1—Luke 14:26

Jesus has the audacity to suggest his twelve disciples love Him above every human relationship, including love of self.

> "If anyone comes to Me, and does not hate his own father and mother
> and wife and children and brothers and sisters, yes, even his own life, he
> cannot be My disciple."

Who is He to ask for that? The Gospel writers are not ambiguous about the claim of Jesus to be God in the flesh. He claimed it and demonstrated it in numerous ways. These are men, so He uses "man language"—hyperbole— to make His point. It would sound a little creepy if He said, "Hey, men, you have to love me a lot more than everyone who matters to you in life." Instead, He captures their attention with an exaggerated way of saying it, *You have to hate* (hyperbole for love less) *all the important "blood" relationships in your life compared to what you think of Me. Blood is thick. Given I am the creator/redeemer of the world, this is thicker. If you don't settle the priority of me being your first love, you cannot be My disciple.*

Condition #2—Luke 14:27-32

> *"Whoever does not carry His own cross and come after Me cannot be My disciple." (v. 27)*

The twelve had no idea yet of Jesus dying on a Roman cross. The image for them would certainly include the known Roman crucifixion, however. A dead man walking: he has no rights, no life of his own. A man guilty, carrying his method of execution in public. As he walks through the public square on his way to crucifixion for crimes against the state, it's as if he is saying, "I'm guilty of such and such crime and subject to Rome to pay by death." It's a powerful image, but again—man language. They owe their lives to Jesus and will no longer walk according to their will but His. They surrender their agenda to Him. Instead of a ruthless state, the disciples are surrendering to the leadership of One who loves them and is a dispenser of good gifts. He will carry a cross for them that will pay their debt against God, erasing a certificate of debt with eternal implications… spiritual death.

He invites them to count the cost by running calculations and by offering illustrations that help them run the numbers in two directions. The parable of building the tower in the vineyard asks, *Can you afford to do this?* The parable of the coming, conquering king with a bigger army than yours asks, *Can you afford not to?* The disciple of Jesus is invited to do the math.

Condition #3—Luke 14:33

> *"So, then, none of you can be My disciple who does not give up all his own possessions."*

If we take Jesus literally, we would walk around naked. That would be extreme asceticism. On the other extreme, He is clearly warning against materialism—being possessed by possessions. So, then, how does He mean for us to take this statement in verse 33? The answer is found in the Greek verb translated "give up." It is middle voice (act on yourself) accompanied by the present tense (keep acting on yourself to give up all your own possessions). It is therefore implied that a person must continue holding the stuff to be able to keep acting to give it up! The word for possession can be literally translated, "all he himself possesses." It, too, is present tense, so I'm to keep giving up all that I possess. Does this sound crazy?

A word picture might be helpful. Imagine the palm of a hand and a symbolic possession—say a precious wedding ring. Ascetism would say, *Let go of the ring... no more ring.* The palm is open and empty.

Materialism would say, *Place the ring on your finger and clench your fist so no one can take it.*

Stewardship (according to Jesus in this text) is saying, *Open your palm and hold the ring or put it on your finger with the palm open.* It is not abandoning or clutching the ring.

Many years ago I heard about the function of a quitclaim deed from Dr. Bill Bright. Before God gave him the vision of Campus Crusade for Christ, he was a businessman who wanted to acknowledge God as owner of all he and his wife possessed. So they symbolically did so with this legal document. A quitclaim deed is a legal instrument by which the owner of a piece of real property, called the *grantor*, transfers any interest to a recipient, called the *grantee*. The owner/grantor terminates ("quits") any right and claim to the property, thereby allowing claim to transfer to the recipient/grantee.

I thought this a powerful statement of God's undisputed ownership and our willing stewardship of all we owned—in the eyes of people. Pam and I recorded all our tangible (and intangible) wealth on such a document and signed it before the LORD. It sits on my desk as a continual reminder. One day I got a little heavenly pop quiz on this. We were driving to Utah and stopped at a rest area. It was gusty. When I opened the door to our minivan, the wind ripped it out of my hand, blowing it forward with an ugly metal crunching sound. I said, "Ooooh! That can't be good." I couldn't believe it. I looked, and the outer metal siding by the hinge was bent. Worse, I closed the door to test it and could only open it again 6 to 8 inches—just enough for my body to squeeze through with some effort. I got furious at how ridiculous this whole thing was. We were on a several-day trip, now with a driver's door that barely opened. And I was obsessed with wondering what it would cost to repair, once we were able to. As I was pulling back onto I-84, I was grumbling to myself when an internal voice (the Holy Spirit, I presume) interrupted and asked, *Jon, whose van is this?* Ah, yes. It too was on the quitclaim deed, I remembered. I wasn't feeling it, but I said, "LORD, I'm sorry about what happened to Your van. What do You want me to do about getting it repaired?"

I passed the quiz and felt burden-free, though still amazed at how stupid the situation was. One day, I passed an auto body shop and asked for God's favor on the repair bill that "His money" would pay for. The man came out, looked at the damage and said, "Wait here a minute." He returned with a tool that he applied to the side of the van. With three quick *thunks* the bent metal was popped out— almost indistinguishable, and the door closed just fine. Nice. It occurred to me that it's easier to hold a minivan with an open palm than with a clutched fist. The minivan is in a salvage yard now. The lesson of putting God first is enduring.

CHAPTER 17

Germination:

God Seeks Valuable Small Ones, Making Them Tall Ones

"'This son of mine was dead and has come to life again;
he was lost and has been found.' And they began to celebrate."
—Luke 15:24

Parents rigorously seek the well-being of their valued children, but often have a hard time thinking God would ever pursue them (the parent). I find this to be a disconnect that leaves them in the spiritual and psychological poorhouse. Much of this has to do with pain, not logic.

Living in our children's pain is an occupational hazard for parents. There are few things worse than watching your children suffer through an upside-down life. We would do anything to deliver them from physical, emotional and psychological pain. Anything that threatens their well-being is our enemy. We are ever watchful for predators, threats, hurtful consequences and anything that diminishes their life. If they are really threatened, we will spare no expense or effort to rescue or deliver them.

Even as I write, I'm observing a young mom trying to carry on a business meeting. She got up in the middle of a sentence and ran outside to speak to two young, grade-school children who appeared to be beyond her watchful eye. She reined them in, apologized to her client, and resumed the conversation as if nothing happened. As "guardians" it's instinctual and done by moms and dads countless times every day.

Why would we think God is less attentive toward us? You remember the question Jesus posed, *"If you then, being evil, know how to give good gifts to your children, how much more will your Father who is in heaven give what is good to those who ask Him!"* Speaking of outside threats, Jesus instructs the disciples:

> *"Do not fear those who kill the body but are unable to kill the soul; but rather fear Him who is able to destroy both soul and body in hell. Are not two sparrows sold for a cent? And yet not one of them will fall to the ground apart from your Father. But the very hairs of your head are all numbered. So do not fear; you are more valuable than many sparrows."* (Matthew 10:28-31)

Two guiding thoughts from Jesus are put forth here:

1. Each one is valuable to God. (More valuable than many sparrows.)
2. Spiritual death is more to be feared than any physical or psychological threat. (Hell is a place of self-inflicted separation from God.)

Lost = Valuable and Missed

Seeking valuable and missed people (children) is the theme of Luke 15. God is concerned about the whole person and their rescue. In response to the Pharisees' question about why Jesus consorts with tax collectors, Luke includes three parables Jesus told in succession to answer their question. They all make the same point: *lost = valuable and missed.* When the lost thing is found, whether a sheep, coin, or a son who cashed in his inheritance and squandered it, all are worth seeking and finding.

Have you ever been desperate to find something valuable and missing? If losing a wallet or your keys isn't bad enough, how about losing a child in a huge crowd?

Our Lost Son

I asked Pam to share her firsthand experience I did not live through in real time. However, her account of it replayed in my vivid imagination, leaves a pit in my stomach every time I think of it. In her words:

One of the most heart-stopping experiences I had when my kids were young was the day I lost Sean at the Idaho State Fair. Sean was around three or four years old. I was with a couple of other moms and their children and we had been taking in all the sights and attractions. We had stopped for a break and I had my friend keep an eye on my boys while I went to the restroom. Unbeknownst to me or my friend, Sean tried to follow me. Needless to say, he couldn't keep up with me. Since I didn't know he was following I didn't turn around or slow down. When I came back, he was nowhere to be found. Let me just say, I can think of better places to lose a child than a state fair! All kinds of ugly scenarios filled my mind. Praying and running around like a crazy woman, I searched frantically for him. But to no avail. Someone told me there was a place where you can report lost children. I headed for that spot and just as I arrived, a security guard, holding Sean's hand, walked to my spot. Oh, my goodness, was I ever relieved! I couldn't lift Sean up fast enough to hug him and cling to him! I really thought I had lost him for good!

Question

When would Pam have stopped looking? (Answer: Never! As long as there was any ray of hope, and beyond that even: never.)

Again, we are arguing backwards, from the lesser to the greater. Being the object of God's pursuit leaves many of us wondering: *Are we worth it? Does He care that much about me?* Answering the why from the standpoint of being a "good human parent" leaves no doubt what will happen on a human level. So, how much more will God pursue His missed and valuable children? When will He quit on us?

He will not.

There is one variable in the Luke 15 story of the lost son that is not present in the first two parables, the lost sheep and lost coin. It's the issue of free agency. The son cashes in his inheritance, effectually saying to his father in this culture, "You are dead to me." He squanders everything, then considers that his father is a good man and might take him back as a servant even though he is no longer a son. He takes a risk. And, for it, he is welcomed home.

The father is watching for his son's return. With the sheep and coin, the seeker goes on the hunt. For the son, he waits, and waits. One day he sees his son's frame in the horizon and runs out to greet him. As he approaches his son he pulls out a concealed 2' x 4' and begins to beat this worthless kid for squandering the wealth and having the audacity to show his face. Sometimes I will be telling this story to irreligious people who are not familiar with Bible stories and they will look at me with the most horrid face. Then I say, "Not really." (It's as if they already know the story should be different than I'm telling it.) Then I give them the story of the father embracing his son, clothing him, firing up the barby for a major celebration. Twice he exults, *"This son of mine was lost and now is found; was dead, but is now alive."* (Luke 15:24, 32) What a picture of amazing grace!

In this case, it's the corrupted and wayward son who has the audacity to return and ask. Could he be a picture of me, the child-of-God, parent? I may not deserve good gifts as a parent, but God invites me to return to Him to ask. I may think I can only return as a slave, but He receives me as a son or daughter. He searches the horizon for my profile, the wayward free agent.

Now He invites me to seek other free agents through waiting. As He waited for me, I stand in His shoes waiting for my children to come to Him. Who knows what it will take to get them to come to their spiritual senses? In this, why wouldn't I be as prayerful, watchful and diligent about their spiritual return to the Father as I am to bring physical or psychological safety as their guardian? Their danger, like mine, is choosing to live without God. I have God-given power to influence this. It must be power rightly used and not abused.

There are winsome things we can do to invite our free-will-gifted children into a life with God. In God's house, as in ours, every ONE matters. But there are two principles (rails) we need to put the "wheels" of our perspective on to keep us "on track":

Rail/Principle #1: Sharing God's amazing grace with our children is a **process**.
Rail/Principle #2: God is responsible for the **results**.

God seeks the missing and valuable, parents and children alike. They are all His children and they are all free agents as His image-bearers. God pursues everyone with what theologians refer to as "common grace." All humanity enjoys some level of God's common grace: air, water, food, family, sunshine, fat rainbow trout on a fishing trip, etc. These are gifts extended to all mankind, belief in God or not, relationship with God or not. God uses common grace to win the missed and valuable into considering His act of amazing grace—His payment for the debt of sin (spiritual death) each of us has rung up on our tab. Reconciled to a relationship with God or not, God still deeply cares about people and their families.

CHAPTER 18

Seed Gifts:
Children Are a Gift from the LORD

"Behold, children are a gift of the LORD,
The fruit of the womb is a reward."

—Psalm 127:3

God subtly seeks to win parents to Himself through the common grace gift of children.

Are children a gift or a reward? The Psalmist appears to say both. Yet, isn't that a contradiction? A gift is not something earned. A reward is earned. Perhaps we can explore the structure and flow of Psalm 127 and resolve the tension. I suggest that children are both a gift and a reward, depending on what season of life parents find themselves in. The larger context of the Psalm presents something vaster than a point in time; it spans a lifetime.

Children and Work: Necessary but Risky Ventures

Working out from the core message of the chiasm (God being the giver of gifts) is the corresponding couplet found in v.2a, *"eat the bread of painful labor"* and v.3b, *"the fruit of the womb is a reward,"* referring to *"the children (sons) of one's youth."* (v.4b) Painful labor is present in both work (such as growing crops in a field) and child-raising. We eat or enjoy the beneficial result of both after a season or process.

Fruit Versus Loss

Reading Psalm 127 in its original setting, one would be more painfully aware of the perils of both crop and child-raising. They are a lot of work marinated in risk. There are no guarantees either will work out with a satisfactory result, reward or payoff. A man's fieldwork could be wiped out by drought, famine, flooding, pestilence, disease, and attack. (Leviticus 26:16-20; Deuteronomy 28:38; Micah 6:13-14) Amos 5:10-15 describes the disappointment of one who does the hard work of planting a vineyard, but does not enjoy the wine of the vineyard. Displacement from one's home due to hostile invasion (Deuteronomy 28:49-57) was also an imminent threat. Deuteronomy 28:33 describes the possibility that others will eat your produce and you end up oppressed and crushed. The risk of parents not having (willing) children to care for their interests in their more vulnerable season of old age is frightening, as mentioned in Psalm 127:5.

Blessed Versus Vain

Two other themes emerge as parallels in the outer edge of the Psalm 127 chiasm. My building, watching and working could be all in vain. The third of the thrice-used "vain" is found in verse 2a stating, *"It is vain for you to rise up early, to retire late…"* Contrasting and parallel to vain labor is the notion of the "blessed" (fortunate) man. Psalm 127:5a states, *"How blessed is the man whose quiver is full of them* (referring to *"the children of one's youth"* in 4b)*…"*

The Point: Live for an Audience of One

God extends common grace to all people, giving them the good gifts of children/home, city/community and work/produce. We can build, guard our stuff and work our fingers to the bone growing things only to lose it all. It is such a huge investment and so much can go wrong. Why ever try it alone when you could do so much with the sovereign LORD by your side?

Solomon, the über-builder, über-vigilant, and über-grower categorically states that it is vain to do this without God. If he thinks this, how much more should the rest of us, not having his resources, pay heed? The prized gifts and our multi-fronted vulnerabilities ought to remind us that we need to build life God's way. There is God's part: He builds, He guards and He gives. There is our part: we build, we guard, we work hard and we sleep while God works for us. Shouldn't

God, then, be our primary audience in life? He's got our back. And our front, sides, flanks, top and bottom sides.

When God becomes my main audience I find that I need to start kicking people out of the room of my mental space. Too many voices and players in my soul will yield a noisy, distracted "Tower of Babel" lifestyle, building up, up, and away... for what? Only God can provide the true shelter, true security and true food. The condition is: *"Unless the LORD builds... watches... gives,"* I am prone to build in vain. Contrast the Tower of Babel in Genesis 11 with the obscure efforts of Terah, father of Abram. Genesis 12:1-3 reveals God saying to Abram that through his descendants God will bless the entire world. God has something big and long-lasting in mind. Nothing short of Messiah will come through this line. It starts with life on life. There is nothing special about Abram that we can see. God's grace visited Him, making an unconditional promise. His part was to trust and obey, letting God build the house and legacy. I mention Terah because, from a heavenly view, watching this play out in his son's life, can you imagine anything more satisfying than watching the effect of your son on human history? Better than that . . . God's history!

Men with big audiences want to build towers. And they do! Men building with God as their audience make the obscure, quiet deposits into lives. Not much applause here in the short run for the Terah's, but they are long-haul people and that requires trust. God made Abraham a rich man, and that's nice, but it's the heritage that matters. A gift (God's covenant with Abraham) becomes fruitful when one lives with a sense of stewardship.

Children Are a "Heritage" (Gift + Labor)

Some Bible translations use the word "heritage" instead of the word "gift." *Heritage* refers to something inherited from the past—a gift. Heritage can refer to practices or characteristics that are passed down through the years, from one generation to the next. It's something you freely received from "up-line" ancestors (no genius of your own) and faithfully transmitted "down-line" to your descendants (with intentionality and effort, work).

Children are a gift we have received up-line from God. We also received practices from our family of origin. Question: Do the "practices" enhance the gifts (valued people)? There are some things to drop from the family portfolio such as corrupted (evil) habits. Sometimes, these things are simply like bad gas: silent, but deadly. They make the offender feel better for a moment, but leave a lingering, unpleasant effect. Room-clearers, they are. Some people are very outgoing about their gas, blasting away and announcing with exultation what they (or others) have done. Gas happens, but what's up with the amplification and public announcements? Perhaps gas is God's creative way of keeping us all humble and humored. Evil is like colon corruption: amplified or hidden is noxious, and passing it on to others is obnoxious.

A large part of our "heritage stewardship" is sorting out practices: some should be passed on; some should be dumped.

This book is full of sorting. You have already read some things to be dumped. Better, you will read of many things in the final "Knock" section to pick up as practices in releasing your children into the world. (I'm resisting any more gas jokes here, but there really are many.)

We will never "perfect" ourselves. Jesus is the author and finisher (completer or perfecter) of our faith. (Hebrews 12:1-3; Philippians 1:6). We are way too corrupted to get it done. We are not as bad as we can be, nor are most of us as bad as we wanna be, but we are bad off as we can be in terms of rescuing ourselves from our respective dirt bags. We need God, the life-giving one, to re-create us. He is at work rebuilding us as we seek God's day-by-day wisdom for life. In our seeking, we may raise the bar on what it means to be human and a human family as God designed it.

Released: The Child's Part

The child has the opportunity to discern and choose what will mark her legacy. Life done with God, a child will return to bless the parents in their old age as Solomon describes in Psalm 127:5. This is a marvelous thing to watch and reflect on. Released into the target, a parent will receive back in their advanced years, mature warrior-defender adult children. They are builders, protectors and givers with God's help. If parents do not prepare and release their children well, they may be stuck with child-minded adults. These live with life patterns that tear others down, attack and take because they, themselves, feel entitled to be taken care of.

Our friends, Dan and Jamie, have set a new standard for me, modeling the warrior-defender. They are very modest about this and rarely share it, which makes them even more endearing. I will be modest in my comments here so as not to expose or exploit them, but from them, we have much to learn. Dan has been a top-level executive of a Fortune 500 company. They made their money, but with Jamie's aging parents needing personal care in their advanced years, they opted to leave the corporate world, move to a smaller market city (death blow for Dan's career) and give themselves full-time to this.

Besides trying to meet the physical and social needs of Jamie's parents, Jamie and Dan also were concerned about something even more difficult. Her parents didn't know God.

In fact, they only would come to know Him through the servant-leadership of their God-fearing, warrior adult-children. Through Dan and Jamie's explanations of God's amazing grace, both parents made their peace with God before their deaths. Was that worth the five years it cost Dan and Jamie to burn through their nest egg? They will tell you, *absolutely*. Going into this situation, they had no idea how long it would go on. Instead of making more money in their peak earning years, they invested it back into Jamie's parents' livelihood. They used their "*worldly wealth to make,*" Jesus said, "*friends for the eternal future.*" (Luke 16:1-14)

Watching several of my own siblings care for my aging mom, enabling her to live on her property, has been inspiring as well. There are many challenges and inconveniences to them at times, but Mom's adult warrior children are doing what they can to honor all that she did for them as children.

> "*Like arrows in the hand of a warrior,*
> *So are the children of one's youth.*
> *How blessed is the man whose quiver is full of them;*
> *They will not be ashamed when they speak with their enemies in the*
> *gate.*"—Psalm 127:4-5

Womb to tomb, life is war. The image of the warrior is carefully selected by the sagely Solomon. As people abuse and neglect babies, people take advantage of the aged. Pathetic, but some people have larger dirt bags than other people and they see vulnerable people as someone to exploit for their own end. Gray hair was honorable in Solomon's culture; the elder at the gate (Hebrew *zaken*) was the wise gray-hair the younger men would seek out for counsel.

At the city gate, business was transacted and legal matters were settled. It was a place for justice and commerce to be worked out. At some point, however, the aged begin to slip mentally and physically and become easy prey. From the Better Business Bureau we regularly hear of schemes (particularly on the telephone) where predators are targeting the fears and vulnerability of the elderly. They need protection: physical, social and fiscal guardians. Ask yourself what people did with their wealth before fund managers, banks and FDIC. We have a lot of built-in protections in our culture, but people were more vulnerable in other times and cultures.

Needed: Warrior Defender Adult-Children

As children come into the world vulnerable, cared for by adult warrior defender benefactors, the table tilts and the defenders become the vulnerable and once-vulnerable become the defenders. *"They will not be ashamed"* because their livelihood and dignity is defended by warriors.

There seemed (to me) ambiguity in the pronoun "they" and to whom it referred. Is it the children in the quiver or the man whose quiver is full? Upon much reflection and discussion, I think the answer is, *yes*. It's both. There is a tipping point when a child becomes more the adult warrior and the adult warrior becomes the aged adult, then the child-adult in terms of needs.

"Getting old sucks," my stepfather O.D. used to say. Indeed. Preparation we give our children will likely come back to bless us on our exit. O.D.'s daughter, Jana, spent extensive time with him in his last days. A hospice nurse by trade, Jana was brilliant and a picture of strength and grace for her father as his health failed from pulmonary fibrosis. The crowning moment in his last breaths were when she whispered into his ear, "Dad, it's okay. You can go." And he did. An adult warrior. I'm reminded that Matthew 7:12 immediately follows 7:11. Think about it.

"If you then, being evil, know how to give good gifts to your children, how much more will your Father who is in heaven give what is good to those who ask Him." (7:11)

"In everything, therefore, treat people the same way you want them to treat you, *for this is the Law and the Prophets."* (7:12)

Using the language of Luke 16:8-9, Psalm 127:4-5 says to use your parent power and worldly wealth (good gifts) to **make friends for your old age—with your children,** as well as for the eternal dwelling place. (Luke 16:9) Now let's all break into song, singing the theme from *The Lion King* about the circle of life. The common grace gift of children is a subtle act of God, who seeks to win parents to His amazing grace. They are won by both the act of raising children (experiencing God-likeness) and through the grace-gift service of believing children.

Children are a gift, heritage and inheritance from God. Children are a reward if we do well in preparing them for release as gifts to the world in front of them. That release finds them returning to us as our defender warriors for our vulnerable exit from this life. This, too, is a good gift from God.

CHAPTER 19

Gifted Seeds:
Children Have God-Given, Special Bents

"Train up a child in the way he should go [lit. "according to his bent"],
Even when he is old he will not depart from it."

—SOLOMON, PROVERBS 22:6

Living on our Lewistown ranch on Spring Creek, we found many ways to occupy our time, including playing Cowboys and Indians, Revolutionary or Civil War, or WWII. Sometimes we had store-purchased play guns, but my brothers were very inventive and we often made our own. We made muskets, pistols, bows and arrows—all out of wood, bent over nails, twine and whatever else ranch kids could get their hands on. Imagination lifted our humble creations made of shop and barn resources to war-worthy weaponry.

Bows and arrows were a special challenge. For the bow, it was key to find a piece of willow that was stout and flexible. We would notch the willow and then tie slipknots on the ends of the baling twine in such a way that there was adequate tension on the bent bow so we could launch our arrows.

I learned to carve a notch into the middle of the bow, or angle a nail into it, to create what I later learned is called a rest. It would stabilize the arrow for a target-bound release. Finding and creating a worthy arrow was the most time-consuming. The need for something long and straight sent us searching into the creekside brush, pocketknives in hand. We would fasten chicken feathers to the arrow (our fletching) to create the appearance of a guidance system. We would whittle both ends, one end cutting the nock, to steady the arrow on the twine for the draw and release; the other end was the point. Occasionally, we might affix an actual arrowhead we found. Very cool! Then came the shooting. We shot at wild game or at anything that we determined might be "the enemy." In our minds, hunters and warriors we were.

Alive in my mind are the dynamics of bows and arrows. Recently I was invited by my friend, John McClure, to participate in a several day bow hunting trip on the Idaho/Wyoming border. Though late notice, I opted to go, but not weapon-bearing because I hadn't been practicing and didn't have time to become proficient. While bow hunting, shots need to be skillful: you only shoot to kill. You never shoot to maim. In this case we were hunting elk. This was a practical and ethical choice knowing the culture of bow hunters. It makes me wonder: what if we were so careful in deciding who should and should not attempt to raise children? Shouldn't the medical creed of Hippocrates, "Do no harm," apply here as well? I wonder if bow hunters have higher standards for elk hunting than our culture has for parenting. Then again, how does one practice for parenting? Even good bow hunters sometimes maim animals after releasing a crappy shot. So, I went to pack meat (hopefully) and do some fishing on the side.

Warrior-Archers and Parenting

Getting to the point of my bow hunting history, I find it fascinating that the smartest man in the world (King Solomon) used warrior/archer imagery to enflame the mind of the reader about child-raising. This works for me even though my personal archery experience is barely juvenile. All of us have watched it; most of us have tried it. Let's seek to understand Solomon's use of this image.

> "Like arrows in the hand of a warrior,
> So are the children of one's youth."—Psalm 127:4

The culture Solomon wrote to lived and died by archery skills. The warrior-archer was essential for a people's survival, both because he could defend them in military conflict and so he could bag game for dinner. The archer was the most diverse skill person in the military because he could be infantry, cavalry or chariot. The preparation of bow, arrows and delivery skills was huge for most people in most cultures in history. The warrior-archer was fundamental to life survival.

The archer prepares his bow. He has a release system in hand that he has the strength and skill to use in releasing his arrows.

The archer prepares his arrows to have integrity for the release into its target. Pun aside, the arrow penetrating its intended target is the point. It must have fletching (guidance system), a weighty point, a nock to hold it in place for powerful release, a straight shaft, etc. These are essential components.

The archer prepares himself. He picks up his bow and arrows and practices his releases as he readies himself for the big moment when his livelihood will be on the line, either gathering food or in military engagement.

Notice a few archer-parent perspectives and action points from Psalm 127:3-4:

The parent comes to grip with the serious nature of his role and the need to be intentional.

Children are essential both to life and to the furthering of civilization. How we build them, battle for them, train them for battle, and bless them (as givers) makes a difference in my family, my community and my nation.

Question: *What do you really want for your children?*

This forces us to ask, *What do I really want?* Again, if God came to you in a dream, like Solomon, and offered, "Ask what you wish Me to give you," what would you say? (1 Kings 3:5) Most of us want our children to do better than we did, flourishing and being influential in their own special way. Parents derive their highest level of satisfaction from this when it happens; they also experience their highest level of pain when their children (of any age) are not flourishing.

The parent identifies the future target(s) and develops a release system (bow) to deliver the arrows.

Question: *What are we trying to do with our children? What are we aiming at?*

Struggling with this question, I got an idea one day while reading Stu Weber's book, *Tender Warrior*. He had a release day for his oldest son that included his whole family. They read a letter to their son, "releasing" him as a man into the world. That's what I had to do! I wrote a "Release to the Target" letter for each of our four (then) young sons. It was a single page and was attached with Pam's and my will should we not live long enough to read it to them at a future "release" date.

Our target letter has been read, as a family, to the three of our four sons who have graduated from college (as I write). For us, that was an opportune time to celebrate who they are, their accomplishments and our belief in them to enter society as their own man (woman). We did this on graduation weekend, choosing a visionary spot to read the letter and bless them.

Bryant: This Is the Place Monument, overlooking the Salt Lake Valley.

Jason: Table Rock, an iconic scenic Boise location with a cross on top.

Jonathan: Riverfront Park in Spokane, next to the powerful, pulsating waterfall.

Sean: We've decided it will be in "The Living Room"—the hills overlooking the University of Utah.

The parent shapes the arrow, making sure it has the essentials.

It has a point/purpose, guidance system, a close connection to the one(s) releasing.

Question: *In the release, what is our part? What is the child's part? What is God's part?*

Our "release letter" contains a description of the division of labor and a firm statement of the child's free will to choose the path they will take in life. Our job is to love, teach through word and model, and pray. They will choose their own master, mate and mission. (The biggies!)

A large part of our letter (Appendix A) is a celebration of each son's attributes, gifts and aptitudes. Through the years, we recorded these observations (descriptive words with illustrations) and used them in ceremonies, especially the initiation into manhood when they were about driver's license age. The meaning of their names (we chose intentionally) and these God-given attributes were listed. We actually added a second page with more detail about these with a statement of what we could envision (broadly speaking) each son's influence to be given his profile.

We wanted them to realize their own giftedness and have a strong sense of God's and our blessing as they moved ahead. If they have a clear sense of their God-given identity and value, they won't be as likely to burn a lot of time and energy trying to be something they are not. Furthermore, they may avoid the pitfall of inventing (or taking on) pseudo-images to gain value and importance in the eyes of others.

The parent practices the release with many mini-releases so the big release will be on the mark.

Question: *What are the strategic, pivotal and developmental moments in a child's life where mini-releases (ceremony or special events) can be employed?*

We employed four ceremonies that served as mini-releases. Really, every day is full of deposits that will contribute to the ultimate release, but these four were seasonally appropriate with special preparation. Contributing to my thought process was a "mentor from a distance," Robert Lewis. He is on my "wall of gratitude." He has helped me turn rubble into a beautiful retaining wall. I met him briefly once at a conference in Dallas, long enough to say, "You've been my mentor on this front for all these years and I just thought I should shake your hand and say thank you." We shook hands, he signed my book and I'm now satisfied for a lifetime. For many years, Robert's books and audio messages have had a profound influence on my thinking and practice as a father and pastor. *The Making of a Modern-Day Knight* was the first book I consumed. Combined with Robert's *Men's Fraternity*, these sources are a clarion voice to me and through me to my sons and men in our community. I improvised on ceremonies Robert did, some things same, some different.

1. Passport to Purity (entering puberty when the voice starts to change, about age 12):

2. Manhood Ceremony

3. Graduation from College

4. Wedding and Rehearsal Dinner

Yes, each of these was a lot of work and pushed me way out of my comfort level. It's hard to do something you haven't seen or experienced for yourself. But I am really glad I did. None of them were perfect, but all were weighty to not only my sons but to all participants. After the manhood ceremony, I regularly hear men utter, "I wish someone had done that for me when I was his age. What a difference that would have made." We have the opportunity to make this difference.

Value the One: Each One Matters to God

Consider the specialness of each individual. Doesn't it feel good to be acknowledged and celebrated once in a while? Would you not agree that our closest friends and relationships are those who know and value us for whom we authentically are? We trust them; they trust us. They respect and honor us as a lifestyle. They may not always agree with us, but they are on our team. We need this and need to be this person to others. These are influential and transformational relationships.

One of my favorite Psalms is 139, authored by David, father of Solomon. David reflects on the omniscience of God (He knows everything, v.1-6), the omnipresence of God (He is everywhere, v.7-12), and concludes that a being with that kind of power is unnerving. (Even more than the NSA!) Everything David thinks, does and says is known to God. Everywhere he goes, God is already there:

> "For you formed my inward parts;
> You wove me in my mother's womb.
> I will give thanks to You, for I am fearfully and wonderfully made;
> Wonderful are your works,
> And my soul knows it very well.
> My frame was not hidden from You,
> When I was made in secret,
> And skillfully wrought in the depths of the earth;
> Your eyes have seen my unformed substance;
> And in Your book were all written
> The days that were ordained for me,
> When as yet there was not one of them.
> **How precious also are Your thoughts to me, O God!**

How vast is the sum of them!
*If I should count them, **they** would **outnumber the sand**.*
When I am awake I am still with you." -David to God, Psalm 139:13-18

This is the God who will "give what is good to those who ask Him." (Matthew 7:11b) He gave good gifts to us in our creation. Each person carries fearful and wonderful specialness. This is the power of Mother Teresa: seeing the value of each person, seeing their uniqueness and value with the powerful vision of a microscope.

Malcolm Muggeridge was an agnostic won to Christ through his journalistic coverage of Mother Teresa. He introduced those of us in the West to her ministry to the dying and destitute. One day, he carried some criticism back to Mother Teresa to get a reaction from her. He said to her, "Twentieth-century man thinks we should provide a 'collective solution.' 'There is Mother Teresa—she saves and helps so many, but this is merely a fleabite; this is nothing; there must be some other way of doing it.'"

Mother Teresa responded, "I do not agree with the big way of doing things. To us what matters is an individual. To get to love the person we must come in close contact with him. If we wait till we get the numbers, then we will be lost in the numbers. And we will never be able to show that love and respect for the person. I believe in person to person; every person is Christ for me, and since there is only one Jesus, that person is only one person in the world for me at that moment." (Malcolm Muggeridge, *Something Beautiful for God*,) I believe the powerful influence of Mother Teresa is her vision for the value of each one, even those who will never be in a position to contribute back.

All of God's creation is special, but at the pinnacle is humanity. Francis Collins, one of the world's leading scientists, was the head of the Human Genome Project. He researches at the cutting edge of DNA study, the code of life. In his book, *The Language of God*, Collins shares a striking feature of the human genome. He writes of our own species that we are 99.9 percent identical. We have low genetic diversity, 98 percent in common with the chimpanzee; and 52 percent in common with the dog in terms of finding similar DNA sequence in the genome of other organisms.

It is estimated that we have about 70 trillion cells in our body (give or take 20 trillion). Each cell has enough DNA information in it to fill the *Encyclopedia Britannica*. This number, multiplied to our .1 percent uniqueness in our own species, is a staggering number in terms of special DNA information. We have special capacities as a species, but multiply the "specialness" by this number and it's a mindblower. I imagine it is part of the vast sum of God's thoughts…which outnumber the sand. Only God can count the actual number, but we can try to imagine it, factoring it into how we see people, starting with our children.

Open the Gifts and Celebrate Them

Parents are like research scientists of the immense uniqueness and specialness of their children. These children are gifts from God and it our job to open these gifts, see the special "bents," and train or guide them accordingly for their special mission and works, *"Prepared beforehand that we should walk in them."* (Ephesians 2:10b)

Pam and Jon are the lead scientists in the Strain Genome Project. It is now out of the lab of our home and has become "field research" as we have moved into the empty-nest season of life. Some people look into microscopes, some into telescopes; parents look into child-scopes. You are the lead scientist in your children's research project.

Do you have the vocabulary and tools to see well and describe with detail and precision what you see? The average educated English speaker has a vocabulary of 20,000 words. With them we construct simple and complex documents. We encourage you to develop your human attributes vocabulary. There are all kinds of human personality or temperament tests to work with. We chose to employ a simple and old one, the Four Temperaments, originated and organized by the Greek physician, Hippocrates. They have been picked up and used profitably by people through the years and are fairly expansive. Imagine the observations Hippocrates made about human beings to come up with such a list of observations.

Remember, Hippocrates is considered the "Father of Western Medicine," from whom we received the still widely observed Hippocratic Oath, "Do [the patient] no harm." Make him a mentor from a distance, by modeling and taking advantage of his tool of temperament observation. Tool in hand you will be on your way to do good, and do no harm, honoring your children by training them up according to their bent, originated in the mind of God for a life purpose.

CHAPTER 20

Cultivation Is a Process:
Patience for Free Agents

"Do you not say, 'Four months more and then the harvest'? I tell
you, open your eyes and look at the fields! They are ripe for
harvest. Even now the reaper draws his wages, even now he
harvests the crop for eternal life, so that the sower and the reaper
may be glad together. Thus the saying 'One sows and another reaps'
is true. I sent you to reap what you have not worked for.
Others have done the hard work, and you have reaped the
benefits of their labor."

—Jesus, John 4:35-38

Anyone who gets a livelihood from crops knows how important the harvest
is. It's the focal point of everything. My early years in Montana were full of
opportunities to work, especially during the wheat harvest. I can still see Louie
Beeler throwing his hat in the air in celebration as the last bit of wheat was sent
from the combine hopper through the auger into the truck. Whew! Danger of
losing the crop was eliminated; livelihood is in the bin. That was the climax, but
there is quite a process of machine and field preparation, planting, praying for
rain, weeding, fertilizing, etc. before that climax.

Harvest drawing near, Louie would have everything ready to go; equipment
double-checked. In and out of the field we would go, cutting samples to check

the moisture content and readiness of grain to be harvested and safely stored in a bin. You'd dare not fill a bin with green (unready grain) or you would likely lose your crop. Once dry enough, it was go-time for the harvesters. It was exciting and my favorite work. Wages are better during the harvest and meals are awesome. Ann Beeler would often bring them to us in the field so that we could work all daylight hours, and occasionally into the night. Seven course meals, three times a day. We gained a lot of weight because we sat in trucks and on combines all day. Ann treated us like harvesters of old who really did hard work.

In farming, it is impossible to skip steps. "Four months more and then the harvest," Jesus said. Louie and my brother, Kim, his year-round employee, worked the process all year. Some of it was very quiet and certainly required much waiting. They did all they could during the process to ensure a profitable yield. This could not be a more fitting metaphor of how God works in the human heart. Like a kernel of wheat, or millions of them, God causes germination and a "natural miracle" happens again. It's the same with humans and their children. In Search Ministries, one of the core principles is, "Evangelism is a process." With the process in mind, let's merge it with the "each one a gift" theme in the previous chapter.

Nurturing the Planted Seeds for a Bountiful Yield

The brutal fact is many well-intended parents violate the vital process of spiritual discovery and ownership. We must give children *"air space"* to move toward God. Remember, our valued children are "free agents."

Seeking to understand our four sons has been an adventure. Each is awesomely packed with quirky specialness. Pulling the wrapping paper off the gift box and exploring their multi-faceted dimensions of raw temperament, bent and style has been an adventure, especially watching their life applications in 3-D circumstances.

But in the midst of these gift-loaded playmakers is free will. We have sought to honor and respectfully guide this part of God's image in them. Trust and respect is our spending capital to keep the relationships flourishing. Resolution of inevitable conflict due to differences has been critical and certainly exhausting at times. If you asked me to categorize each of our sons in one word (certainly an overgeneralization) I would describe each of them, oldest to youngest, this way:

Bryant is pastoral.

Jason is sales-adventure.

Jonny is a writer-humorist.

Sean is a scientist.

Perhaps Sean has taught us the most about the process of seeking God and truth. We highlight his journey as it best illustrates the point of free-will agents requiring margin as we engage them.

All of our man-sons are very good students, but all of the older three will tell you Sean is "the smart one." They good-naturedly call him "our last hope." He sizes things up quickly and remembers everything. (Yes, he's the guy you hate when test scores are returned in class; he blows up the curve.) He always has approached life, relationships and information differently than the rest of us. He puts ideas and claims through a vetting process and is not afraid to stand alone in his findings. In some ways, one could say he has been a spiritual holdout. It's not that he doesn't believe; nor does he have a reason not to believe; nor is he trying to gain attention from the hope that he might believe. He simply cannot assume that just because he's had a positive family experience, it makes our belief system right or true. He has integrity.

Pray, Wait and Watch for Open Doors

One day, Sean was reading some things and expressed to Pam his interest in exploring what I call the "great questions." Search draws its paycheck from exploring these questions with people of alternative worldviews, using street language. She asked, "Sean, you know that's what Dad does, don't you?" He said, "Yeah, I know that." Next question: "Why won't you talk to him about these questions?"

I know why. He's aware of my views, and a "scientist" will widen his source material, plus cross-examine what's in his possession. At this stage he didn't need more Dad; he needed an opportunity to do what I encourage men to do all the time: I invite them to look at what's on the *larger life* map, think it through, explore it with others and come to their own working conclusion. Sean is the guy that I like to meet and reach out to in the business community! It was a strange irony that I, his pastor-dad, could not be the one to assist at this time. (Since he's been in college, we are engaging on a lot of topics and he's been very receptive to my reading list. Armed with new ammo, he is re-examining mine.)

"Holdout" and "integrity" were the words I used earlier in describing Sean's spiritual journey. His three brothers, on their own initiative as grade-schoolers, approached Pam and me about being baptized. It was offered periodically at our church so each son in his own time and readiness expressed intent. We discussed what it meant and discerned right reasons; I got to do the "dunking" honors. Sean never expressed interest. My instincts and training told me to leave it alone. He has his reasons. We gave him space. More importantly, he had some "God experiences" over time and was enjoying the youth group friendships. He especially enjoyed a working-mission trip to an Indian reservation in Wyoming several years running. We trusted that God and Sean would work it out; both are capable and have integrity.

Frankly, I admire his integrity and marvel at his patient approach to the process, even though it makes him a minority of sorts. His brothers certainly show interest in his spiritual life, but they have embraced him where he is at. He says he believes; he just isn't "all-in" (yet), though he anticipates being so at some point. He is not flaky; he's an all-in kind of guy, which is my point. He is very selective about his relationships and time commitments. When he decides he's all-in, he will be.

Unexpectedly, in a moment of Mother's Day honor, Sean delivered a handwritten card to Pam. It captures the heart and soul of relating to free-agent children, neither dominating the child's will, nor abnegating influence toward God. You will perceive that "gratitude" is the best word to describe Sean's affirmation of our "free-agent" approach.

Margin, or "air space" I like to call it, is a posture of respect. It's one of the greatest gifts we can give another human free agent, especially our children. Sean agrees and gives hearty consent to share with you his thoughts.

(Believe us: he would have said no if he didn't want it in here!)

Sean's Mother's Day card to Pam, originally handwritten (age 20, two years into college):

Mom,

I know that sometimes it seems like I am not the most responsive son (I'm not, sorry), but I wanted to thank you for all the hard years of work you have put into making/molding me into who I am. It is dawning on me more and more that had I not been raised by you and Dad, I would be an entirely different kid—and not for the better. You love and nurture me as any mother would dream to do, but not in some standardized way. You learned and understood early on that I didn't necessarily respond to prodding of asking how I was or what my day was like—and most importantly you didn't force the issue (another thing I don't respond well to.) Your love language to me was repeatedly telling me you loved me, back scratches and making food I liked (to name a few tangible examples).

Know that when I say the following, I mean it from the core of my being: **I would not trade ANYTHING** from my childhood. I grew dissatisfied in high school. I knew it. You knew it. You continued to treat me the same.

I admit, I feel like I should expect you to expect things out of me, but you don't. I frankly don't get how you did it. My narrow mind still can't wrap around the idea because everywhere I look I see weak/distant/non-existent mother-child relationships. Sometimes it might seem like I don't respond or reciprocate. Once again, sorry. It's not you, it's me. (No we are not breaking up. That line has always been humorous and true to me.) Despite it all, you continue to meet me on my level—something no one else can do, Dad excluded. I hope you have some idea what that means to me.

As a kid who lives behind a veil, it is nice to know you won't think worse of me if I expose whatever ugliness is inside. I might not do that often, but the option is what's important to me…

Happy Mother's Day!
Love, Sean

Being "C"easonally-Appropriate in the Process

In the home, until graduation from high school, we will have about 6,500 days; 8,000 until college graduation. These are days of primary influence. Throughout developmental stages, how we engage our children in the process will change. Here is a way of looking at each season and what a parent's role is.

Age	Parental Description	Parental Action
0-5	Comforter	Nurture
5-12	Coach	Instruct
12-17	Cheerleader/Counselor	Show/Model
17-25	Consultant	On Call
25-90	Colleague	Call

Different things are required during these seasons of a child's development. In their seeking process, we need to be appropriate.

During the first few years, one can hold a child on their lap and read to them. They are highly interactive with us, wanting to know everything. Hungry for our full attention, it's hard to get them to bed, but what a window of influence during each day. We had family devotionals, which we tried to make fun and engaging. That went well for a while, but then they became laborious. Our sons started to rebel against the instruction no matter how many bells and whistles we threw in. We tried every trick but they were on to us and grew tired of our efforts. Pastor Dad, who has a Master of Divinity and a Bachelor's in Speech, never faced a more challenging audience. It became humiliating to lead "family devotionals."

It wasn't what I imagined, but the "gut call" was to acknowledge we were in a new season, what I call the "show me; don't tell me" season. We quit doing family devotionals and approached things more on the fly. This meant we had to be on our toes and living it.

This was a good call. We didn't get to teach systematically what we hoped, but we didn't bruise the fruit or try to harvest it "green." The house did not burn down as other people became more important in their development, widening the wall of mentors. All good. We continued to pray, love them and vigilantly capture teachable moments.

CHAPTER 21

Produce Harvest:

Relaxed Vigilance—It's Between the Child and God

"What after all is Apollos? And what is Paul? Only servants through whom you came to believe—as the Lord has assigned to each his task. I planted the seed, Apollos watered it, but God made it grow. So neither he who plants nor he who waters is anything, but only God who makes things grow."

– THE APOSTLE PAUL, 1 CORINTHIANS 3:5-7

*"What after all is **Mom**? And what is **Dad**? Only servants through whom **children** came to believe—as the Lord has assigned to each his task. (5) **Dad** planted the seed, **Mom** watered it, but God made it grow. (6) So neither **Dad** who plants nor **Mom** who waters is anything, but only God who makes things grow."*

– PARENTS' TRANSLATION OF 1 CORINTHIANS 3:5-7

"You offended me last time we were together." My friend, Paul, is always forthright; it's one of my favorite things about him. After preliminary small talk at our lunch meeting, he brought up my shortcoming. Sad that he had been carrying the burden of my offense since I last saw him. I was glad he raised it now.

"What did I do to offend you?" I asked.

"I shared a very important moment with you, the baptism of my [infant] granddaughter and you were flippant about it. That offended me." My flippancy was about baptizing infants. Guilty.

I asked his forgiveness for the offense (certainly not intended) and he readily forgave me. Then I asked if we could explore this a bit. Clearly, my attitude about infant baptism was much more casual than his. We shared the same denominational upbringing, but I had departed from this practice. I explained to him that my early-life baptism didn't "take" as it was done *to me*, not something I *chose* to do. I did choose to be baptized as a believing adult. It stuck because it was my choice and not one imposed on me.

The humorous part, I explained further, is that those of us who read the Scripture to teach and model "believer's baptism" have devised another ceremony to secure things with God on behalf of our children. On behalf of our four sons we practiced "dedicating them to the Lord." We are still driven by the same desire (that our children know and be with God), but such a dedication is really for the parents hoping to benefit our children. We parents dedicate ourselves to do our part. We know that Jesus wants the children to come to Him and we should not be a stumbling block to them. (Matthew 18:1-6; 19:13-15) We will raise our children in the fear and instruction of the Lord (Ephesians 6:4).

Good intentions, again, but research consistently reveals that a majority of these evangelical children (many "dedicated to the Lord") will abandon the fear and instruction of the Lord as soon as they leave home, if not earlier. We certainly know that is true of churches that practice infant baptism. Parents have an insatiable desire to "close the deal" and secure their children's standing with God. They cannot. But, there are things they can do to be a significant influence and not a hindrance.

Explaining myself to Paul, I summarized my flippancy as rooted in some cynicism about our well-intentioned practices that don't seem to stick—at least in the short run. Worse, they may create a false security and therefore a deathly passivity about our actual God-given role. Paul knows I am far from flippant about this. Intentional parenting is a serious-minded theme in my life and our ministry. That said, though, while I'm not a proponent of infant baptism, it certainly doesn't offend me. I believe God will honor the parental intention. Really, it's almost the same with a baby dedication. More important to me is the need to respect the division of labor and honoring of each role: God's, the parents' and the child's.

Ultimately, God is responsible for the results and how things will settle up with each child free agent. As discussed in the last chapter, what we parents need to set our mind to is *engaging the process* of winsomely introducing our children to God, loving, explaining, showing and praying for them. (I include "winsomely" because I regularly meet adults who were tortured in a religiously confused Christian home [versus a Christ-filled home] and they often end up the most hostile opponents of Christianity!) Doing our part, we can be patient. Since it's ultimately between God and the child, we can practice "relaxed concern."

Parents are all over the map on how to impart the spiritual/religious dimension to their children. Some don't engage it at all; some seek to teach all views and let their children decide when they are of age; some expose them only to their church or worldview; others ram-it-in, cram-it-in until the child about suffocates and emotionally quarantines them. What is our part with these amazing, highly gifted and valued ones who share God's image and ours? It must account for *free will*.

Discerning Our Goals and Our Desires

How do we navigate between the rock of our *desire*— that our children know God—and the waves of free-will reality? Some of us are crushed by the waves smashing against the rock. But don't forget, we don't control the situation; it's ultimately between the child and God! It's possible that I can use parental power to manipulate my children, tying my approval or disapproval to God-pursuit. No one likes to be obligated.

Dr. Larry Crabb, author of *The Marriage Builder*, offers some helpful advice about differentiating between goals and desires. A goal is an objective under my control. ***I can take responsibility for goals:*** I can love. I can model/explain things. And, I can pray. I can be a winsome influence on free-will agents.

A desire is an outcome I may fervently and legitimately want, but I cannot control it through my effort. *I can pray for my desires*. God is the master influencer with infinite resources and boundless creativity.

God's Desire Is for Children to Come to Him

Does it need to be said? Let's be clear because not all cultures treat and view children the same. Like my stepfather said, "Don't bug God with the little things." What if those little things are children? This was apparently the view of the disciples, the hand-picked men of Jesus. Matthew was among these who rebuffed some children brought to Jesus. He amended his viewpoint and records the Lord's response in Matthew 19:13-15.

> *"Then some children were brought to Him so that He might lay hands on them and pray; and the disciples rebuked them. But Jesus said, 'Let the little children alone, and do not hinder them from coming to Me; for the kingdom of heaven belongs to such as these. After laying hands on them, He departed from there.'"*

God wants to be bugged with little people. They bear His image as much as big people. Moreover, Jesus said that the greatest in the kingdom of heaven were those who came as little children. They are the model for those who want to come to God. To receive a little child in His name is to receive Him; to make one stumble is worthy of a death sentence. (Matthew 18:1-6)

God is at work in the lives of children. This is our assumption. This must be our assumption if Jesus is telling it straight.

Jesus Models What Parents Can Set As Their Goal

A goal is something we can do. Jesus embodies what parents can do with children in Matthew 19:13-15. First, He loved them by enthusiastically welcoming them into His presence. He physically touched them.

Second, he taught them (though indirectly) by standing up for them and modeling God's value of them. He commanded the attending adults to back off and not hinder them coming to Him. Can you imagine the powerful lesson for the children, His secondary audience, in this teaching moment?

148

Third, he prayed for them. (This is implied in verse 15, based on the intent stated in verse 13.)

In the next three chapters of this book, I will discuss each of these three goals but also the corresponding "stumbling block" or barrier children experience in coming to God that is most often presented by the words and actions of adults and parents:

Stumbling block #1—We create an emotional barrier when we ignore or abuse our children. Jesus lovingly welcomed and touched them. He highlighted their value.

Stumbling block #2—We create an intellectual barrier when we teach and model things in conflict with God's values. The men were engaged in an important debate about divorce when the children arrived. One wonders if the same "hardness of heart" expressed toward vulnerable wives (19:6-8) is also expressed toward the children.

Stumbling block #3—We create a volitional barrier (the will) when we perpetuate a hard heart culture. When we don't value, model what we say and pray, people (children) grow hard. They mistrust because they are mistreated.

The words of Jesus are severe and jolting for parents who ponder being a stumbling block to children in Matthew 18:6:

> *"But whoever causes one of these little ones who believe in Me to stumble, it would be better for him to have a heavy millstone hung around his neck and to be drowned in the depth of the sea."*

Woah! Woe! "Woe" is exactly the next word of Jesus.

> *"Woe to the world because of its stumbling blocks! For it is inevitable that stumbling blocks come; but woe to that man through whom the stumbling block comes!"* (18:7)

Stumbling blocks are inevitable because adults have dirt bags, full of darkness. In verses 8-9, Jesus recommends adults take radical steps to address their own darkness and dirt bag, lest they find themselves in the place where waste is taken (*gehenna*, the place where waste perpetually burns—translated "fiery hell"). It's a metaphor for the place where God is not and a life is perpetually consumed.

When the thing(s) that makes us stumble causes a child to stumble, that's serious business. It's important to each "one." Every *one* matters.

> *"See to it that you do not despise one of these little ones, for I say to you that their angels in heaven continually see the face of My Father who is in heaven. For the Son of Man has come to save that which was lost."* (18:10-11)

Each child, each one, is so valuable to God that all have angelic representation in God's presence.

Each child is worth pursuing and rescuing. To despise, stumble or disregard them is to fast-track an adult out of God's presence. To illustrate, we have another version of the parable of the lost sheep. This time, it's the parable of the "straying sheep." Luke 15 uses it to show the value of each "missed and valuable" person, no matter his label and lifestyle. Here, the search for strays seems to cover the one stumbled ("little ones" v.14) and the stumble-maker (18:15-20). Both are valuable and worth chasing and searching for to rescue them from their vulnerable place. However, the adult stumble-maker can choose the place of a wasted and consumed life apart from God if he doesn't rescue himself with radical action (v.8-9), or allow others to talk him off his darkness-ledge (v.15-17). Though this adult is living like a person who doesn't know God and is not drawing on the resources of God, a dignifying process is taught by Jesus to restore him or accommodate him ultimately to live apart from God and His community. The stakes are high; the language is strong.

There is no limit to forgiveness. Nor should anyone get on their high moral horse toward another because we are all debtors! The stumbled and the stumble-makers alike are candidates for search and rescue.

Dignity, Destruction and Free Will

God is the ultimate judge and is responsible for the results. Therefore, we live with relaxed concern.

In the meantime, there is a messy challenge in the process of helping others find their way to God. Stumbling blocks abound because darkness in each one of us abounds. God values each one, each free agent, providing tracks and boundaries that protect our dignity even when we aren't behaving constructively:

"So it is not the will of the Father that one of these little ones perish." (18:14)

"For it is inevitable that stumbling blocks come" (18:17) and "your brother sins" (18:15)

"And the lord of that slave felt compassion and released him and forgave his debt." (18:27)

BUT,

"You wicked slave, I forgave you all that debt...Should you not also have had mercy on your fellow slave, in the same way that I had mercy on you?" (v. 32-33)

THEREFORE,

". . . whoever causes one of these little ones who believes in Me to stumble, it would be better for him to have a heavy millstone hung around his neck, and be drowned in the depths of the sea." ". . . and be cast into the fiery hell." (18:6,9)

"If he refuses to listen...let him be to you as a Gentile and a tax collector (unbeliever though named among believers). (18:17)

"And his lord, moved with anger, handed him over to the torturers until he should repay all that was owed to him. My heavenly Father will also do the same to you, if each of you does not forgive his brother from your heart." (18:34-35)

We live with the consequences of our free-will choices. On Planet Earth, we may experience an internal torture of isolation or broken relationships when we choose a response that doesn't value children or the community of valued people. Hell, by definition, is a place where God is not. In *The Problem of Pain*, C.S. Lewis wrote, "The doors of Hell are locked on the inside...they enjoy forever the horrible freedom they have demanded, and are therefore self-enslaved..." It is the choice of free-will agents who choose to live apart from God, expressed through our pursuit of our darkness and dark choices.

God is a free agent, too. He is free to create a space for those who don't want to do life with Him. Our day-by-day choice is to live with God or without God. To stay the course living without God and set it on a continuous trajectory going forward into eternity is hell. Hell begins here, locking God out.

It is not my job to play the "hell card" on people or my sons. Never have. We want to persuade my sons and all people it's much better to live with God. People who persist in living without God should know that God will accommodate their wish in the long haul because they are free-will agents. He will turn them lose to chase their desires, forever. Jesus gives a depiction of Hell that seems to say, "They will get what they want but they won't like what they get." They were made to be in community with God and others. The language is strong for a reason: to give us a warning.

Those of us with God would like to secure everyone we care about in the same status—most especially our children! We can seek to influence them; but we can't choose it for them, not even by infant baptism or a baby dedication. We must love, winsomely persuade and pray.

The results are ultimately up to God, yet we decide for ourselves as God granted us the amazing gift of free-agency. It all comes down to what we love ultimately. He gave each of us that choice.

CHAPTER 22

Sprouting Seedlings:
Handle Parental Power with Care

*"The **emotional barrier** consists of negative feelings people develop when they have bad experiences with Christianity, Christians or religious people in general. It isolates people from one another and even from God. Our responsibility is to build relationships and cultivate loving, non-manipulative friendships wherever we find common ground."*

—SEARCH MINISTRIES (A CORE PRINCIPLE)

Observing greatness is a treat; we pay big money to hear gifted musical performances or witness professional sports. Sometimes greatness ambushes us in small ways. Just this morning, Pam and I were running in the Boise foothills. We were passed from behind by a mountain biker who handled the moment with class. I was impressed. He gave us a clear warning of intent saying a crisp, "Left!" As we crowded right and he passed us, he softened the "crisp" by thanking us and saying something about the beautiful day, which offset the speedy intrusion we might have experienced. He gave us good space and was clearly under control, but swift. We spend a lot of time in the foothills, running, hiking and mountain biking so we see everything. It's a small thing, you might think, but there is plenty out there to ruffle feathers. He classily and powerfully commanded the trail as a biker. Shortly after he passed, I thought to myself, "His voice sounds familiar." Then seeing his body frame and biker clothing it confirmed to me that it was Bill

Reed, owner of Reed Cycle. I said to Pam, "Bill Reed is a great Christian even in the foothills." One certainly gets that in his cycle shop. It's no wonder he has been awarded Eagle City's Small Business of the Year—twice I believe! I doubt that he recognized us coming from the backside, plus wearing sunglasses and hats, we were anonymous to him. Yet, in the anonymity he treated us with great dignity while commanding the hill. When it comes to biking, Bill has power—in knowledge and skills. Greatness is when one uses his power to serve and value others and not to dominate them.

Parents generally don't intend to harm their children, but the brutal fact is they can cause their children to stumble through ignoring or abusing them. Feeling despised, children experience an emotional barrier to the faith of their parents. Parents are given power to serve and show value to their children. But will they use that power, like "Bicycle" Bill Reed, to value and honor their children and not dominate them?

Great Parents (People) Use Their Power to Serve and Value Children

Recording the teaching of Jesus on this very powerful principle (Matthew 18:1), the apostle Matthew was clearly impressed with the greatness definition Jesus gave his men. Mark and Luke record the greatness teaching as well. They also record how each of us must become like a little child to enter the kingdom and the notion that we need to receive children in Jesus' name. Matthew includes this in 18:1-5, but only he develops the principle by taking it to another level in relating to children in verses 6-14. Why this resonated with the former tax collector (a hometown Jew employed by the occupying Romans) is uncertain.

Introduced in our last chapter, let's quickly review how Matthew develops the notion that *greatness is revealed by how we treat the less powerful.* Jesus warned His followers:

- Not to look past the powerless, the children (v.1-6)

- Not to look past inevitable, destructive stumbling blocks (to children), but take radical action (v.7-9)

- Not to look past or despise "one of these little ones," for angels represent children to God (v.10)

- Not to look past the value of each one and to do whatever it takes to rescue them (v.11-14)

- Not to look past the destructive behavior of adults, but respect dignity while disrupting it (v.15-20)

- Not to look past one's own God-debt while demanding justice for another's social-debt (v.21-35)

We have brainstormed and led brainstorms with parents on ways parents can be stumbling blocks to their children. After coming up with the list, we noticed that these are all human issues, and Matthew vividly illustrates them or provides instruction of Jesus about them.

- Unresolved marital conflict, largely due to "hardness of heart"
  Matthew 19:1-9

- Abusive anger, including discipline
  Matthew 5:21-22

- Hypocrisy, saying/teaching one thing and doing another
  Matthew 6:2, 16; 23:13-33

- Using (parental) power to coerce/obligate religious externals
  Matthew 5:21-48; 12:1-14; 46-50

- Showing favoritism or partiality
  Matthew 5:43-48; Genesis 27

- False gods, pursuing lesser things to lift stature or extend life
  Matthew 6:19-34

Diamonds on Black: Love Deposits Draw Children to the Love of God

Reading about the seriousness of stumbling blocks leaves the discussion quite dark. The negative is stark reality. Diamonds are often displayed on black cloth to make them stand out more. We are going to explore several diamonds-on-black approaches that enable you to love your children into the love of God. Love covers a multitude of sins, including inevitable stumbling blocks.

Moving forward, let us recall the model of Jesus in Matthew 19:13-15.

"Then some children were brought to Him so that He might lay hands on them and pray; and the disciples rebuked them. But Jesus said, 'Let the little children alone, and do not hinder them from coming to Me; for the kingdom of heaven belongs to such as these.' After laying hands on them, He departed from there."

Stumbling block #1 is the emotional barrier we create when we ignore or abuse children. Jesus stood up to this by loving the children, enthusiastically welcoming them into His presence. Jesus touched them and prayed for them. He highlighted their value. He defended their right to come to him, and He verbalized His desire for them to come near. It's important that we sense the Jesus vibe before we read through our eight-fold love list. He was in the moment with these children. Most of His time was spent putting the oxygen mask on the adult parents.

In the following chapter, we will share eight things we have done to communicate love to our children, thus disarming the "landmine" stumbling blocks that blow up healthy spiritual formation in the home.

Here is an overview of the eight:

#1—Love Your Children by Loving Your Mate

#2—Love Your Children by Knowing Their "Bent" and Love Language

#3—Love Your Children by Making a Million Deposits with Your Presence in Time

#4—Love Your Children by Finding Common Ground and Doing Special Things

#5—Love Your Children by Discerning the Real Need in Their Failure

#6—Love Your Children by Disciplining Them in Love

#7—Love Your Children by Asking Forgiveness When You Blow It

#8—Love Your Children by Listening & Giving Them "Air Space"

A third chapter on the emotional barrier will follow addressing the biggest bully stumbling block that comes at the hands of well-meaning religious people. It's been labeled "A Religiously Confused Home." We will contrast it with "A Christ-Filled Home" so that you can discern the subtle, but profound differences.

CHAPTER 23

Watering:
Eight Ways Parents Show Love

*"We are hard-wired to connect to other people and to moral
and spiritual meaning… Good parenting can be passed on to future
generations at the cellular level."*

—Hardwired to Connect:

The New Scientific Case for Authoritative Communities

When parents lack perspective and practices that show love to their children an emotional barrier results. The tangible love of parents creates a strong basis for children to experience the love of God. As we observed in the previous chapter, greatness in parents should be measured by how we use power to value and serve others who are vulnerable and not dominate them. Reality is, we are a mix of good and bad. Children don't need perfection, just honesty. Much of what we communicate will be from a position of weakness—half of the diamond principles are provided by soul-darkness opportunity. Our love in dark times will be an experience of contrast for our children.

Diamonds on Black: Love Deposits Draw Children to the Love of God

Diamonds are often displayed on black cloth to make them stand out more. We are going to explore several diamond approaches to really love your children into the love of God. As we mentioned, love really does cover a multitude of sins, including inevitable stumbling blocks.

A few principles, perspectives and best practices will provide some edges to this important topic. Our stories are meant to illustrate what this looks like. Stories help us learn vicariously when we can't be there in real time to observe. We hope you can sense the culture of love and how it disarms and dispels stumbling blocks—the emotional barriers that keep children at a distance from God.

#1—Love Your Children by Loving Your Mate

The culture and quality of your marriage completely determines the culture and quality of your home.

For husbands, this means you cherish and nourish your wife. She is a co-heir or co-regal in the grace of life. (1 Peter 3:7) For wives, the man's word for love is "respect." When a woman isn't feeling loved and a man is not feeling respected, they are suffocating relationally. It's hard to function and give when you are air-depleted. Emerson Eggerichs describes this as "standing on one another's air hose." We highly recommend his book, *Love and Respect*.

There is a tendency for a man to be work-focused. He's made for this, but not at the neglect of the most important relationship in his life, the woman to whom he made his vows. Likewise, there is a tendency for a woman to be children-focused. She's made for this, but not at the neglect of the most important relationship in her life, the man to whom she made her vows. The sacred oath precedes the having of children. It's not either/or, it's both/and, yet in balance. The most destructive stress your children will experience is when Dad and Mom cannot resolve conflict and they live in the prolonged stress of this. Conflict will happen—a lot! Children need to see us humbly work through it and prayerfully figure out solutions. They need to see us enjoying each other and having fun. They actually experience more security when they know your spouse has higher priority to you than they do. While a man can have an extra-marital affair with his work and recreational pursuits, a woman can have an extra-marital affair with her children and their pursuits.

#2—Love Your Children by Knowing Their "Bent" and Love Language

We have already discussed the focus and intention of discovering our children's bent. We are students of our children, looking for keys and insights into the DNA packaging to affirm and guide their life mission. Love language is part of that. All people have a primary love language, says Gary Chapman. Chapman also co-authored a book on this topic with Ross Campbell, entitled, *Knowing Your Child's Love Language*. There are five primary love languages: physical touch, words of affirmation, quality time, acts of service and gift-giving. We all tend to love others with the way we want to be loved. The million-dollar insight for spouses and parents is that we should learn what makes another person feel loved, especially those closest to us. It opens up their heart even if we don't fully understand why.

I heard a man describe to me one time that the most endearing thing his wife could do for him was to clean his eyeglasses. (His love language was acts of service.) His mother used to do that for him and it really made him feel special. I didn't get that at all. I thought he was being goofy, but then I realized he was totally serious. To each his own. While it matters not a whit to me, this is a very important thing for his wife to know. She does, and it really opens his heart.

Knowing Jason's love language in a discipline situation was huge a few years back. He was about ten years old. Neither of us can remember the issue, but we both vividly remember the situation. I recall being very firm about standing on a principle that Jason was challenging. We were totally sideways with each other about it. It was a hill to die on for me. As I stood ground, he thought I was being unjust or unreasonable. I sensed his heart growing dark toward me. It is one thing to disagree, but another when someone really questions your sanity and your love. Walking out of his bedroom, I felt a sense of urgency about standing ground and communicating my heart and love for him. I asked God for wisdom and to show me a way to let him know I loved him even though we were at a total impasse.

I knew Jason's love language was gift-giving. I also recalled that in the King's Store toy section, he was really eyeballing a little gumball holder in a Yankees baseball glove. I needed to go purchase it and present it to him as a gift, saying, "I love you, son." So, I did. I wrapped it up and knocked on his door. I said, "Jason, I know we don't see this thing the same and maybe never will. That aside, I got you this gift and want to say, 'I love you, buddy.'" He had a stunned look on his face and received the gift.

Nothing else was said until ten years later. Jason was studying abroad in Italy for a semester. It was my 50th birthday and Pam set up a Voice Quilt account for me where people could call in and leave voice message greetings and say kind things. Jason called on Skype and expressed some very special things. Then he called again, saying, "Oh yeah! I almost forgot to relate a story to you. I never told you this, but it had a very powerful effect on me." He recounted the discipline story and said, "Dad, that experience is the most powerful experience I can point to of realizing the unconditional love of God for me. It was totally unexpected, but when you brought me that little gift, I felt so loved." He recounted my words and the effect, very choked up as he was saying it. I could not have received a more powerful birthday gift. To be a teaching agent of the love of God in a very dark experience is the utmost. Again, I didn't know what to do, but I asked God. He reminded me of my son's love language and of a gift. (It was not expensive at all.) For a guy who does not have the gift of gift-giving, I was totally transcended. It left a forever mark on my son's heart.

#3—Love Your Children by Making a Million Deposits with Your Presence in Time

Parenting can be exhausting, but think of all the things we do to serve our children: playing, shuttling, feeding, training/teaching, disciplining, watching them at all kinds of events, praying for them, scheduling them, worrying about them, on and on. There will be some negatives. Overwhelm the negatives with the positives. This leads us to #4.

#4—Love Your Children by Finding Common Ground and Doing Special Things

A friend of mine told me the other day, "I have virtually nothing in common with my son. We couldn't be more different." He jokingly wondered if he should do a paternity test. Worse than lacking common ground, they clash. It isn't even neutral. He's trying to enter his grade-school-aged son's world, but has little aptitude for his son's interests. I asked him, "What is your son into?" He named some things, among them, comic books. I said, "Why don't you take him to one of those comic book conventions? It would be a loud statement of, 'I love you;

I will do anything to enter your world.'" I don't think he scheduled it after our discussion, but I think it got him looking at things in a new way.

There was a season in my youngest son's life where I felt like I was hitting dead ends as well. I initiated a lot of things but was coming up empty-handed. Besides school studies, he wasn't showing a lot of outside interest. I began to pray about this as he was nearing the age (getting his driver's license) where I would hold an initiation into manhood ceremony. I felt we needed a special outing of some kind. I happened to notice (and was always amused by) the fact that he was a rabid Philadelphia Eagles fan. He spent a good deal of time on their website and could tell you just about anything going on with them, including what mouthwash DeSean Jackson gargled with that morning. I happened to be a lifetime Washington Redskins fan in the same division, so there was some rivalry banter. My energy for the NFL was about 10 percent what it was for much of my life, but it was common ground.

Amazingly, I had never attended an NFL game in my entire life of fifty years; and neither had Sean. It was spring when I went online to check the Eagles schedule for the following season, looking for West Coast games the Eagles might be traveling to. There were three; one date was out, one was in Oakland (no way!) and the last was in San Diego—perfect! "Father, would you allow me to get tickets to surprise Sean with?" They weren't for sale yet, but I was satisfied having a plan and being ahead of the game. I couldn't believe it: within the week, Sean said to me, "Dad, do you know what would be really cool?"

"What?" I asked.

"What would be cool is if we could go to an Eagles game when they are playing on the West Coast next fall."

I couldn't believe it! *What are the odds of this?* I thought to myself. *Someone is looking out for me, prepping me to be ready to be the hero-Dad! Thank You, Father!* I said to Sean, "Amazingly, I had the same thought a few days ago and went online to check the schedule. There's a game in San Diego that looks perfect. We can stay with Aunt Sharon and Uncle John, neighbors to Philip Rivers—San Diego's quarterback."

The next trick was getting tickets as soon as they were available. I hadn't a clue how all this worked and quickly got over my head. I'll spare you the details, but after several confused approaches I sat, shoulders slumped, staring at my laptop screen wondering what to do. The phone rang.

"Jonny-Be-Good. What are you doing?" Only Skip Hall calls me that.

"Skipper, I'm sitting here perplexed about how to purchase NFL tickets for a special father-son trip with Sean." Skip asked, "What are you looking for?" I said, "Philadelphia at San Diego in November. The Eagles are Sean's team." He said, "Well, let me make a call. I happen to know Marty Mornhinweg, the offensive coordinator for the Eagles, and I helped him get a coaching job some years back."

I was stunned. I couldn't believe it. Then again, I could because Skip had coached college football for thirty years and knew everybody in the coaching fraternity. What I couldn't believe is that he called at that very moment. Skip's call couldn't have been more on cue. *Father, thank You! Wow.*

Skip said, "It'll probably be three days before he gets back with me. I'll let you know." Apparently, the Father was using the situation to bless a father who was trying to bless his son. The Father would bless two sons, plus continue to raise a father doing it.

Sure enough, Skip called back within three days; he scored the tickets—Marty's personal allotment, usually used by his family if they traveled. "Jon, Marty asked me three times—'Skip, are you sure this is a really good friend?'"

I said, "Skipper, seriously… you lied for me three times? You really *are* a good friend!" The pot was really sweet now: not only were we going to an Eagles game, we had Eagle coach family tickets, they were free, AND we had to pick them up at the hotel where the Eagles were staying, which meant we could do some player spotting!!!! I could not have dreamed up a better plot.

Imagine the specialness my son felt when I related this story of God the Father's provision and the quirky circumstances. I asked for help and He gave so fantastically beyond my request. I prayed my son would be affected by the prospect that two fathers, one heavenly and one earthly, were pursuing him through this. Talk about being transcended. In my desperation to value my son tangibly, I asked the Father for help and He delivered. Two sons were feeling very special.

#5—Love Your Children by Discerning the Real Need in Their Failure

As will happen, there were a couple of occasions when our sons got busted for looking at things on the Internet that were "forbidden fruit." No one is getting thrown under the bus here; this is every man's battle and every woman's perplexity—especially a mom. In this case, Mom walked in on the crime scene and well…

As soon as I walked in the door I knew a world crime had been committed. I knew this day would come. I was ready for it and already decided what my response should be. Our family is not into "sin management." We are into authentic relationships, grace, truth, health and living for things and not against things. They knew what they did was wrong; they didn't need me to blow up and grind on them about the moral travesty at hand. They know that. What they needed was grace.

I immediately hugged them and said, "Son, I'm sorry you had to experience this. I know the power of this and now you know why we have taught you to respect the boundary."

Consequently, we have "no shame, no blame" culture in our relationships.

#6—Love Your Children by Disciplining Them in Love

Each of our sons required "custom-fit" discipline. They all respond differently to things because of temperament and birth order. For example, Bryant and Jonny were quite conscientious by temperament and Bryant, being the oldest, was "the responsible one." Jason was a mischief machine and litigator-in-training. It was a three-parent job to reign in his antics. He could argue and spin things so well he would have us doubting our own reality—together! We compared notes a lot and then double-teamed him. Sean was the smart one not only because he was the youngest, but he also was a born observer. We rarely disciplined him because he learned about "Dumbville" watching his three older brothers (especially Jason!) and decided their antics were not worth the effort. By temperament, Sean was a straight-shooter and would tell you exactly what he thought about things. I cannot recall a time that I ever questioned his truthfulness or integrity, though his youthfulness might not have been fully informed.

#7—Love Your Children by Asking Forgiveness When You Blow It

One thing I admire about Pam is her ability to own her shortcomings. The following story illustrates the effect of owning our part in relational failure.

A prideful parent will not do this—and with long-term consequence to the relationship(s). It has been our practice, spiritually, to keep short accounts with God, claiming His forgiveness as stated in 1 John 1:9, "If we confess our sins, He is faithful and just to forgive our sins and cleanse us from all unrighteousness." My observation is this carried over into our marital relationship where she has owned her stuff when I have felt offended or alienated. And, likewise she does so with others. It is a grounded (humble) and relationally empowering discipline to ask forgiveness even when you don't believe it's only one person's fault. We could use our parental power to "win" every conflict, but that is a losing strategy, relationally. Why not use our power to win a heart? We think we will lose control, but we don't—we illustrate the way of Christ. I asked Pam to share one incident that vividly illustrates this. In Pam's own words:

> There were several times when I found that I needed to humble myself and ask my boys for their forgiveness. Usually it was because I "reacted" instead of "responded." As you can imagine, with four boys being 6 years apart, there was a lot of commotion in our home. Some days were extremely exhausting! I felt I needed to wear a striped referee's shirt and blow a whistle at all the arguments and punching that occurred! Usually, it was when I was tired that I blew it—and I'm not referring to the whistle!
>
> On one such occasion, I clearly remember an encounter with Jason. You may have figured out by now that he was our negotiator and litigator. He could very quickly have Jon and me all twisted up in what we thought we were saying and the position we held on any given subject. He seemed to have a quick defense statement at his beck and call. He used words quite creatively and knew how to push my buttons. There was one such time (and I don't even remember what we were debating about) I got exasperated and said, "Jason, don't be such a smart ass!" To some of you this may seem harmless, to others you are gasping! We carefully guided our kids in the proper adjectives and nouns they could use, or in other words, we did not

allow swearing. "Ass" was not an allowable word! Nor was calling each other something demeaning!

Jason's nonverbal expression pierced me immediately. His countenance fell, his defensive posture weakened and he proceeded to ask me why I said "that word." I knew I had to deal with this immediately although everything in me wanted to run away. I was embarrassed on one hand, but on the other, part of me thought what I said was true! Yet, I have seen so much damage in the names we call our kids and how we can easily demean them and cause them to withdraw. I went to him and said something to the effect of, "Jason, I am extremely sorry that I called you that name. I sincerely don't mean it. I spoke without thinking. Although I was not happy with your behavior and how you were responding to me, I had no right to respond to you that way. Will you forgive me?" I can assure you I was crying because that's what I do in emotionally painful situations! He, of course, willingly gave me hugs and acceptance!

#8—Love Your Children by Listening and Giving Them "Air Space"

Sitting with Wes and Karine, we listened to their story for the second time. This time, though, they were explaining it to a much larger audience. Their skepticism and subsequent departure from their church was no small thing. They were quite open and vulnerable over the three-hour period we met. And even though they shared a few viewpoints I wanted to pounce on, I sensed that it was not the right time. I bit my tongue hard at least three times; it was truly a conflicted gut call. Toward the end of the conversation, Wes addressed us: "Jon and Pam, I want to thank you for the air space you have given us tonight. You can't possibly imagine what that has meant to us. We are not where we will be in time, but it's just where we are now."

"Air space." What a great way to say it. And, boy! Am I glad I didn't say anything! It was huge to Wes. I knew Wes was writing out his ideas and reasons, and I thought to myself that I'd ask him to share the best of those with me down the road. He would likely ask for my reaction and I knew I would get my opportunity then.

Everyone needs air and space. When we listen without judgment (condemnation) and hold our discernments to ourselves, we allow air to enter the lungs of others. People like to breathe, I've noticed. Our listening is oxygen for the one sharing, and this includes our children. Listening shows respect and builds trust. Listening is also really, really, *really* hard work. People have a huge need to express their minds and hearts on their own terms.

Listening also gives you time to think and to consider things in context. One can always share his thoughts later on; it's better when we are requested to do so instead of backing up the dump truck, delivering unsolicited and maybe unwanted words. Air space wins respect. Air space wins trust. Air space wins a hearing and an open spirit to receive our counsel.

One Sunday morning, Sean's senior year of high school, I overheard an exchange between him and Pam regarding his attendance at church that day. Sean loved going to youth group on Wednesday night, but church on Sunday was a different experience. As I heard his reasons for not wanting to join us, I thought to myself, *I cannot disagree with anything he is saying.* It would have been total hypocrisy for us to sell him on attendance. We had a couple reasons we thought he should consider coming anyway, but at what price? Pam had already articulated the official parent reasons, playing the "bad cop." It was time for the "good cop" to enter the room.

"Sean, you will be out of the house in a few months. You will be at college calling your own shots. No one will be waking you up for church. We would love to have you come with us, but I get why you don't want to. I actually agree with your assessments, but we have other reasons that are more important to us and likely not that important to you. Given coming reality, you have a standing invitation to join us. We leave at 9:30 a.m. if you want to ride with us and save gas. Or, come at your own speed and drive. Or, don't come…and you don't need to explain to us if you are coming or why you are not."

This "air space" disarmed the situational tension of parents letting go of control of an emerging adult son. We were saying, *"We respect and trust your judgment to make decisions about your life you can live with. We are here for you, and here is how you can be your own man and have a place with us."*

If memory serves right, he did not come very often. Two years later, he is coming on his own volition on a regular basis and we enjoy the experience together as mutually respecting adults.

Beginning the chapter, we posited that **greatness is when one uses power to serve and value others and not dominate them.** A few principles, perspectives and best practices later, communicated through some of our stories, we hope you can sense the culture of love and how it disarms and dispels stumbling blocks, emotional barriers that keep children at a distance from God.

We need to make you aware of a lethal stumbling block that comes at the hands of well-meaning religious people. It's been labeled "A Religiously Confused Home." We will contrast it with the "Christ-Filled Home" so that you can discern the subtle, but profound differences.

CHAPTER 24

Weeding:

How to Discern a Religiously-Confused Home from a Christ-Centered Home

"Research shows clear correlations between religiosity
and good outcomes for young people."

—Hardwired to Connect:

The New Scientific Case for Authoritative Communities

This chapter will be a game-changer for many who were raised in a "Christian home." You may discover you were raised in religiously confused home with a Christian label on it. There is a dramatic difference between a Christ-centered home and what many perceive to be a Christian home. It's subtle when one is in it, especially when the parents are well-meaning. But there must be truth in labeling and that's what we want to do here.

I've learned to be a careful label reader when it comes to packaged food. My discernment has grown over the years. Many ingredients listed are beyond my knowledge. Then I read an article or book discussing the benefits or liabilities of these ingredients and my estimation of a given product grows or diminishes. Many things I thought were healthy for many years have been exposed to be fraudulent. Sometimes I become a bit infuriated by the labeling games. It's marketing run amok and downright dishonest. We are including a list of ingredients to help you discern between what is Christ-centered and what is labeled Christian, but lacking healthy substance.

Indulge me for one more metaphor for the comparison you are about to observe. A Christ-centered home produces the fruit of the Spirit because it draws upon the resources of Jesus Christ as described in John 15, Jesus' metaphor of the vine and the branches.

> "Abide in Me, and I in you. As the branch cannot bear fruit of itself, unless it abides in the vine, so neither can you unless you abide in Me. I am the true vine, you are the branches; he who abides in Me and I in him, he bears much fruit; for apart from Me you can do nothing." (15:4-5)

Contrast this picture, or any fruit tree (apple, orange, peach), with another kind of tree—a Christmas tree. It has been cut down and hauled into a house. It's now dying, though we may trim an inch off the stump so that it will drink a little water for a few days. This dying (and maybe already dead) tree is then hung with lights and ornaments. Suppose on the ornaments is written words like "love," "joy" and "peace." The tree is pretty and shows well for a while, but soon becomes a fire-hazard. This is "Christian religion," not Christian life in Jesus. We may hang religious activity bulbs on our Christian tree, such as church attendance, Bible study, prayer and evangelism. We may include Christian morality bulbs. These are not the fruit of the Spirit, which come from a life continuously "rooted" in Jesus Christ.

One of the most helpful distinctions in discerning the difference between a "Christmas tree home" and a "fruit-bearing home" has already been written. The title of this chapter comes from Aphesis Group's *Immersion Experience* handbook written by my long-time friend and founder of Aphesis Group, Tim Rule. He enthusiastically gave us permission to include the following description of these two homes, "Religiously Confused" vs. "Christ-filled." If the inclusion you read from here to the end of the chapter resonates with you and describes the kind of home you grew up in, you will benefit from exploring more of Aphesis Group's *Immersion Experience*.

The Religiously Confused Home

We might assume that if a person grew up in a Christian home where Jesus Christ was daily lifted up as being of supreme importance to the family's values, the home would naturally be healthy. It would be a home where Christ's lovingkindness and grace would be acknowledged during most meals together, along with words of gratefulness about God's unfailing provision for the family. Both the father and mother of the family would be seen reading their Bibles on occasion, and even family devotions would be done on a weekly basis, at least when the kids were younger. Of course they would rarely miss church on Sundays or midweek Bible studies. The kids would be required to attend Sunday school, and as they grew older, they would also be required to attend youth group meetings. Dad may serve as a church leader and mom as a leader on several committees or the chairperson of the women's ministry committee. Often in the home you would hear phrases like, "What would God think of you doing that?" or "Now, Jimmy, what would Jesus do?" Clear statements of right and wrong would often be said, but not explained. The neighbor next door, known to be a divorced alcoholic, would often be lifted up to the children as an example of what *not to be*. Television viewing would be highly scrutinized along with what the children were viewing on the Internet and in books and magazines, saying words like, "Would Jesus watch this?"

A person would assume that if someone grew up in this type of environment, automatically they would be from a healthy home. However, our experience tells us a different story.

Imagine a home that was like the home described above, but the love and grace of God that was often talked about was not felt among the family members. As a matter of fact, Mom and Dad did not seem all that happy. Regular displays of joy and laughter seemed to be oddly missing. This was odd to the children because their divorced, alcoholic neighbor, to whom their parents referred to as a poor role model, seemed genuinely happy. His laughter was real, along with his kindness toward the children. The majority of the time when the parents did show emotion, it was usually emotions of anger and disappointment in the home. It's not that the parents didn't smile, laugh or be joyful at all, but the majority of the time, they were not happy. They would often talk about the grace of God but they seemed very performance driven when it came to their relationship with each other and the children. If the children behaved well, everything would be at peace; if they behaved poorly, swift and sure discipline occurred, along with emotional displays of anger. This was confusing to the children because when they displayed anger, they were quickly disciplined for it. Often the words, "I love you" were said to the children, but said almost mechanically with very little warmth and affection. Sometimes they would pray and talk about lost people, those who don't know Christ, but the children would never see the parents talk to people about Christ. The parents often talked about their trust in God and how He always provides for their needs, but often when Mom was paying the bills, she would cry, and the parents would have tension between them.

The mom often seemed stressed or depressed. Sometimes when she was acting depressed, the kids would ask her if she was all right. She would then seemingly force a smile and say, "Yes, dear, everything is fine. God is in control." Most of the time Dad seemed oddly stoic and emotionally distant, pre-occupied with work, and uninvolved with the family members. The exception to this is when he would be called upon to discipline or correct the children. These things were true until they arrived at church or church functions; then they would almost magically change. They would begin to smile and laugh and seem quite happy. The children began to realize this is what is normal for the Christian. Even though there was pain and tension at home, you smile and say, "Everything is all right," and even say things like "God is good," when people at church ask how things are going.

The "Religiously Confused Home" is one involved with church and religious activities, but God's love and grace are *not* something that is deeply felt and displayed among family members. Can you imagine how confusing it would be to children growing up in this home? Incredibly important Biblical truths are read and talked about but they seemingly have no effect on the home. God's love and grace are often referred to and lifted up as gifts, but love and grace are not daily practiced or displayed among the family members. Instead, rule keeping or keeping the law seems to be the highest value. What seems to be the strongest value is not the person, but what the person does religiously. People from these homes are strongly confused because all the things that normally make a home healthy are talked about and lifted up to be of extreme importance, but different instinctual behaviors are being lived out in the home, instinctual behaviors that are driven by fear, guilt, and shame.

A Christ-filled home is different than the religious home. The great truths of the Bible are not only talked about among family members, but they are instinctually lived out by the parents and deeply felt by the children in the home.

Comparing the Religiously Confused Home with the Christ-Filled Home

The following illustrates the differences between a religiously confused home and a healthy, Christ-filled home.

Make a special note that the descriptions given are referring to *the parent's* beliefs, attitudes, and behavior, not the children's. *The parents* are the ones who must first actively believe and instinctually model these things to their children. The children simply respond to what they see in their parents. This by no means guarantees the children will come out of the home as model citizens. It will, however, improve the chances that they will not be confused about what a Christ-filled home is. The list defines general tendencies and is not meant to be exhaustive. It does not refer to what is *talked* about, but what is most strongly *sensed* or *felt* by the family members.

Comparisons between a Religiously Confused, Dysfunctional Home and a Healthy, Christ-Filled Home

Religiously Confused/ Dysfunctional Home	Christ-Filled Home
God's love and grace are talked about, but are not strongly felt among family members.	God's love and grace are not only talked about, but strongly felt.
Rule keeping is the highest value.	Persons are of the highest value.
The Christian life is emphasized and lifted up to be of the highest importance.	A personal relationship with God is emphasized and lifted up to be of highest importance.

What a person does is more important than who they are.	Who a person is, is more important than what they do.
Environment is heavy with unmet expectations	Environment is one of peace and people feel free to be themselves.
Environment is unsafe and produces a *"false self." The false self* is lived out and daily exemplified by parents.	Environment is safe and produces realness. Realness is lived out and exemplified daily by parents.
Good behavior is of high priority.	Good character is of high priority.
Boundaries are established by the Law and maintained by rejection of behavior and the person.	Boundaries are established and maintained by rejection of hurtful behavior, but NOT the person.
Displays of emotions are discouraged and not talked about.	Displays of non-manipulative emotions are encouraged and talked about.
Gratefulness for good behavior is what is most often expressed.	Gratefulness for people and how God has uniquely made each family member is what is most often expressed.
The Laws of God are lifted up and touted as of highest importance.	People are lifted up and touted as of highest importance. God's law is taught and talked about and actively trusted to be His way of protection and providence.

Doing the right things and being nice is strongly taught	Right doing and kindness is lived out by the parents and loving others like God loves is strongly taught and modeled by parents.
Parents are proud and self-centered. Authority and rules are overused to influence children.	Parents are broken and humble and use modeling, servanthood, and good communication to influence children.
Parents point out wrongdoing by others, but hide their own wrongdoing in order to appear righteous.	Parents are quick to apologize for their own wrongdoing and ask forgiveness from others in the family.

You likely quickly discerned if you were raised in a religiously confused/ dysfunctional home. More importantly, you have some "truth in labeling" to discern with and choose your future. To those still setting their course on the Christ-centered life, marriage and household, we say all aboard. We now turn to overcoming a second stumbling block: the intellectual barrier.

CHAPTER 25

Balanced Nutrients:

Teaching Children the Path of Life

"Then some children were brought to Him so that He might lay hands on them and pray; and the disciples rebuked them. But Jesus said, 'Let the little children alone, and do not hinder them from coming to Me; for the kingdom of heaven belongs to such as these.' After laying hands on them, He departed from there."

—MATTHEW 19:13-15

Inviting the little children to come to him, Jesus softly rebuked the disciples for hindering them. He showed them their value by standing up for them. Not only did Jesus invite them; He made models out of them for their status as children. Everyone comes into the kingdom of God as a little child. This was a teaching moment for adult and child alike.

Teaching is both explaining and doing. Jesus showed us what it meant to be a stand-up guy for God's values. More was done than said, but something very powerful and simple was stated. Matthew was impressed by the occasion of Jesus giving children access though He was in the company of the contradicted disciples. Here, a second stumbling block is featured.

Stumbling Block #2—The Intellectual Barrier

We create an intellectual barrier when we teach and model things in conflict with God's values. It's not that anyone intends to do this, but we just don't know our own darkness, blind spots and ignorance, both individually and culturally.

Just prior to this event, the men (including religious leaders) were engaged in an important debate about divorce. Then the children arrived. One wonders if the same "hardness of heart" expressed toward vulnerable wives (19:6-8) in the wife-throwaway culture is also on display here toward the children. It's almost like Jesus was ready to get out of that conversation but then found the little children coming to Him, simply and vulnerably, refreshing.

Shame fills my mind recalling an incident that modeled the "south end" of what Jesus taught. We were playing a family game with nieces and nephews at my mom's house several years ago. We were having fun until my brother baited me into a theological discussion. (Not uncommon.) He and I see a lot of things similarly, but we have some differences. As my brother, he knows how to punch my buttons. I couldn't resist letting his "facts" go unchecked. I chased the carrot and our conversation escalated. I was playing the game with a mix of cousins (my nieces and nephews and sons) while he was watching. Increasingly distracted, I was getting "off my game" in more than one way. My conversation style and attention to the board game were both coming undone. Eventually the children were waiting as my brother and I got lift-off into a full-throttle disagreement. I have no idea how much time elapsed, but the fun environment that was shared soon dissipated. The game ended, but without a winner; there were two losers who barely noticed the game ended. Seriously. It was pathetic. Up to my axle in social mud, I dismissed myself from the conversation and went outside to decompress. My part in this was so very wrong. We had become a stumbling block to precious young lives. I would never allow an exchange to degenerate professionally. Why would I allow less for our children?

Standing by my mom's woodpile shed, it became symbolic of God's "woodshed" to discipline me. The Holy Spirit brought to mind Paul's words to Timothy, *"…solemnly charge them in the presence of God not to wrangle about words, which is useless and leads to the ruin of hearers."* (2 Timothy 2:14) God convicted me about the culture of exchange we (pathetically) modeled. We ruined young hearers. He reminded me of what it should look like. I'm the guy who trains people in a higher model of idea exchange—for a living! As I said, *pathetic.*

"The Lord's bond-servant must not be quarrelsome, but be kind to all, able to teach, patient when wronged, with gentleness correcting those who are in opposition, if perhaps God may grant them repentance leading to the knowledge of the truth." (2 Timothy 2:24-25)

As brothers do when pulled apart to break up a fight, I complained. I complained that my brother picked the fight and was relentless in his position. It was as if God said to me, *"Son, you are not responsible for your brother. I hold you (a pastor!) to higher standards and you are responsible for yourself. You get back in the house with those precious children and own YOUR junk. You confess your wrongdoing and ask for their forgiveness. No blaming...no throwing your brother under the bus; just own your part. You are a stumbling block to your children, his children, all the cousins and every other adult listening in."*

So I did. I gathered everyone who had been in earshot and apologized for ruining the game and being such a poor model of what an exchange about truth could look like. I asked their forgiveness. No one really said anything, but I could tell that it was important that I did it. Their eyes said it. A little dignity was restored. It was awkward, but I'm really glad I did it. It deflected the stumbling-block shrapnel from a bomb dropped.

Immersing the Family Culture in God

Fortunately, the culture of the Jon and Pam Strain household has not been like the situation I described with my extended family. We have had plenty of disagreements, but have learned to bring into balance all of the important things. Let me reiterate. . . we have *learned* this. This is what the family is for. We teach, through modeling and explaining, what our life should be lived for, and how.

Truth matters. People matter. Relationships matter. The challenge is to keep all of these things mattering at the same time, as much of the time as possible. Families fight about all kinds of things, but it's especially distasteful when it has to be religious or spiritual in nature. Love, trust, respect, honoring free will, allowing process, and raising children—that's all we're trying to do! This is a lot of work.

I recall hearing someone say, "We are just one generation away from barbarism." This statement is well understood by parents of sons; no explanation needed. If you ever came to our house for dinner when we had children at home, you know.

Our youngest, Sean, wrote a paper for a college class entitled "Men of Virtue." It's about our family dinner table. We are including it in the "KNOCK" Appendix of the book because it illustrates a fairly good outcome for our sons as they have been released into the world. The double meaning of the KNOCK section is this: Let's knock Dad around for all the dumb things he tried at the dinner table. Yes, Sean's paper is a mild roast on Dad. I was simply trying to do my job by teaching our sons manners—and other things—at the dinner table. (At the time it didn't seem to work, though they seem to do well as adults at other people's houses. Two are even married.) Sean gives me credit for trying and seems to say that just the attempt, though misguided in tactics and methods, seemed to catch hold for the most part.

On the other hand, another kind of knock which, as I said, I spell "nock," refers to the end of an arrow that grips the drawn bow string before it is released. Sean's point: though awkward, these dinner table training sessions served as a "gripping nock" in our child-arrow delivery system into life. The nock has prepared them to knock on doors of influence and opportunity. A chance to train men of virtue was earned because we actually ate dinner together—around a table. So, I'm flattered that there is something (someone) to roast! Kidding aside, the dinner table was a huge part of what we have called our "full immersion home." This idea came from the book of Deuteronomy, particularly 6:4-9.

Full Immersion Home

Turning our attention to the educational and truth-imparting culture of a home built with God, the book of Deuteronomy has fueled our focus, style and substance. I would like to delve into these few verses, but also comment on the larger contextual themes of Deuteronomy. Parents know they are supposed to educate their children, but the point is to educate in a way children will embrace for life—in order that they might have life. Moses has a lot to say to this as he envisions God's treasured people entering the Promised Land. Moses doesn't get to go in, but 120 years of experience gives him an idea of what has staying power.

The Qualification of Moses in Home Leadership

Moses experienced leadership on the extremes. Forty years of association with the top leaders in the most powerful nation on Earth, Pharoah's palace in Egypt, puts a little edge on a guy's leadership blade. He murdered an Egyptian who was beating a fellow Hebrew, which caused him to flee from Egypt to Midian. Here he takes a wife and starts a family. In Egypt, his education level was likely on par with West Point and Wharton School of Business. However, for the next forty years he will be looking at the backside of sheep in mundane Midian.

At the end of the 40-year Midian season, God calls Moses to his life's work in delivering Israel from Egyptian slavery to the Promised Land. It's apparent his leadership level is at an all-time low, both in public and at home. From palace to pasture, he lost his edge. After a dismal response to his calling to deliver the people of Israel in Exodus 4:1-13 ("I am slow of speech and slow of tongue," vs.10), God is ready to put him to death (4:24), but not for his speaking skills. Evidently, he has not yet performed his head of Jewish household responsibility of the covenant-circumcision of his oldest son, Gershom. Going to Egypt to deliver God's people, Moses' wife Zipporah manned-up and took care of covenant business for him. It's hard to tell who wanted to kill Moses more, Z or God. Her fury is revealed when she throws the bloody circumcised foreskin at the feet of Moses. The text indicates she saved her husband's life, an interesting inclusion if we accept the fact that Moses was the author of Exodus and therefore reports third-person this humiliating moment of passivity.

Let's just say Moses is not ready to share the message of Deuteronomy yet, the lofty pre-game sermon to send the Israelites into the Promised Land; that will be in another forty years. One hundred and twenty years of training—40 in excellence-based Egypt, 40 in mundane Midian, and 40 in the wandering wilderness of Sinai—will find him ready. In the heart of this great sermon, we note a section (Deuteronomy 6:4-9) known as "the Great *Shema*." *Shema* means "listen." It defines the home of the covenant people.

"Hear, O Israel! The LORD is our God, the LORD is one!

You shall love the LORD your God with all your heart and with all your soul and with all your might.

These words, which I am commanding you today, shall be on your heart.

You shall teach them diligently to your sons and shall talk of them when you sit in your house and when you walk by the way and when you lie down and when you rise up.

You shall bind them as a sign on your hand and they shall be as frontals on your forehead.

You shall write them on the doorposts of your house and on your gates."

There are six imperatives that dominate these verses. They define the perspective and practices of an inside-out, full immersion home. Prior to writing these commands, Moses places them into the historical context that reveals the LORD's demonstrated love for His people, Israel. In Deuteronomy 1-3, he shows the LORD to be their creator, deliverer, provider, leader, protector and the initiator of the covenant. He starts at Abraham and walks through Isaac, Jacob, Joseph, then 400 years of slavery in Egypt and a great deliverance. Now, 40 years later, they stand on the edge of the Promised Land ready to go in.

To summarize, Moses raises a question (4:7), then summarizes the answer (4:20, 35):

"For what great nation is there that has a god so near to it as is the LORD our God whenever we call on Him?" (Deuteronomy 4:7)

"But the LORD has taken you and brought you out of the iron furnace, from Egypt, to be a people for His own possession, as today." (Deuteronomy 4:20)

"To you it has been shown that you might know that the LORD, He is God; there is no other besides Him." (Deuteronomy 4:35)

He will sandwich the beef of 6:4-9 between two whole-grain facts:

1. The mighty acts of God on behalf of His treasured people, Israel.
    "For you are a holy people to the LORD your God; the LORD your God has chosen you to be a people for His own possession out of all the peoples who are on the face of the earth." (7:6)

2. The grace and faithful love of God for his people.

   "The LORD did not set His love on you nor choose you because you were more in number than any of the peoples for you were the fewest of all peoples, (8) but because the LORD loved you and kept the oath which He swore to your forefathers, the LORD brought you out by a mighty hand and redeemed you from the house of slavery, from the hand of Pharaoh, king of Egypt. (9) Know therefore that the LORD your God, He is God, the faithful God, who keeps His covenant and His lovingkindness to a thousandth generation with those who love Him and keep His commandments." (7:7-9)

One could say Moses has been around the block 120 times. These two passages and corresponding points show two essentials in parenting – leadership and love. It's almost as if every child has a love-meter testing the responses of their parents with asking two questions. Who is in charge? (Leadership) And, Am I loved? Both questions must be answered in balance by parents in the home. Parental leadership is always answering these questions in tandem. The teaching environment is a big part of the life-leadership parents give. How do parents go about that? Consider the six imperatives of Moses. He's learned a thing or two.

CHAPTER 26

Feeding:
Six Imperatives for Teaching Children

*"It is not within our power to place the divine teachings directly
in someone else's heart. All we can do is place them on the surface
of the heart so that when the heart breaks they will drop in."*

—HASSIDIC ANECDOTE

"I have learned that our background and our circumstances may have influenced who we are, but we are responsible for who we become." These are the wise-beyond-years words of a 25-year-old. Some people never make the pivot. Have you?

Would the audience of the live sermon, we now know as the book of Deuteronomy, be found with such wisdom? Wandering 40 years in a wilderness, witnessing the death of an entire generation, and yearning for a promised home could create sober-spirited openness never before known. The physical view of the land of milk and honey may yield a teachable moment. Perhaps the heart has been broken and is now open to a new way to live—and live well. There is certainly a little more life-texture for the message Moses has in mind for the Hebrew home in the new land.

When Moses says, "HEAR O Israel," it's emphatic! It's loaded with historical significance. Coming through his voice is 120 years of gravitas, 40 years of world-class leadership training in Egypt, plus 40 years of humble grounding as a sheep herder, and finally another 40 years of wilderness wandering leadership several million Israelites will give life and leadership perspective. He will begin with "first things first,"—God's preeminence in life (6:4-5), then explore what it means to love God at home—the real trench work in life. These six imperative verbs found in Deuteronomy 6:4-9 come across like commands in the tone of a strong *"Do this!"* They provide an educational pathway for a child to flourish in. They have informed us all these years. Perhaps you will see the relevance to your future home, too, as I share them in principle and our present-day practices.

Imperative #1: HEAR THIS! The LORD is our God — our one and only. Our love for Him is to be absolute in terms of loyalty and our life bedrock.

Moses is saying foundationally that the LORD our God *is our one and only, above all others* because of our history with Him. He created us, called us, delivered us, provided for us, endured with us, showed us grace and has a terrific future for us and a great place to be. We are God's own possession and His treasure. We make God wealthy.

This is a repeat of the first commandment: *"I am the LORD your God who (history) brought you out of the land of Egypt, out of the house of slavery. You shall have no other gods before Me."* (5:6-7)

As a father to four boys, my greatest challenge (and fear) is that I will be overtaken and distracted by other things. In the KNOCK section of this book there is a letter written to our four sons for their manhood ceremony passage. The essence of my letter (personally read and hand-delivered to each of them to carry for life) contains a summary of what I believe is the most important thing in being a man—committing one's hearts completely and exclusively to God. There is no god but God, and the single most important thing I can do as a man is command my drifting heart to grasp this reality. It is a daily, even hourly, intentionality. To not do this is to sell out to lesser things and be found with a divided heart, just as Solomon was; his tragic choices brought tragic results.

This brings us to the second imperative that comes through the swinging doors of the first.

Imperative #2: LOVE GOD! He is your God, so this is your response to Him being one and only.

Our love for Him is to be all-in, total *(heart, soul and might).*

More than making God our "one and only," I invited each of our four sons to embrace my best statement of loving God totally: being all-in. This is addressed to Sean, the last son to receive it. Along with my sons, I shared the substance of it with many other young men in like ceremony:

> What I've already written to your older brothers is still fresh. I have no revisions. It's overwhelmingly clear what I should commend to you, Sean: *Let your heart be completely God's.* Love Him preeminently. Live for Him exclusively. Leave everything for Him for the duration. (Luke 14:25-33). It will define everything you are. There is nothing else in the world to be so fully immersed in, and defined by, than the pure, holy and magnificent nature of God.

Soren Kierkegaard wrote, *"To be pure in heart is to will **one** thing."*
Jesus said, *"The pure in heart will see God."*

> There are a myriad things less worthy to occupy the precious and all-defining center of your soul. People, ambitions, things, and ideas will compete daily, even hourly, for your primary affection and attention. Though many of these things are valuable and good by themselves, they can become false gods. False gods are like candy in that they taste sweet and satisfy us at first, but rot our teeth and pollute our system. They can turn into a raging animal within us and devour us. They are subtle and require constant vigilance to ward off. I have learned to place *sentries at the gate of my heart*, watching for *anything* that challenges my fidelity to God -- anything that would replace His primacy in my heart. These sentries are **the word of God**, His indwelling **Spirit**, a tender **conscience**, and the **counsel of trusted friends and family**.

> I did not place these sentries at the gate until my first year of college, and thus, my boyhood was extended beyond the years it should have been. Without these guardians of my soul, the early years were lost to foolishness and vain pursuits, making choices that brought both hurt and shame to me and to others. Though I have every reason not

to be, I am still very capable of forsaking the One who is my very life and nurture.

David and his son Solomon provide both positive and negative examples of the benefits and consequences of giving (or not giving) ones heart completely to God. Most of David's life was characterized as "a man after God's heart." No doubt, David would like to erase one year of his life that was full of sin (adultery), cover up (deception and manipulation) and evil choices (murder) to save his reputation. It all started when he allowed the sentries of his heart to sleep at the gate while he sought to feed an appetite apart from God. David started well, slumped, but finished well, yet not without pain-filled years brought on by those slumping sentries. Solomon started well, too, asking God for wisdom. God blessed him with wisdom that led to unparalleled affluence and influence.

Pathetically, the historian and writer of 1 Kings (11:4) summarized the condition of Solomon's heart, not his wealth and affluence, with these chilling words: "His wives turned his heart after other gods; and *his heart was not wholly devoted to the LORD his God.*" Solomon, the smartest man in the world, finished foolishly.

To make God our one and only is to love Him above all others. This is not easy. It is an intentional path each individual must become preoccupied with, as we will see in the third imperative.

Imperative #3: IMPRESS ON YOUR HEART the commands of loving God absolutely first.

Our love for Him is to be internal, *weighty, and concerned to the inner core.*

This takes away our tendency to lay the responsibility at another's feet, such as the underwhelming worship and preaching at a church, the busyness of my work world, the demands of a busy family schedule, especially the millions of hours we spend supporting our children in sports. There is no excuse for my wandering heart. I am responsible for my heart—period!

My letter to my sons finishes this way, emphasizing the personal responsibility to make sure our heart is rightly focused:

Regarding the heart, consider the following two defining passages:

"For the eyes of the LORD move to and fro throughout the earth that He may strongly support those whose heart is completely His." 2 Chronicles 16:9

"Watch over your heart with all diligence, for from it flow the springs of life." Proverbs 4:23

My son, embrace the *discipline* of turning your heart fully toward God. Make the sentries I've mentioned your friends, too, for the duration of your life. You have been given an excellent start as Solomon had. For the sake of God, your well-being and the lives of those you influence, *choose* to let these guardians speak truthfully to your inner man throughout your life. Their words and influence are *life*. I commend to you Psalm 16:11 and Psalm 37:3-6 for your memory and continual meditation. The pleasure of God is at the heart of everything I am (and do) as a man, a husband, a father, a leader, and a pastor.

The first three imperatives put responsibility on heads of household. You cannot impart what you do not possess. Your teaching comes completely from who you are and what you are committed to. Remember: they know. Then again, it doesn't end in my heart. Moses adds the priority of sharing the focus with the entire covenant community. The last three imperatives address how we influence others, starting at home.

Imperative #4: TEACH the commands of loyal love diligently to your sons/children. Our love for God is to be communal (my family), all-day and in all situations.

The verb translated "teach" represents the mental image of inscribing with sharpness and precision. For example, the engraver of a monument, chisel in hand, painstakingly etches a text into the face of a slab of granite. "Diligence" implies a constant focus and repetition. Sitting (inactivity) and walking (activity) covers everything spatially. *From the time one rises in the morning until he goes to bed at night* covers the time scope of such diligence. The parent-to-child etching goes on in every life situation (resting or active) and every waking hour. It is all-encompassing, in 3-D totality, and life's preoccupation teaching "the words." First, I am intentional in loving God as my one and only; then I am intentional in teaching those I love more than any about God, who loves them even more than I.

Before Pam and I had children, and challenged by these commands and images, we tried to imagine what this would look like. We wanted to be all-in communicating the life of God to our children. This was part of our motivation to homeschool the first few years, which we did up to the fifth grade. It was my hope to use the Bible to teach theology, Christian life essentials and on and on. Pam did a great job integrating this, choosing from many homeschool curriculums. During pre-school and grade school years, we had significant access and opportunity to make age-appropriate deposits. Our sons would sit on our lap and we could read to them or they would read to us. I looked forward to the day we could engage them on a more sophisticated level, putting the pieces of a Christ-centered worldview into their mental space.

But something was shifting. We would learn to exercise less control in coming years. Let me reiterate: we would learn—and in the nick of time.

We had family devotionals (Bible reading, discussion and prayer) and these became "labored." I worked hard at preparation and creativity, but one could feel resistance. Aside from content, I worked at keeping these times fresh with all kinds of change-ups and fun. From dinner table placemats with creative discussion questions on them to "Dr. Pepper on the Deck" to "Dessert and Devo," we did whatever it would take to gain and keep our young audience. I invented material and I watchfully surfed for anything that might hold their attention, but the resistance grew. (*Maybe it wasn't about material,* I thought.) It was the toughest small group I have ever led. They would slice and dice "Dad the family shepherd."

You may recall my earlier reference to our challenged family devotions. No kidding, Jason would stick his head into the corner of the couch, as if trying to escape our living room to enter another dimension through the couch cushion passageway. I thought to myself, *I work as hard as anyone I know at this. And I'm many times more trained in this than the average guy, but I'm getting my head handed*

to me on a platter every time I watch my son stick his into the corner of the couch. I
became exhausted and beaten down. So, finally, I took the hint: I quit and turned
in my resignation. It was one among several times I resigned as dad. The Father
reminded me that I was their only human father. Ultimately, they belong to God.
I had been praying and working hard (all good), but this was a season where the
Father would parent me up in my capacity to be "watchful." We learned regularly
to ask, *Where are we at?* And, *What is God doing?*

Instincts (and cold, existential reality) told me we were moving out of one
stage and into another. We were leaving the "tell me/teach me" stage to the
"show me" stage. It's as if the boys said, "We have heard enough. Now we only
want to see it in action." We terminated the family devo and heightened our
watchfulness for real-life teaching opportunities. Pam contributed a great dinner
table conversation question we got a lot of mileage out of, asking, "What was the
highlight and lowlight of your day?" This generated some interesting life-sharing
and spontaneous teaching. We also were able to use the time to explore and
debate whatever came to mind. We listened to their perceptions and they heard
our way of looking at life. Mostly, they observed our intentionality and reactions
to challenges.

In retrospect, we were more ambitious on content than was necessary, so we
did a course correction. The volume and focus of content is really quite relative.
Time, interest and life will take care of content volume, especially beyond the
family. Instead, we gave our sons perspectives, practices and skills to build
on. Their hearts are open to others who will come after us to give specialized
contributions in areas where we have limited ammunition. The greatest learning
gifts our sons received were love, joy of learning, problem solving tools, and, at
a young age, discipline. (Being chained to their mom during homeschool days
taught them to complete their work efficiently so that they then could enjoy
free time.) They are all good students and self-motivated. Credit goes to Pam for
creating the learning culture: balancing task and play and developing both sides
of their brains in concert with their hearts.

Beyond formal and organized learning opportunities, Pam and I were vigilant
about teaching moments. Bedtime ("as you lie down") is one routine thing parents
and children do, but it's a goldmine of heart to heart teaching opportunity. Bryant
was four or five years old when he started asking "God" questions. Most of these

happened at bedtime for several nights. As I answered his questions about God, I tried to explain the gospel in terms he could get his five year old mind around. He wasn't ready to explore "justification by faith" out of the book of Romans, but he was ready to hear something of the following (as I recall): "Jesus died for the bad things we have done and wants to forgive us. We can receive Jesus into our heart, be forgiven and go to heaven to live with God forever." That was it in a nutshell, enough to understand how Bryant interpreted it and how it actually became an intellectual, emotional and volitional (will) barrier.

His persistent curiosity led me to ask him one day, "Bryant, are you ready to receive Jesus into your heart to be forgiven and go to heaven one day?" He said, "No." I was a little perplexed about his quick and firm response. I asked, "You're not? Why not?" He said, "I don't want to go to heaven. I want to stay here with you in our house." I didn't know whether to laugh or cry. I had no idea he was thinking he would have to go to heaven right away if he received Jesus. He was not sure about a place he couldn't see, but he liked where he was— so no Jesus and heaven, thank you. Yes, we did some clarification about the timing of such things. My point: a series of spontaneous bedtime conversations gave Dad and son a chance to explore the meaning of the gospel and clarify misunderstandings. Most nights, we did fun things as we tucked them into bed like reading favorite books and making up stories. And there were nights when we were just exhausted and goodnights were brief. But once in a while, great questions emerged and clarifications were offered by Mom or Dad. We are glad we were there and watchful enough to capture such moments. We prayed for such moments.

Imperative #5: BIND the commands of loyal love to all you put your mind to. Our love for God is to be public and evident in our influence.

When I see a person with tattoos publicly displayed, I figure they are inviting me to ask about them. Over the years, I have learned two things about all that ink: 1) there are usually some detailed and dramatic stories behind all that body art, and 2) I need to allow plenty of time for an answer. This is possibly a contemporary parallel with what Moses had in mind when he said, *"You shall bind them* [the words/commands] *as a sign on your hand and they shall be as frontals on your forehead."* (Deuteronomy 6:8)

A favored interpretation of this suggests something metaphorical, not literal. The hand represents all one does; the forehead (between the eyes) represents all one thinks. If you want to go literal, like some Jewish people, you can don a little box (phylactery) containing written commandments and stick it on your forehead and forearms. In these days of tattoos, one could literally put some messaging artwork on these areas so others could note and inquire. Frankly, many people can't relate to this and may find it weird and distancing, which is the opposite effect Moses had in mind. More attractive to me (and I think many others) is a life well lived. People are either attracted to or repelled by what you do and how you do it. If the words of God are benefitting me, others will notice and, eventually, be curious.

Paul well summarizes this in Colossians 4:5-6: *"Conduct yourselves with wisdom toward outsiders, making the most of the opportunity. Let your speech always be with grace, seasoned with salt, so you will know how you should respond to each person."*

Salty and gracious living in proximity to people will yield curiosity and questions. These are teaching and revealing moments. The questions aren't always in the form of questions. They might be statements to provoke a reaction. If you attach duct tape to a little box to your forehead or wrist, you will get stares, questions and reactive comments all day long. (I don't recommend this.) I do recommend that you allow God to be firmly placed as your first love, living an intentional plan to keep things that way all day, every day. Stares, questions and comments you will get; especially from your children, who will tend to be less inhibited. But you then get opportunities to describe and define what is in the box of your life. Pray about this, plan for it, but prepare to be ready and watchful for any opportunity. By the way, if you don't have contact with people, or more importantly your children, they will have less to ask about and fewer opportunities to ask. Little contact, little impact. Both quantity and quality of time with children matter.

What we do and think matter; we ultimately reveal who and what our God/god is. Children are smart. As the man said, *"They know!"* When children (and anyone) see hand (what we do) and heart (what we think) compatible with both home and public life, we have a clear and powerful signal. The final of the six imperatives shows how.

Imperative #6: WRITE the commands of loyal love where they can be read by family and public.

Our love for God is to be transmitted from generation to generation.

> "You shall write them on the doorposts of your house and on your gates." (Deuteronomy 6:9)

The doorposts of the house would remind family members of their loyalty going out and coming into their dwelling place. For the Israelite community, the term "your gates" speaks of the city gates, the public location where business and law are transacted. In a God-ruled covenant community, these words were to be present in writing so as to govern the market and social justice.

What does this mean for us who live in a pluralistic culture? Is there a salty and gracious way to go public? Certainly, we can write on our own walls and those of the covenant community of faith (church), but I may go about work and social situations a little differently.

Writing adds specificity and precision to a message. Again, the talk without the walk is hypocrisy; the walk without the talk (precise explanation) is a mystery. What does this mean exactly to write the commands of loyal love where they can be read by both family and public? Does it mean placing a Ten Commandments sign in my yard? Writing Joshua 24:15 on my front door, "As for me and my house, we will serve the LORD"? The answer is, *whatever it takes* to transmit the message permanently. If imperative verbs dominate the text, then these commands must dominate the life. If they don't dominate the life, why would anyone export them? If they aren't working for me, why would I put them on someone else? Teenagers live in the "show me" state; so does most of our culture.

Consider this: in our information-saturated society, I may wisely live more out of Imperative #5, earning the right to be heard. I'm also prepared to hand off helpful, relevant and credibly written information when asked. Books, articles, invitations to message-oriented events, audio-visual presentations and Internet resources are all ways to share written explanations revealing our life in God.

In a round-about manner, this book is a precise way for us to keep transmitting the command to love God inside out, both in our household and public. Though our sons will be contributing, it's still a distinct reflective statement of our household. We all will learn and be honed by the exercise. The book may have limited circulation, but the exercise is eternally valuable and a possible record to generations to come, minimally to our sons.

Even if our home is full of grace, love, total fairness and well-communicated truth, and thus there is no emotional or intellectual barrier or stumbling block to the gospel of Jesus (or Moses!), my children may still opt out or be slow to respond. What do we do with the barrier of the will? Some people just simply want to run their own life—without God! What is the parent's response to that?

CHAPTER 27

Crop Busters And Dusters:
Bring in "Air Support" and Cover Much Ground

"Ask…seek, and you will find…and he who seeks finds."

—Matthew 7:7-8

"Devote yourselves to prayer."

—Colossians 4:2

Though all of us have innate darkness, parents can make it worse in children by living out a hard heart culture, causing children to stumble. Prayer—devoted prayer—is our response because only God can penetrate the cracks of a hard, dark heart.

"Devoted" Has Diverse Faces

Devoting ourselves to prayer is a multi-faceted adventure. Some of the "multi" has to do with our faith models and spiritual gifting. The role of prayer in the Strain household for the first thirty years (as we write) vividly illustrates this so you will reflect on both styles. Jon and Pam are both "askers." How we roll in our asking is distinct, a very complementary different.

Jon is more "Nehemiah" in style: faith-risk, reacting to circumstances and opportunities with arrow-prayers on the go. Pam's style is more like what Paul described his communal (ministry team) prayers to be in Colossians 1:9: *"Since the day we heard of your faith, we have not ceased to pray for you."* She persists in daily and weekly petitioning, pounding the throne of grace on behalf of (and for the sake of) others.

Some of this might be gender-oriented. Allow me to use Psalm 127 language to characterize our prayer focus and contributions. Men are action figures and do more conversing on the go as they do projects side by side. Generally speaking, men are work-focused and break more toward a Prayer Warrior, "take ground" model, while women tend to be more face-to-face with special "you and me" time. They are more secure home and child-focused and seem to break toward a Prayer Warrior, "hold ground" model. Jon has to be moving about with eyes open when he prays; Pam can sit with a Bible and prayer journal in hand, recording petitions. Jon prays for work/ministry expansion, money and serious issues/challenges with family. Pam leans toward praying for children and relationships, and she does so with other women.

"Overgeneralization" might be the criticism of the previous paragraph. We both pray about all of this stuff, but it seems we tend to lean into it with gender-based foci. We would like to think we are both "devoted to prayer." Each one's devotion looks different. We hope both models (and there may be others) will widen the reader's thinking about prayer and its applications in all of life. It's too easy and debilitating to get down on oneself and others for not praying enough, or the right way. The important thing is that we ask, seek and knock a lot!

Prayer table set, let's explore what both prayer styles look like, or have looked like: Jon will speak to the "take ground" model, then Pam will describe her world and the "hold ground" model.

Prayer Warrior: "Take Ground" Style/Model

Considering how I came to faith, the following story should not be a surprise because we tend to do what was modeled to us. Earlier chapters described the role of prayer in salvation. My mom, practicing the "hold ground" model, continuously interceded for all of her children before the throne. Hearing her petitions, God the Father "made me an offer I couldn't refuse" in that Palm Desert studio apartment in 1978. It was my big pivot… a surprise to all of us! I began to pray for my dad that same year, joining my "ask" with the petitions of other family members. One year later, seated at his dining table in Shreveport, I shared my story of coming to faith and explained the gospel of grace to him. This opportunity was large in my trust development, realizing that through prayer God would open doors for the word of Christ to be shared. You may recall his story of coming to faith two years later in a Lewistown, Montana diner in 1981.

A few days before that conversation with my Dad, I spoke to the graduating class of 1979 at my high school. I felt compelled to write Henry Badt, the principal, and ask for time to share my faith story at the religious portion of the graduation ceremony. He and I had a good relationship when I was a student, so he became my advocate and persuaded the committee to allot me ten minutes to share my story, which turned out to be a Gospel presentation to a packed Hamilton High gymnasium. I believe God whispered to me to ask Him and Mr. Badt this ridiculous request. I had many friends in that class and was burdened for them, spiritually. I couldn't believe it when the invitation came from Mr. Badt and the graduation committee. I was sick to my stomach and thought to myself, *What the heck have you done?!! Now you have to follow through.* I never prayed harder and worked harder on a ten-minute speech. It was surreal standing in front of that class and their parents, telling my story and offering a challenge to consider the unique claims of Jesus.

Faith-Risk Finds Its Grounding in Prayer

God opening doors with the graduating class of '79 and shortly thereafter with my dad, fanned the flame to ask God for a lot more. The next fall at Idaho State, I challenged a football player, George, to open his home for a spiritual discussion with teammates. We were scared to death, but marinated it in prayer and stepped out trusting God for the outcome. We couldn't believe these guys came, nor could we believe that they were willing to engage the discussion with so much openness. I knew about these guys and how they rolled.

Wrapping up, one player, Bill, bee-lined over to me, peppering me with questions. I liked him from the word go. He was one of the most sincere and forthright guys I had ever met, and he was hungry for answers. I was only a year and a half into my walk with God and on the fast track to learning ministry skills on the frontline. Even though I was green, I also was a risk taker who learned things on the go, in leaps and bounds. I did my best to answer Bill's questions, but knew my answers were God's, not mine. (My answers were better than I was capable of!) Bill and I arranged to meet again and again for the rest of our college years. Raw and green made for a healthy dietary combination; Bill was raw and I was green. Both of us were moving toward God; neither of us would comprehend why, but we are glad for it.

Twenty-five years later, while recounting the story of Bill coming to faith in Jesus, I had an overwhelming "a-ha" moment. How could I have missed it? Midway through 1979, two young men went up on two different nights to pray: Jon on Red Hill; Bill on Water Tower Hill. There is no way to know if it was the exact night, but it was during the same season and certainly right before the football player outreach discussion at George's house.

Climbing Red Hill at night, I scurried up to stand on a bench in front of the Greek pillars to pray. Usually it was stress and the need to commune with God about my challenges that prompted this behavior. Overlooking the campus of Idaho State and the city of Pocatello, I would always shift my focus from my needs to those of others, asking God to move in hearts of students and folks to hunger for God and come to know Christ. I know I was praying a lot for the football player outreach because it created a fair bit of anxiety. That meant I was on Red Hill between the scheduling and hosting of the football players outreach.

Little did I know that Bill was climbing Water Tower Hill on his motorcycle, too. He describes how frustrated, empty and lost he was feeling at the time. Things came to a head that night. Bill was at a party with a girl under one arm and holding a beer can with the other hand. It came on him like a wave—the emptiness of his life. He crushed the mostly full beer can with his hand and flung it aimlessly, spraying beer on other party attenders. He stomped out, jumped on his motorcycle and started riding. On top of Water Tower Hill and through tears he cried out to God, "God if you are there, what is it all about?" Shortly after that evening, George's roommate, Bob ("Big Geek"), would invite "Little Geek" (Bill) to his house for the football player event. Many conversations later, the following spring, Bill would attend an Easter weekend retreat in West Yellowstone, Montana, where he chose to stand with Jesus for good. Teaching from Josh McDowell in the Book of Romans, supplemented by observing the dramatically changed life of another football player he knew at Boise State, was too much to put off any longer.

God in His "big sky" sovereignty brought two college guys, crying out to Him from two different hills in Pocatello, together for a pivotal, life-altering conversation at George and Bob's house. Raw and Green were going in the same direction then, and still are today. Our lives would rendezvous for pivotal alterations, especially on my part, many times. Four years after the Water Tower Hill and Red Hill experience, Bill and I were on Red Hill talking and praying. This prayer was immediately answered when I met Pam a few days later. Bill and I have spent our lives helping guys like us take the next step toward God. We have even served on the staff of two organizations for many of those years, Campus Crusade for Christ (now CRU) and Search Ministries in Nashville and Boise. Bill prayed and recruited me onto the staff of both organizations.

From the beginning, Pam and I have prayed for our sons to lay claim for themselves a saving faith in Jesus Christ. We also, from day one, have prayed for their wives-to-be. God has answered our petitions early on most fronts. This has brought us immense satisfaction knowing the parents of our two daughters-in-law did the same.

While I've explored what is behind our "asking big," it is time for Pam to describe her style of asking often, and for everything—also known as the "small stuff."

CHAPTER 28

Crop Disasters And Insurance:
Let's Get Praying

"Be anxious for nothing, but in everything by prayer and supplication with thanksgiving let your requests be made known to God. And the peace of God, which surpasses all comprehension, will guard your hearts and your minds in Christ Jesus."

—PHILIPPIANS 4:6-7

This final chapter is the final inning of our message of social and spiritual wealth, which we are privileged to pass on to our children. Praying together secures victory. In this final inning I'm looking to the Strain bullpen to bring in the Ace to get the save. I've thrown quite a few pitches, but the reader must know this chapter is the game-saver. Step into the parenting batter's box and concentrate intently on the heat the Ace will bring—Pam's pitches are few and fast. You are in your stance; here is Pam's wind-up—in her own words…

If you are around me for very long, you will often hear me say that prayer is not so much about the answers God gives (although I love that part!) but what it does in me. Many years ago I heard someone teach on Philippians 4:6-7. *"Let your requests be made known"* has the idea of continuous action. In other words, I don't stop praying until I have the peace of God. There's a good chance if I am still sitting there with clenched fists, worry and fear, I'm not experiencing the peace of God.

Well, if there's one thing moms do best, it's worry—which leads to our attempt at controlling our children. A helpful piece of wisdom I heard recently is, "Worry can be our lunge for control," or, "Worry is the façade of taking action when prayer really is." Everything in me wants to take control of my children's lives—to protect them from pain, to lead them around the hurtful consequences of their poor decisions and to put it plain and simple, to decide what's best for them!

As previously stated, we homeschooled our boys until they entered fifth grade. Upon releasing Bryant, my firstborn, into the scary (to me!) public school system, I knew I needed to elicit help from other moms! I had heard of the international organization called Moms in Touch (now called Moms in Prayer). This group exists to rally moms to stand in the gap to pray for their children and schools. I began leading my first group when Bryant hit the public schools and am still praying with other moms for my adult children and their wives.

Praying with a community of moms has done several things for my children and me. First and foremost, I am able to relinquish my fear, worry and control into the safety of other moms who share my "momma's heart." Another huge benefit is to see how many specific prayers God has answered in my children's lives as a result…character development, college choices, mates received—to name a few. An unexpected joy has been to team up with other like-hearted moms who pray things for my children, sometimes having never met my kids, and have them be exactly what I needed them to pray for without me even knowing it! I love how God does that!

What does this look like? We meet weekly and follow a Scripture-based outline to lead ourselves through an hour of praising, thanking, confessing and interceding for our children and their respective schools, teachers, and concerns. We follow a simple guideline of "what is prayed in the group, stays in the group," to instill confidentiality and safety. We carry the burdens, in prayer, of a variety of topics. Some of our kids simply need to do well on a test, others might be far away from God, while others are making destructive life choices. We also pray for our kids' purity, friendships, leadership and a variety of other topics.

I remember that over a period of 2-3 years I had been praying with my "moms" for Jason in a particular area. Even though his name means "healer," he had been using his words and actions toward his brothers in a harmful way. A dear friend of mine said of Jason when he was a toddler, "He's not naughty; he just likes to have fun!" That very well may be, but it was often at the expense of others. He was a master at knowing what everyone's triggers were. A little footnote here…he followed in his mom's footsteps. I take full responsibility. During my childhood, I was known to have a particular torture method for each of my three sisters. They only wished a group of moms had prayed for me! Anyway, I found myself praying regularly for Jason to see what his words and actions were doing to his brothers. We prayed that God would cause a change in Jason. I kid you not; one day, after this period of regular prayer, I noticed that Jason was being kind to his brothers. The abusive language had stopped; he was becoming their advocate and cheerleader. And it has continued to this day! Coincidence? Possibly, but I really can't describe it any other way than God doing His work in Jason using our faith-fueled prayers.

Do we always see specific answers to our prayers? No, but then again, sometimes God answers in ways that only He knows and we embrace by believing He will work it out in His own timing. To this day, my group of praying moms has been praying for the daughter of one of our group's members. She has wandered away from her relationship with God. It is so encouraging to me to see her mom, a friend of mine, continue to come back week after week and allow us all to intercede and beg God to bring the daughter back to Him. We have seen her making better choices and still believe for her full return to God. And believe me, we will be throwing a huge celebration praise party when that happens!

There was another instance when we prayed specifically for a local middle school teacher who had a tendency to yell at her students. We prayed God would protect those students and do what He needed to do to correct the situation. One day the teacher showed up with a strange microphone attached to her head. She had been advised by her doctor to quit straining her voice and this device monitored her voice levels and her yelling stopped. A very creative answer to prayer!

I do pray on my own and on the move for my children. I have learned that God does a much better job than me in parenting. But praying in the previously described manner by joining hearts with my mom friends has been so powerful that it is one of the first things I put in my schedule each year—that is how important it is to me. Sometimes, I just need the community of other believers to carry my parenting burdens by praying for my children and their needs. I seem to be able to draw great strength from hearing in a collaborative fashion how God is working in every request and plea…the big and the small.

PART III:

Nobly KNOCK on Doors of Opportunity and Share the Wealth

"What is your most embarrassing moment?" For a good time with friends, this is a fun question to throw on the table. I've done this several times and generally it turns into an ab workout due to uproarious laughter. But what if I changed the question slightly? *"What is your most humiliating moment?"* This may not be so funny. For me, it's a very painful memory. Then again, it has become a sweet-and-sour memory because it turned into a door-opening event.

Walking out of the small seminar room in Reed Hall, I was stunned by the unexpected. The head of the History department and seven other students at Idaho State University had just reviewed a paper I had written for a history seminar class. This class completed my history minor requirements—if I passed. Weeks prior, I attacked the assignment, chasing down primary sources to explore the spiritual life of former President Woodrow "Tommy" Wilson. I poured myself into the research. I enjoyed the discovery process and formulating my findings in the research paper. I felt good that I had done capable work—for an undergraduate. Unfortunately, I did not leave enough time to have someone else proofread the paper. It will be okay, I thought. This was before word-processers were available for easy edits. Not smart.

Reviewing my paper with disdain and disgust, the professor highlighted my repeated grammatical error throughout the paper. It was same error, over and over. The professor ripped into it, into me and went off on an endless rant about how pathetic it was that someone with my writing proficiency could be found in a senior history seminar course. I sensed the entire seminar group felt humiliated for me, which added more humiliation and shame. I took it.

Apparently, realizing she had "deep-sixed" me, the professor started shoveling dirt off my shallow grammatical grave. "Well, it's really not your fault. It's a sign of the failing education system," she added. Her attempts to resuscitate me would turn into another rant that continued on for several more minutes. I welcomed it. It felt better that every schoolteacher in America had joined me in the grammar grave. She never commented on the content and research. Later, I learned I received the letter grade "B" for the course, which was based almost entirely on the paper and 10 percent on class participation. Yet, the moment I walked out of the room, it felt like it was going to be an "F."

Humiliation teamed up with its dark soul-cousin—anger—and started excoriating me. *Sixteen years of formal schooling and you blew it. It's too late to go back. You missed your opportunity,* I said to myself. The self-talk whipping continued, *Sad for one heading into a communication-based profession. You have failed and now you will be stuck this way for the rest...*

Wait a minute! I thought, catching my own verbal fist in mid-air. *Why are you assuming you can't get this right?* I asked myself. *You have the rest of your life to become a capable writer,* I counseled. I resolved to work on improving my writing skills (especially grammar) the rest of my life. *I can be a life-learner.* Over 30 years following that Reed Hall discussion with myself, I'm still writing—and with good effect. I have worked hard, practicing through emails, letters, messages, newsletters, tributes and...even a book.

Writing is a huge part of my life. Why did the "rubble" voice (my self-talk informed by my brokenness) back down to the "mortar" (building bonding material) voice? The mortar voice, God's rebuilding of me through His Word and His mentoring people, exposed lies and established truth. Five years prior, I would not have had the tools to turn that mental conversation for good. I would have gone into GPTS (grammatical post-traumatic syndrome) retreat and not risen to my God-given destiny to write.

The appendices to follow are a testimony of door-opening opportunities and destinies. Many are my written documents for the purpose of shaping the valuable lives of my sons. The others are written documents by our sons who are far superior to Dad in skill, especially considering their age. The water has risen, generation to generation. This is just the beginning, for they have just begun.

These are game-changing documents for us—historically speaking. They are testimonies, templates and tools to fuel your imagination of what could be, should be and by God's grace will be if we do our part and trust Him to do His part. We have learned to ask; we have sought to seek; now we will explore noble knocking on doors of opportunity.

We begin with Appendix A—the clear-eyed target. Shifting metaphors, it can serve as a blueprint from our house construction, useful for creating your own. Sights set, Appendices B-F provide useful tools and testimony exhibits.

Seed for Future Planting I:
Template for Parenting Target Letter

Jon and Pam's letter to our son, Jonathan. Similar letters were written to each son when they were in pre to early-grade school.

Our dear son Jonathan,

"Children are a gift of the LORD; the fruit of the womb is a reward. As arrows in the hand of a warrior, so are the children of one's youth. How blessed is the man whose quiver is full of them…"

—Psalm 127:3-4

In God's gracious character and sovereign plan, He entrusted you into our care, to be shaped under our tutelage. We are deeply grateful for the privilege of having nurtured you from conception in your mother's womb till now…the day we send you into the world as a man. This letter, written so many years ago, seems like yesterday. What was future tense all these years is now present tense.

From the start, we realized there have been many things about preparing you for this day that we could control and many that we could not. We could control the example we give you (though imperfect and limited by perception). We chose to live obedient to God's instruction and be strategic in our thoughtful training of you. Day by day and minute by minute we have sought to make many mini-decisions to show you how valuable you are as a person—declared so by God and affirmed by us. We chose to show you acts of kindness through listening, serving, playing, instructing, disciplining, modeling and praying for you.

What we knew we could not control is your life path. We have sought to point to the path of life as we have come to understand it, but you are choosing your own pathway and steps. We have sought to tell you of, and point you to, the God we know, love and serve. You, however, have decided for yourself that He would be your Master too. We've sought to train you in social wisdom, character and values, but you are deciding with whom you share this wealth—most importantly being the life-mate you may select. We have spoken of, and seek to live consistently for, what is important in life, but you are discovering and choosing which life-mission you will serve. While we have labored to bring you to full maturity as a person, today we once again surrender you to be your own man. You have chosen your own Master, you're choosing your own mate and have discovered your own mission. We can only hope and pray that we have done all we could to prepare you for the war zone of planet earth and opportunities ahead.

Jonathan, you are fulfilling the meaning of your name with each passing year. *Jonathan means "Gift of God" or "God Gave."* You are certainly God's gift to us. Now you are proving to be such to so many whom your life touches. Your valuing of every kind of person, accompanied by your good-natured and empathetic demeanor, accents the glorious image of God in each individual you encounter. You are a contagiously enjoying soul whose joy is a refreshingly soft mist on a hot day. You have always made us laugh, even when you are not even trying. Your creative humor, whether in your own head, written, reactive to a situation, or a spontaneous burst of fun, is always measured with kindness and respect and not at the expense of another. You have such an honorable heart for people, the effect uplifting. *Stephen means "Crown"* in the sense of a laurel wreath, the champion athlete's reward for competing according to the rules. You are a regal-minded man, forthright, just, and committed to do the right thing. More than sitting on top, you use your platform to lift and serve others. As you honor those made in God's image, you honor Him. Your aspirations are measured by organized thinking, living by priority, personal discipline and strategic intention. This is *who you are!* What a gift of God you have been, are, and will be to our world.

Watching you and your brothers grow has been like opening a gift continuously. Now that you are a man, it still is. There are still nuances and fresh expressions coming forth, always new surprises or ways which your uniqueness is expressed. Jonathan, you are a blessing to us and have filled our lives with so much delight. You are a message and blessing we now release to a world, much of which we may never see, but will enjoy the fruit of for all eternity. As an arrow is meant to be released into the heart of its target, so we now release you, our honorable and noble-minded son. Though you are not a little boy anymore, you will always be our cherished son. And therefore, you will always have our unconditional love, commitment, loyalty and friendship.

Co-founders and lifelong members of your fan club,
Dad and Mom, Jon & Pam Strain
Original Draft, Spring 1994.

This letter shared in the family's presence, May 18, 2013 at Jonathan's special place, overlooking Spokane city and the river that runs through it.

What We See in Jonathan Stephen Strain
Shared by Dad and Mom

Funny/Creative/ Sense of Humor/Self-Entertainer/Author
("Far Side" sense of humor; plays games in head; tells his own jokes; written his own comics and satirical student newspaper column)

Rounded/Balanced/Good-Natured (easy rider: doesn't take self too seriously; laughs and lets go)

God-Loving, God-Pleaser

Obedient/Prudent/Wise

Strong Sense of Fairness/Justice/Equality

Does the "Right Thing" (pleasing to people, but not a people pleaser)

Loyal/Dependable/Faithful/Conscientious

Honest/Authentic/Straight-Up with people ("man without guile," like Nathaniel)

Values Relationship (intentional and doesn't settle for surface, e.g. roommates)

Sensitive/Empathetic Spirit (hurts when others hurt; enters their joy)

Vulnerable/Trusting/Open (shares the deepest parts of his heart)

Kind/Respectful (Good boundaries; not imposing, but will ask)

Organized Thinker/Good Decision-Maker (e.g. point guard & soccer)

Author/Architect/Builder (e.g. writing and Legos)

Analytical/Detailed/Thorough (a processer and reflective)

Creative, Imaginative (loves books, stories and good ideas)

Confidence

Aspires to Excellence/Work Ethic/Hard Worker (school, soccer/sports, piano, chores)

Lives by Priorities/Disciplined (School work, work-work, scheduling, piano and drums)

Sacrificial (but lives for good reward)

Great team player, but also can work independently

Personal Observations from Brothers and Fiancée (shared May 18)

Bryant: Great maturity observing bookends of college experience… dropping off and attending graduation. Ready for adventure and investment; Vulnerable openness is not "normal;" Quick conscience, raw, sensitive, humble confidence in God. Networker… hugs for every other person we walk by. Has a heart for the "have-nots."

Jason: Humility: handsome and amazing but doesn't know it. Things that were disdained by me many years ago are now highly respected. Used to pick on Jonny, but now respect and brag on you about everything. Not intrusive, open, confident and accepting.

Sean: We have a special connection as roommates growing up. You have rubbed off on me… good because I always wanted to be like you in so many ways: no judgment whatsoever.

Christina: If you were an animal, you'd be a golden retriever: full of purity, kindness and joy.

What We Envision for Jonathan

Using all of the gifts and abilities mentioned above, Jonathan will empathetically envision ways to help others walk on a noble life path, discovering their God-given value and gifts.

Jonathan Stephen will fulfill his name by giving and investing his life as a gift of God to others. His crown will be authentically and vulnerably helping them discover their identity as sons/heirs of God and live like it—by the grace-gift of God.

Seed for Future Planting II:
Jon's Man-Ceremony Letter

This letter was shared with our four sons around the time they got their driver's license. Entering the world of adult responsibility and privilege (such as driving a car) seemed a good time to give a clarion call to manhood. This was the second of four timely ceremonies that served as rites of passage. Accompanying the letter was a gift—more symbolic than expensive. The keychain contained a summary of a four-part definition of a man I used as a "hitching post" for communicating what a man is. I adopted the definition from Dr. Robert Lewis, who also instructed me on the power of ceremony.

A real man:
Rejects passivity
Accepts responsibility
Leads courageously
Invests eternally (lives for God's greater reward)

At a special dinner, I invited several men to join me in reading similar but unique letters to each son. These were men who my son knew, respected, and who I thought would care about making such a significant deposit. (Over several years, many of us did this for one another's sons.) Still more letters from men who could not attend the event were included in a Dad-made "man book" that celebrated each son as a uniquely and wonderfully made person. Celebrating them as a gift of God and their giftedness from God is a powerful affirmation, while a circle of men welcomes each son into the community of men.

The symbolism of the keychain I shared is summarized this way:

- The metal containing the four-point definition is the unchanging substance and character of a man.

- The leather backing on which the metal rests shows that a man is both tough and pliable.

- The ring attached to the leather/metal is the circle of men who help connect the substance to his life responsibilities.

- The keys symbolize the responsibilities a man will bear in his life, such as a car, house or office key.

A man will palm his keychain several times a day—a continuous reminder of the noble man he aspires to be.

Here is the original letter to our oldest son, Bryant. The letter to each son is the same. It's noteworthy that virtually every man who participated in all four ceremonies shared with me afterward they wished they had such a ceremony.

My Dear Son Bryant,

In welcoming you into the community of men, I have been calculating that which has been defining in my own life journey to manhood. Actually, it's overwhelmingly clear what I should commend to you: *Let your heart be completely God's*. Strive in your inner man to make Him your pre-eminent passion. It will define everything you are and there is nothing else in the world to be so fully immersed in and defined by than the pure, holy and magnificent nature of God.

Søren Kierkegaard wrote, "To be pure in heart is to will *one* thing." Jesus said, "The pure in heart will see God." There are myriad things less worthy to occupy the precious and all-defining center of your soul and being. People, ambitions, things, and ideas will compete daily, even hourly, for your primary affection and attention. Though many of these things are valuable and good by themselves, they can become false gods. False gods are like candy in that they taste sweet and satisfy us at first, but rot our teeth and pollute our system. They can turn into a raging animal within us and devour us. They are subtle and require constant vigilance to ward off. I have learned to place sentries over the gate of my heart, watching for *anything* that challenges my fidelity to God, anything that would replace His primacy in my heart. These sentries are the word of God, His indwelling Spirit, a tender conscience, and the counsel of trusted friends and family. I did not place these sentries at the gate until my first year of college, and thus, my boyhood was extended well beyond the years it should have been. Without these guardians of my soul, many years were lost to foolishness and vain pursuits, making choices that brought hurt to others and myself, not to mention shame. Though I have every reason not to be, I am still very capable of forsaking the One who is my very life and nurture.

David and his son Solomon provide both positive and negative examples of the benefits and consequences of giving, or not giving ones heart completely to God. Most of David's life was characterized as "a man after God's heart." No doubt, David would like to erase one year of his life that was full of sin (adultery), cover up (deception and manipulation), and evil choices (murder) to save his reputation. It all started when he allowed the sentries of his heart to sleep at the gate while he sought to feed an appetite apart from God. David started well, slumped, but finished well, yet not without pain-filled years brought on by slumping sentries. Solomon started well too, asking God for wisdom. God blessed him with wisdom that led to unparalleled affluence and influence. Pathetically, the historian and writer of 1 Kings (11:4) summarized the condition of his heart, not his wealth and affluence, with the following scathing words: ". . . his wives turned his heart after other gods; and *his heart was not wholly devoted to the LORD his God* . . ." Solomon, the smartest man in the world, finished foolishly.

Bryant, embrace the discipline of turning your heart fully toward God. Make the sentries I've mentioned your friends, too, for the duration of your life. You have been given an excellent start as Solomon had. For the sake of God, your well-being, and the lives of those you come into contact with and influence, *choose* to let these guardians speak truthfully to your inner man as a way of life. Their words and influence are *life*. I commend to you Psalm 16:11 and Psalm 37:3-6 for your memory and continual meditation. The pleasure of God is at the heart of everything I am and do as a man, a husband, a father, a leader, and a pastor. It is my observation that God has given you a great mind and a heart of integrity. With Him you are destined for greatness. I believe in you and heartily welcome you to the community of men.

Your earthly father and eternal brother,
Jon Strain
May 9, 2002

APPENDIX C

Crop Yield I:
Sean's College Paper—"Men of Virtue"

This is an analysis of the family dinner table by our youngest son. It illustrates that even awkward, intentional attempts to make a deposit in our children's lives has a pay-off, eventually. Sean throws poor ol' Dad under the bus with satirical humor, but graciously chooses to vindicate the sacrificial labor of love when he's had his fun. Humor aside, the inclusion of this college paper is to encourage you to take risk (though awkward and misunderstood for a season) in this messy adventure called parenting. Furthermore, the dinner table provides an extremely valuable nurturing and educational opportunity to parents. Have as many family dinners as possible! Name another time each day when the whole family sits face-to-face conversing. Though we feared we were raising barbarians some days, the socialization that happens at mealtime will eventually chase the Vikings, Vandals and Goths out of the camp. You may misfire occasionally in attempts at meaningful exchange, but be intentional about figuring it out. And have as much fun doing it as possible. Watch for the man-definition. He got it!

Men of Virtue

I hated the placemats. They severely limited my creativity and freedom of expression: more rules I had to follow. Nonetheless, if I ever have children I will probably make table-manner placemats as well.

I strode into the kitchen, the floor transitioning from stone slabs to white linoleum, slippery under my socks. The new placemats sat on the trusty dusty table beneath our dinner plates, covered in diagrams and words. I was young, but I knew this was a bad sign. Up close, I saw the placemats outlined proper table etiquette. My dad deemed it necessary that my brothers and I learn our manners; we weren't sloppy or impolite kids, but we were in need of refinement. Sometimes when I felt like I wasn't being paid enough attention or had valuable information, I stood up on my chair and announced my thoughts like a doomsday preacher. According to the placemat, my soapbox was unacceptable behavior.

My dad created the placemats to not only teach my brothers and me superficial table manners, but also to be decent men. I'm sure he was concerned that we didn't embarrass ourselves in front of guests, but he cared more about us being agents of respect. When the placemats were no longer necessary for our family dinners, I didn't recognize the subtle impacts they had on me. After all, I was just a child.

I have since forgotten most of the rules on those placemats, or even rules that we were taught but weren't explicitly written out. One of the rules standing prominently in my mind was before taking our seats we had to wait for my mom to sit down. This rule was the most difficult for me to follow. It was second nature for me to sit down and heap piles of food onto my plate before everyone was seated. I wasn't allowed to serve myself, let alone sit down, until my mom did. Even when she was seated, I couldn't serve myself and begin eating until she had taken her first bite.

Other rules stated that we weren't allowed to put our elbows on the table, though I thought it was easier to eat that way. We were to sit up straight and not cross-legged in our chairs. We were to respect one another. We were to ask to be dismissed from the table. We were not to stand on our chairs; this wasn't actually on the placemat but I'm sure it was implied. The rules described were similar to those followed by previous generations when manners were more important.

The table also survives from a bygone era. The smooth, brown, and faux-wood surface has seen better days: suffering twenty-six years through the abuses wrought by homeschool children and countless family dinners. Many times I strayed off of my paper with a sharpie or pen and left a trailing smudge. I frantically licked my finger and rubbed the blemish, trying to remove the mark before it became permanent.

We spilled syrup, bread crumbs, milk, and every other imaginable food over the surface, leaving little deposits over time. I consider it a minor miracle that the rickety old table still stands. The legs of the table are only an inch and a half to two inches thick and don't have any support other than the nails connecting them to the table top. I wonder if it would still be standing if we had swept the crumbs from the cracks that cemented together the sections.

My parents sat at the ends of the table while my brothers and I filled in the middle. We fought with our feet under the table for the limited space, which to this day I will say was *not* footsie, but rather a form of physical prowess. Being the smallest and youngest, I didn't fare well in the arena. My spot was with my back to the wall facing the kitchen. If I went to the table early, I could watch my mom boil chicken noodle soup, mix up salad, or chop fruit on the cutting board. I stewed there in the atmosphere of cooking and let the garlic and onion fragrances fuse with the hearty odor of barbequed meat. Garlic enticed my appetite as I was able to smell it from almost anywhere in the house and my favorite meals usually required it. Its dominant tangy flavor could spruce up any lacking dish.

Conversation and family bonding mattered more than getting nutritional sustenance. We played board games, asked questions of the day, and told stupid puns or jokes. An often repeated joke was when someone asked to pass the honey or sugar. My dad would pipe in, "Pass the sugar, sugar. Pass the honey, honey. Pass the tea, bag."

I find myself repeating his phrases, which I refer to as Dadisms. He also used the phrase "just to be polite" when offered a dessert. A lot of people express shame at the weird things their parents do. I've learned to embrace them, because as I get older, their quirks seem funnier.

My parents often would ask what our highs and lows were during the day. I didn't like answering those questions because I didn't like talking much; I'd moved on from my chair standing days. This question commonly popped up on Monday and I would facetiously say, "My low of the day is that it is Monday."

But when I did decide to mention something that was bothering me, especially if it was a serious issue, my family would listen and offer advice. Dinner time was where I refueled physically and emotionally. As I grew up, I learned that if I had any concerns I could bring my issues to either my parents or my brothers and expect honest concern. Family unity grew from our family dinners.

Much like the graying crusted food in between the sections of our table, the unity built up and hardened over time. This bond between us is now inseparable. No matter how much time passes, our bond will only grow stronger. My parents made little deposits, like the manners depicted on the placemats into our lives, hoping for a payoff. As a result, we try to be strong men of virtue.

I still find myself resting my elbows on the table in the college cafeteria and I slide them off slowly so my friends won't notice any change in my behavior. As I do so, I imagine my elbows sticking on the laminated placemat and my dad's eyes peering at me from the end of the table.

Crop Yield II:
Jonny's letter to Sean, delivering him to college

This piece is about a brother who man-mentors his college-bound younger brother on what to hitch his carabiner to while in college. It was unprompted by us—a complete and delightful surprise. Jonny traveled with us to Salt Lake City to help Sean move into the University of Utah residence hall his freshman year. Carrying the final load in, Jonny asked me, "Dad, I have a letter for Sean. When do you think would be a good time to give it to him?" Curious, I asked him if I could read it, which he graciously allowed me to do. I was blown away. What a thoughtful, intentional and caring thing for an older brother to do—as if it wasn't enough to make the trip to deliver Sean. Again, watch for the man-definition. It's become their own. Perhaps it's contagious, especially between brothers.

Brother!

In exquisite Strain fashion, I have written you a letter built around an expansive and highly complex extended metaphor. It is my honor to introduce, *"The Carabiner Letter."*

THE CARABINER
A carabiner is a metal loop with a spring-gate used in rope-intensive activities, like sailing, caving, construction, window cleaning, or climbing. This simply complex piece of equipment is the pinnacle of safety and the hinge upon which such adventuring relies. As you embark on your new adventure in this next phase of your life, it is

essential to make sure that you are equipped—physically, spiritually, and emotionally.

There are three distinguishing characteristics that define the nature and function of the carabiner (besides being a cool thing to clip on to your water bottle).

Security in Adventure
The carabiner is designed as a piece of safety equipment. It sustains great weights and is used to keep you alive as you traverse life's craggy rock faces. But that's just it: while it is a tool for safety, it is meant to be used on a cliff face, up where it is dangerous and frightening to be. God does not call us to sit on our butts. He calls us out to go forth into the world. Sean, your world starts at the U: the cafeteria, classes, even your dorm room. He calls us to go where we are afraid to go, to do things we are not capable of doing. He calls us to ask our friends uncomfortable questions, to act like we know what we are talking about, even though we really have no idea. It is frightening, and most people cower from this call. But he calls us to harness up, and promises to be there as your security every step of the way.

"Then Jesus came to them and said, "All authority in heaven and on earth has been given to me. Therefore go and make disciples of all nations, baptizing them in the name of the Father and of the Son and of the Holy Spirit, and teaching them to obey everything I have commanded you. And surely I am with you always, your carabiner, to the very end of the age." (Matthew 28:19-20)

Strength
The carabiner (this one in particular) is designed to sustain a force upwards of 24 kilonewtons. For those of us without a background in physics, that is about 5,400 lbs. A single carabiner is strong enough

to suspend a mid-sized car in the air. In these next few years, there are going to be some tremendous forces pulling you around, vying for your attention and your heart, pulling you down. You will be utterly convinced that you are worthless, incapable, and weak. Nowhere, at no point in time, has this ever been good news—until Jesus came along. "But he said to me, 'My grace is sufficient for you, for my power is made perfect in weakness.' Therefore I will boast all the more gladly about my weaknesses, so that Christ's power may rest on me…For when I am weak, then I am strong, for Christ is my carabiner." (2 Corinthians 12:9). Theologian Karl Barth described our role as Christians in this way: "The job of Christian Community is a negative job only—to seek to be a "void" in which the gospel reveals itself, as you scale a cliff face."

What this means and how it is to be lived out in your own life is yet to be determined. I just know that it is one of the most important lessons that I have ever learned. God calls us first and foremost to be *free*. The joy that comes from truly understanding this freedom will then result in good works, in living the kind of life that Christ has for you. Do not do anything out of guilt, even if you are helping blind orphans. Because if you feel guilt (which is made apparent anytime you think you "should" do something), then you are not living in the freedom Christ has already given you. Your job? Remain in the vine (John 15). You do not have to do anything else. Your job is not to produce fruit, but to abide in the vine, meditating on how Christ has already done it all. Your life is a void that Christ then fills with fruit. Easy, right? No. But that's ok, because Christ is your strength.

Diversity of Function
It is this characteristic that makes the carabiner such an unbelievable piece of equipment. There are a million different ways to rig up a rope, to tie off knots and build anchors. At the center of all this is the carabiner. It is never used just one way. Do not live

with the expectation of "the way" your faith should be lived out, because you will always be disappointed and frustrated. Your faith and understanding of God will be stretched in a million different directions. Let this simple metal ring be the symbol of your faithful response to these forces: it does not bend and give into pressure, but it can be unclipped and rigged up in a different position so that it is more useful. Strong faith adjusts and adapts, but it does not bend.

These are the three primary characteristics of the carabiner and how it is supposed to be used, but I do want to add one more thing. While an amazing tool, one carabiner will not get you up a mountain. It is meant to be used within an entire working system of ropes, harnesses, and other carabiners. Seek out good friends who pour into you, who help share the load. We were not meant to journey alone. Find people who make you laugh, who challenge you, and who you genuinely enjoy sharing life with. "A friend loves at all times, and a brother is born for adversity, like a carabiner" (Proverbs 17:17).

Sean, I am excited to see where life takes you these next few years. You are a tremendous brother: steadfast, generous, intelligent, and incredibly good looking. Know that I love you and that I am always here for you. I will keep you in my thoughts and prayers, and wish you the best. Now go forth and rip the U a new one.

Love,
Jonny

Crop Yield III:

Jason's "Case for Marrying Jenna" Letter

After asking Jenna's parents permission to propose to their daughter, Jason sent them a detailed letter that any parent of a daughter could only dream of receiving from a prospective son-in-law. We include it here because it illustrates (one more time) the positive outcome of the man-definition. Amazingly, asking Jason for permission to include this, I learned that Jenna hadn't yet seen it! She needs to—and so do you! If you are single and reading this—pray and wait for this kind of excitement about a potential spouse. They dated six years before they were in a position for Jason to propose. That was on purpose. It pays to wait and do it right.

Bob and Pam,

I am writing this letter with an attitude of humility, respect, and admiration toward your relationship with your second born, Jenna. I wanted to take the time and craft a letter that will, and most likely not even come close to, explain to you both what it is that I see in Jenna that makes me want to spend the rest of my life with her. I have never had the opportunity to explain to you two the way that I view, value, and feel about the young woman that you have both raised. Our relationship has steadily grown from casual high school sweethearts, to a more serious, unclear college dating relationship, to a full grown, ever-maturing relationship with long-term expectations and desires. You are reading this during the tipping point of what is about to become one of the fastest, euphoric, and exciting times of our lives. You both have gotten to know me very well during the past 6+ years that I have spent dating Jenna and spending time with your family. What you haven't gotten to hear from me firsthand, however, is the way that I feel about Jenna and how I am aspiring to be the man that she deserves. I hope and pray my love for her is evident through my actions, but here it is from my fingertips....

I was listening to a new song by John Mayer the other day called "Something Like Olivia," where he sings, "There's only one man in this world who gets to sleep with her by his side." I got the chills as he sung that line as it hit me (and not for the first time by any means) that through divinity and amazing fortune that I will be that "one man in this world" who will someday soon sleep with Jenna by my side. It's stunning. I have done nothing in my life to deserve a woman like her, but God has for some wild reason, chosen to bless me immensely.

Jenna is, bar-none, the most incredible woman that I have ever met. She models what it means to live a life of loving, valuing, and caring for others. Her vibrant, bubbly, sweet, and most of all, sincere, personality has nothing but a positive impact on everyone she comes in contact with. From the way that she treats and loves me when I am not exactly deserving, to her sincerity in rejoicing in my successes and making me feel like a million bucks, she models what it means to be empathetic. She lives her life in such a real way. Since I have met her, she has known who she is and what she stands for, and has never once wavered from that. She is genuine. To me, that is the most attractive and beautiful thing about her. She lives her life in such a way that many are often too afraid or incapable of doing. She lives a life with no walls, is vulnerable and honest, and is quick to both receive and accept love. Because she is not spending time accounting for insecurities and covering the bases to keep up a certain persona or image, she is the go-to in all of her social circles for counsel, advice, understanding, and acceptance. She is VERY slow to judge, and VERY quick to extend love and understanding to those she comes in contact with. In our relationship, she is constantly affirming me, building me up, listening, supporting, and putting me in touch with areas of sensitivity and self-realization that I did not know were there. This is all because she knows who she is as a woman created in God's image and values herself in that. This is the most attractive thing about her. (Might I add that this is matched by an external beauty as well, but that goes without saying.)

All clichés aside, Jenna has become my best friend. As frustrating as a long distance relationship has been at times, it has made me value the details of my relationship with Jenna more than ever. Whether we are making dinner, watching a television series, hot air ballooning, building gingerbread houses, leading Young Life, or traveling the world there is never anyone I would rather share those moments with than her. She matches my zeal and enthusiasm towards life and all the adventures it holds and often takes it a step further. She lives passionately and fully. She balances me in areas that I need to be balanced (sensitivity, thoughtfulness, patience) and enhances the areas of my life that are most important to me (my faith, serving, ambition, loving others). Our values are completely aligned and continue to mold together more and more as we continue to put God at the center of our relationship, put each other's needs before our own, and simply live life together. Jenna has a heart for serving people that is inspiring. This is evident in the way that she treats her friends, leads high school girls in Young Life, and like the rest of your family is an amazing host to guests. She has a hilarious sense of humor that clicks with my own and I am continuously cracked up by her blunt attitude towards life. She has never stopped challenging me to grow in my faith, career, and as an individual. At the end of each day, I can honestly say I am a better person because of her, and I aspire for her to be able to say the same of me.

I want you both to know that I am open to any guidance, advice, and accountability that you may want to offer along the way. Like I said, it is by grace that I have Jenna in my life, and want to treat our to-be marriage with the due diligence that it requires. I look at your relationship, as well as my own parent's relationship, as the prototypical examples of what a marriage should look like. You have set a high standard for your children and have shown us what real love and commitment looks like. Because of this, I will be very receptive to any counsel, advice, and recommendations you have for us along the way. What I can promise you both is that I will submit myself before both God and Jenna, while rejecting passivity, accepting responsibility, and leading courageously in our relationship. This is the outline of a man that I am always striving to be, and the man that I see in you, Bob, and my own Dad. I can only hope that I would be held accountable anytime this is not apparent.

I love Jenna by the world's definition and am making the constant effort to love her by the Bible's definition. Jenna makes me giddy, still gives me butterflies, and brings out the romantic in me, and I would do anything for her…this is the world's definition of love. The Bible's definition of love is a much bigger feat and something that I have to work for because it is developed over time. I am sure you have come across this passage (1 Corinthians 13) countless times, but it still hits hard every time:

"Love is patient, love is kind. It does not envy, it does not boast, it is not proud. It does not dishonor others, it is not self-seeking, it is not easily angered, it keeps no record of wrongs. Love does not delight in evil but rejoices with the truth. It always protects, always trusts, always hopes, always perseveres."

It is my promise to you both, as the ones that brought Jenna into the world 23 years ago, that I will take action to live up to this definition of love. I am full of the world's definition of love that revolves around a feeling, and aspire to be full of the Bible's definition, which is centered upon action. We all know equally well that this is not a hard thing to do with Jenna. I almost feel like these verses were written to describe her.

Thank you one more time for welcoming me so graciously into your family and for entrusting me with the wellbeing of your daughter. At the core of it all, this letter is just to say that I am a lucky, lucky guy. I am beyond thrilled for my future with Jenna and to "officially" join the family. Life just continues to get more and more exciting and I wouldn't have it any other way.

With love,
Jason
10/16/2012

Crop Inspection:

Bryant's analysis of this book and key applications

The oldest, Bryant, is self-labeled the "family test dummy."
A lot of mistakes are made on the oldest. Just when parents
start figuring things out, they run out of children and try to
make up for it through grandchildren. It's only fitting we have
the "last word." We are out of words.

What an interesting experience it is to read a book written by your own parents on the topic of parenting and it is specifically targeted to me. Talk about an unsolicited attempt to offer my brothers and me advice! Really? They think writing a book will finally get us to listen to them?

As the eldest son, I have joked with my parents about being the "guinea pig" or "test dummy" of the family. In raising a family, someone has to go first and be the subject of all the parental experimentation. This is partly why we joke about Sean (the youngest) being our "last hope," he's definitely the smartest of us all and has the most up-side to actually become a productive citizen of society. From my quasi-limited perspective, I look down the line of my brothers and it only gets better as you go from Jason to Jonathan to Sean. I relate with the Apostle Paul when he calls himself the "Untimely Born," the only difference being that he was late and I was early. This is why I get the last say!

In all seriousness, this book cannot have come at a better time for my wife Christina and me. We are in our early years of marriage, starting the conversation about what it would look like to have kids and raise a family. Both of us have been captured by God's fatherly love for us and have surrendered our lives to him for his service and glory. We have a desire to be parents, but also see a need to be intentional on the front end, while we have some time. Especially recognizing this before the tyranny of the urgent of raising children takes over and we are left without a plan, only responding rather than initiating.

Currently, I work with 6th-12th graders as a Youth Minister at Evangelical Free Church of Salt Lake City. In this context, I have been granted the opportunity to come alongside parents in their ministry to their children. What a window this has provided into the challenges and ups and downs of parenting volatile, at minimum culturally Christian kids who are maybe, possibly regenerate? What a tough place to live as a parent! Wanting the best for your children. Wanting your children to know the Lord, to love their brother/sister/neighbor as themselves, to be morally and ethically conscious, to be productive in society, etc.

As a product of the parenting approach outlined in this book, I'd like to comment on two felt tensions and my experience of how those played out in the home:

1. What is God's role, the Parent's role and the Child's role?

2. If God is the one who saves, why do I need to be intentional?

God Is Good. Parents Are Evil. Children Are Evil.

God is good. The obvious reason anyone would read this book is because they are interested in parenting. If we think about it, the end goal of parenting is to parent well and (as a Christian) see to it that your child is walking with the Lord. If you noticed, the topic of parenting immediately turns our attention to the child and it is very easy for the parent to become fixated on what they must do in order to solve a problem that they are ultimately not in control of. I think this is the wrong starting place. There is a reason the first half of this book is centered around the idea of ASK and first addressing the need that the (evil) parent be parented by the One and Only Father.

God is the creator and redeemer of the world. God was intentional in creation. He was intentional in sending Jesus to provide a way for His children to be with

Him forever. God is the model parent and initiator, He has been doing this longer than any earthly parent. Not to mention that He is all-powerful, all-knowing, all-loving, and in complete control of all things. Nothing is outside of His will and plan. This means that as we begin to think about parenting, we must first go to the Model Parent and submit ourselves to Him as children. How could we ask our children to do something we are not doing ourselves? If we are to learn something about parenting, we must first be parented by God. Growing up, my parents did this. Before they were parents to us, they were children to God. They entrusted themselves to God's plan and purpose, even with their unpredictable, stubborn, childish children! My parents were model parents by being children of The Model Parent. This is what set the tone of our home environment. We knew. We knew my parents were trusting children of the One True God.

Parents are evil. So what is the parent's role in all of this? As I noted above, they must first be children to God. But does that mean that they just sit back and watch as God does His work? Not at all. We can all think of situations where a lack of or harsh parenting provides terrible results. There is general Proverbial wisdom all over the Bible for how to parent, which my dad has spoken to much of. Proverbial parenting wisdom comes from the base assumption that if you follow the ways of the Lord and His guidance, things will generally go well for you. Yet, there is no promise that if you do X, Y and Z that your child's future will be secured. A parent is left in a position of influence, but not ultimate influence. The only hope for this depraved world of evil parents and evil children is that God would work to secure and restore. It is out of this that the parent is led to seek ultimate influence from God by asking, seeking and knocking. That God would parent by means of their parenting.

Apart from God, there is no perfect parent, hence Jesus referring to parents as evil in Matthew 7. My parents were by no means perfect in their parenting, but they know someone who is. Heeding the truth that their Father in heaven gives good things to those who ask, they asked big and they asked often for my brothers and me. All the while trusting that God's ways and timing are perfect. They modeled the Christian life of ongoing repentance and faith; with God, with one another and with their sons. Mistakes were made, but they owned them. Character flaws were real, but that didn't keep them from going to God and continually affirming their love for their children. All that said, God must work and parents are to ask big and ask often. I, for one, am thankful that my parents did this!

Children are evil. The children! What to do with the children?! God help them! I am not a parent, but I can imagine this is a recurring thought running through any parent's mind. This has got to be one of the most rewarding yet frustrating jobs on this earth. I have been fortunate enough to spend time with a number of young children in the context of family and church. One thing I am amazed by is the default heathen (what my dad would call "dirt bag") in each child. I often find myself torn with my own nephews thinking, "You are such a heathen…but you're so darn cute!" It's cute when a 2 year old farts, but when he is 12 and blatantly farting at the dinner table to the point that you have to charge a fart tax of cleaning a bathroom every time one "slips" (true story), you know you've got a problem! There is no question that children need instruction, molding, modeling and ultimately a Savior. Yet, each child stands with the reality that they have two kingdoms competing for their attention and devotion. The kingdom of God and the kingdom of the world. At the end of the day they will choose one or the other, whether actively or passively. A parent can only prepare and encourage their children to do this and actively trust God through the means of ASKing.

When I was a child still in the home, I prayed to receive Christ, was baptized, was involved in church/youth group and showed many of the cultural fruits of a Christian. But, it wasn't until college that God, in his wonderful timing, truly opened my eyes to see his glory and love, and at that point I was "all-in." My parents had done everything they possibly could, but at the end of the day, their dirt-bag eldest son had to surrender his life over to the Lord. I personally cannot point to the specific time that I think I was saved, but I know that God had used my parents throughout the entire process (and continues to use them still). Sure He brought along some other people at different key times, but no one has prayed as big and often as my parents and for that I am eternally grateful, for the Lord heard and answered their prayers! Praise God, I once was lost but now am found!

Intentionality

Intentionality starts with a desire that manifests itself in a plan. Good intentions not acted on still leave you and the one whom you intended good, empty handed. If you don't have good intentions, then there is a heart issue that must be addressed, but as we saw in Matthew 7, even evil parents have good intentions for their children. I have been learning that if things aren't going well in my marriage, it is most likely because I am not being intentional with my wife. Of course I love her and will lay down my life for her…but if I don't show my love to her in the small things or big things then what good is my love? Our actions reveal our desires and priorities. If no action is taken, then ultimately the question of love is on the line. It's not enough to say, "I married you, therefore I love you" or "You are my child, of course I love you." While those things may be true, they will still leave the connected party questioning your love. If you say you love someone and you are not intentional with them, your love will be seen as hollow.

If God is the one who saves, why do we need to be intentional? We need to be intentional because God is intentional. He was intentional in showing us His love by sending Jesus to die in our dirt-bag place. He has been intentional to build His church, make the gospel go forth and open our eyes to receive Him. He wants to affirm His love for us through His actions. God has been intentional to make parents the means through which He parents His children. We love because He first loved us. We are intentional because He is intentional.

In Chapter 23, my father outlined some great examples of how to go about being intentional with your children in some of the smaller ongoing ways. What I would like to further comment on is the significance of some of the ceremonies we had, the biggies! The Passport to Purity Weekend (~6th grade), The Manhood Ceremony (~15-16 years old), Graduation Launch (could be high school, we did after college), and the Marriage Launch (at the wedding). These have been significant and influential events for my brothers and me. Through these it has been communicated that we are valued and loved. They were strategic platforms to affirm us verbally and also for us to receive a bigger picture calling for our lives. I look back at all of these with great fondness and much thankfulness for my parents' intentionality with me. I have no question of their love for me as their son. Their intentionality has primarily been a model of God's intentionality with me. His love has been manifested through their love. I desire to replicate much of what was modeled in the home and written down on these pages because I have seen its very blessing in my own life.

This book is not a parenting formula, but an invitation to embark on a relational parenting adventure with the Father, trusting in His parenting of you as you parent His children. Ask big. Ask often. And trust in his all-powerful, all-knowing and all-loving plan.

ACKNOWLEDGMENTS

We are social and spiritual billionaires because we stand on the shoulders of fathers and mothers, literal and spiritual. There is no book without the countless deposits of "spiritual seeds" from the guiding hands of these generous image-bearers of God mentioned below. Most of them were enabled because they entered the vast treasury of God's amazing grace ahead of us. Through them opening their lives to us, risking sacrificial deposits in us, making liberal deposits of love, instruction and prayer, we have big checks to write to the next generation—our physical and spiritual children. We would be spoiled rotten apart from the fact that our Lord said, "To whom much is given, much is required." But it doesn't feel like a requirement—we give forward out of full hearts. It's impossible to name everyone we have been blessed by, but imperative that we name the weighty ones and the most pronounced (among many) contributions we remember them for. Jon has a list; Pam has a list; some are on (or could be on) both of our lists.

Jon's Acknowledgments:

Robert D. "Bob" Strain—Dad, a trainer of race horses trained-up a trainer of men. Huge deposits: how to exercise, discipline, work, nutrition, wicked humor and excellence in craft. We didn't get enough time together; then again—it was enough.

Norma (Strain) Hill—My mom, who twice labored to "birth" me: physically in 1960, then nurtured me to the day of my spiritual regeneration in Christ (1978). You stood in the gap fighting for me and my siblings through vigilant prayer, modeling Christ, engaging in forthright discussions and sharing books showing God's path of life.

O.D. Hill—My "step-up" father: generosity, reflective wisdom, frugality and stewardship

Bob & Nadeen Boettger—father/mother-in-law: devotion and homestyle servant-hospitality; generosity; four really swell daughters – and one for Jon! Thank you!

241

Patti (Strain) Burt—sister and "second mom," giving crucial life-nurturing amidst a large family

Bob Harmon, Sr.—for noticing me in a life season of feeling lost and falling through the cracks; pitch by pitch (literally) coached me up to a place of getting big wins under my belt

Louie & Ann Beeler—wheat farmers who modeled generosity and contagious joy in the Lord

Mark Moselle—intentional disciple-maker; foundational cultivation for a spiritual sprout; fun

John & Dayle Rogers—encouragement; models of marital mutual respect; strategic leadership

Pastor Bill & Sue Knepper—sense of humor, faithfulness, how to mine the treasures of the Bible

Dr. Bruce Loebs—skills in rhetorical criticism and thinking

Jim Sylvester—first to put the cross-hairs on the target of "real masculinity" modeled by Jesus, I observed you boldly and winsomely present it to college athletes, fraternities and dorm rats.

Bob Monaco, Bob Francis & Marty Brown—formative "bosses" imparting wise leadership; purposeful living

Bill Howard—never let me settle for less; a clear voice in every major life choice

Pastor Scott & Sara McKinney—showing high-value hospitality to the Mormon people

Dr. Robert Lewis—clear vision and transferable definition of noble manhood; annual "man plan"

Search Ministries staff & board members—in a season of life when mentors thin out, I live in a palace with a band of brothers, surrounded with life-wealth, generous teachers and to-be-envied camaraderie. You men have the

Acknowledgments

"eye of the tiger" living fully intentional lives. Through the Search "give it away" culture, all of you have modeled and mentored me in everything this book teaches—especially Part Two (Seek). There is no Search Boise without you. You have given us your very lives and withheld no good thing. Forgive me for not naming you all, but you're gracious and humble enough not to care about it. However, two of you need to be named because without your role there is no book.

Gary (& Judy) Long—your "spiritual seeds" catalyzed the project in three ways: 1) the seed of Gary's suggestion that we write about this was not only caring and practical in our quirky circumstances (too involved to explain here), but powerfully confirming of something we thought we might do one day. And, the notion was birthed in a Search National prayer meeting - wink. 2) The seed-gift (call it 1099-misc) was serious affirmation to hit the "go" button. But only after 3) certain seedy-persuasion tactics you (Gary) must have used to get Search President Larry Moody's blessing.

Larry (and Ruth) Moody—Joking aside, we are profoundly grateful for your affirmation and trust in us to represent Search well with this project. Search is not a "publishing ministry," per se, but rather an "eyeball to eyeball" relational ministry. And yes, we are mindful and affirming of your ongoing prayers for a twenty-five percent "offering of our offspring" to Search staff in due time—wink. You should pray for a higher percentage.

Phil & Caryl Altmeyer—emulated conviction and made life deposits preparing me for "Pam"—and so much more.

Pam's Acknowledgments

Bob Boettger—The God-dependent farmer who took in this 2-year-old and her 4-year-old sister and my mom, not having a clue how three women (with the addition of two more later) could change his life! My memories of you, Dad, and Mom praying at the kitchen table every morning are forever etched in my mind.

Nadeen Boettger—The forever gracious farm wife, who happens to be my mom, who has blessed many through her gifts of hospitality. I am forever grateful for all those years you "stayed home" and nurtured me and built into my life.

Chuck and Ruby Andersen—A loving husband and wife team, servants available to shine their light, who moved into our small town and greatly impacted it. They were instrumental in leading my parents and myself and many others to Christ. I am forever grateful for you.

Karen Hilgenkamp—A woman who availed herself to myself and many other teen girls, imparting God's Word and necessary life skills to us.

Lois Snyder Jacobs—A woman who loves God who just so "happened" to be there my freshman year in college. You were a life saver, Lois!

Nancy Croll Johnson—My mentor, discipler, counselor and friend! Nancy taught me how to be vulnerable, love God and how to give my life away to other women.

Renee Rule—My Mom mentor and heart friend who was there when I was in my black cloud, wondering if I could pull off this motherhood thing. Thanks, Renee, for always being my cheerleader and encourager and for forging the way ahead of me.

My Moms in Prayer Friends (you know who you are)—Thanks for praying with me for my kids and "being there" for me! Oh, the volumes we could fill with God's faithfulness!

Jon Strain—Loving husband and completer of 31 years. You have imparted to me like no one else what it means to be loved unconditionally. You have loved me well and made my world secure. There is no one else I would have wanted to raise children with. We make a great team! As Rocky Balboa said to Adrian, "I got gaps, you got gaps, together...no gaps!"

There are significant contributors to the practical matters of writing of this book:

Kirsten Holmberg—At the perfect time, you generously offered crucial and wise coaching about the editing process. From you and your resources, we learned there is nothing to fear and how to let the editing process be our friend.

Maryanna Young (Aloha Publishing) and Robert Sweesy (Endurance Press): You are good friends with wise counsel. You both are kingdom people first, publishers second.

To Mark Russell and his very capable team at Elevate Publishing, you have been a pleasure to work with. Business-wise, you are very professional and diligent. Yet, you are kingdom people, foremost. You have understood and thoroughly supported the nuanced nature of our ministry motivation for this book. You have given the book every chance to succeed.

A special shout-out to two Elevate staff we worked very closely with for several months:

Anna McHargue—our not-much-like-an-English-teacher editor. You have been a delight to work with, slashing through a lot of word-brush only to shape up a beautifully landscaped book. (Yes, Anna, I couldn't resist one more metaphor! I get the last say.) Ever upbeat, nourishing and dignifying, you gently nudged us to the finish line. Your orange vest is in the mail—wink.

Bobby Kuber—The "millennial marketing guy." We have had a special relationship this year working on this book, plus your participation in my IronMen group. You are both the marketer and the target audience. From the moment we made eye contact I had an immediate confident sense about you, your abilities and your perfect fit for this role. You were the tie-breaker to go with Elevate and you have delivered with style. You have given heart, soul, mind and sweat equity to the project. We are very proud of you; you have what it takes.